THE IMAGE OF LINCOLN IN THE SOUTH

PERHAPS THE MOST FAMOUS OF ALL THE ADALBERT J. VOLCK CARTOONS, "THE PASSAGE THROUGH BALTIMORE," PUBLISHED IN 1863, ILLUSTRATES HOW SOUTHERN PROPAGANDISTS "DAMNED AND RIDICULED LINCOLN THROUGH ALMOST EVERY MEDIUM KNOWN TO THE AGE" (PAGE 69).

THE IMAGE OF LINCOLN IN THE SOUTH

By Michael Davis

UTP KNOXVILLE : THE UNIVERSITY OF TENNESSEE PRESS

LIBRARY OF CONGRESS CATALOG CARD NUMBER 73-158115

INTERNATIONAL STANDARD BOOK NUMBER 0-87049-133-4

FIRST EDITION.

Frontispiece reproduced through the courtesy of the Huntington Library, San Marino, California

FOR MY MOTHER

AND THE MEMORY OF MY FATHER

Contents

THE IMAGE OF
LINCOLN
IN THE SOUTH

Introduction

It is not surprising that Abraham Lincoln became, after his death, the North's supreme hero. He saved the Union and guided his people through the Civil War, the nation's most deeply felt historical experience. Lincoln's words gave meaning and purpose to the sacrifices of millions of common folk. He freed the slaves, thus easing the burden of hypocrisy upon the American conscience. He was a man of the frontier, a man of the people, "the Great Democrat," according to the Brahmin aristocrat John Lothrop Motley. His assassination on Good Friday, after the humiliation of his enemies, was burdened with a religious symbolism not lost upon a people who, if they had given up attaining the Puritan's Holy Commonwealth, still saw the hand of God in the affairs of men. If Yankee ministers hesitated in their Easter sermons to draw the analogy between Lincoln and Christ, millions of their parishioners did not. Lincoln's sudden and dramatic death at the hour of his greatest triumph provided for his people—numbed by the enormous casualties of the past four years—the occasion for a national catharsis. They saw in him both the savior and the incarnation of American virtues. "The hero is he whom every American should wish to be," observed Dixon Wector. "His legend is the mirror of the folk soul." Significantly, the American folk have made Abraham Lincoln—nationalist, emancipator, man of the people, martyr—their greatest national hero.

It is more surprising that the South should accept Lincoln as a hero. There was a time when the South fiercely hated Lincoln's name. He was the architect of Confederate defeat, the destroyer of the South's dreams of independence. His armies killed her sons, destroyed her property, ravished her land, and crushed "the fairest civilization the sun ever shone upon." After his death Lincoln's party fastened upon the South a Black Reconstruction second in horrors only to the war itself. Countless Southerners carried to their graves their damnation of Lincoln because he refused to end the killing and let the South go in peace. He was the crude, heavy-handed frontiersman, the spinner of coarse yarns, the author of the daemonic Emancipation Proclamation, the spear-carrier of the party of greasy mechanics, tight-fisted small farmers, and shrewd Yankee tradesmen. He was the very antithesis of the Cavalier ideal. The South remains the most fertile source of anti-Lincoln jokes and anecdotes ranging from the humorous to the vulgar. Those vestals who guard the temple of Southern tradition still deny that Lincoln may be mentioned in the company of Jefferson Davis and Stonewall Jackson; certainly, Lincoln cannot approach Robert E. Lee in the Southern pantheon. Of the states of the old Confederacy, only Tennessee has proclaimed Lincoln's birthday a holiday. His statue is seldom found in the South, and only a few communities in the states of the late Confederacy are named for Lincoln. Few schools below the Mason-Dixon line bear his name. The South, more than any other part of the nation, has remained immune to the apotheosis of Lincoln.

But if the South has not surrendered wholly to the Lincoln legend, it nevertheless has accepted Lincoln as an authentic American hero, and in some cases, as a Southern hero. There were certain qualities in the Lincoln legend which appealed to the Southerners who yearned for sectional peace and a share in American prosperity and nationalism. These men of the New South praised their late enemy as a great democrat, a great humanitarian, a friend of the South, and an embodiment of American virtue. Lincoln's Kentucky birth and his attitudes toward race made it easier for many Southerners to accept Lincoln as a Southern hero as well as an American one. Countless Southerners still reviled the memory of Lincoln, but by 1909, the centennial of Lincoln's birth, there existed genuine and substantial affection in the South for the martyred President.

A more liberal estimate of Lincoln's character and deeds was bound to come as the South slowly merged into a broader American nationalism which found a symbolic expression in Lincoln. But because the symbolic Lincoln represented the finest human ideals of American nationalism—ideals which Southerners as well as Northerners could appreciate and seek to realize—the Lincoln legend acted as a force attracting Southerners back into the Union of their fathers.

Surely, one of the most interesting stories of the postwar South is that of how Lincoln assumed a place among the lares and penates of his former enemies. The object of this study is to explore and document changing Southern attitudes toward Abraham Lincoln, to examine certain elements of the Lincoln legend to which Southerners responded favorably, and to speculate on the reasons for the South's softening of heart toward her old enemy. This evolution of attitude toward the memory of Lincoln contributed to the rebuilding of a national consciousness necessary to heal the wounds of civil war and make America one nation again. The story of the image of Lincoln in the South is part of the greater drama of war, reunion, and reconciliation.

Throughout this study I have tried to remember Douglas Southall Freeman's observation that he never knew what was in the mind of General Lee unless Lee himself wrote it down. If it is dangerous to speculate on the thinking of an individual, it is still more dangerous to construct an abstract model of a composite "mind," be it the "Southern mind" or anything else. Such an attempt does violence to the rich variety of human experience and response, and few regions are as rich in variety as the South. Consequently, I have tried to avoid generalizing about "the Southern mind" and have sought instead to discover more or less commonly held attitudes toward Lincoln reflected in certain selected writings by Southerners. I have assumed that memoirs, letters, newspapers, magazines, drama, poetry, music, and fiction reflect attitudes working in a culture.

Because I am interested in the South's changing attitudes toward Lincoln as representing and at once contributing to the sundering and the rebuilding of the Union, I have confined this study to the Confederate South—those eleven states which seceded in 1860–1861—and to individuals who cast their lot with the stars and bars and thus shared in the Confederate experience. For the same reasons, I have pretty much restricted this study to a consideration of the white South. Certain opinions expressed by blacks have been introduced to help illustrate the way Lincoln's alleged views on race were incorporated into the pattern of Southern segregationist thought. A systematic examination of Southern Negro attitudes toward Lincoln is somewhat tangential to the problem I have tried to come to grips with here and is complex enough to deserve a study of its own.

The centennial celebration of Lincoln's birth in 1909 supplies a convenient point at which to conclude this study, lest it grow to Brobdingnagian proportions. This is not to suggest that Southern journalists, public men, scholars, and litterateurs ceased thinking and writing about Lincoln after 1909. But the reunion process, in the context of which changing Southern attitudes about Lincoln must be seen, was over. The Democratic party had regained respectability, Southern men had returned to national office, the race issue was submerged in party politics, and former Yankees and rebels had fought together under the old flag in a foreign war. For better or worse, America was one nation again, and the old sectional heroes Lincoln and Lee had become national ones.

I began this study as a doctoral dissertation at Rice University in 1965 under the direction of Frank E. Vandiver, and I owe much to his advice and encouragement. Most of the research was done in the Fondren Library, Rice University; Henry Horner Collection, Illinois State Historical Library, Springfield; the Chicago Historical Society; Library of Congress; and the Richter Library, University of Miami. Charlton W. Tebeau and Raymond G. O'Connor helped secure for me two small grants from the University of Miami for traveling and typing expenses. Albert E. Lowey-Ball's hospitality in Washington sustained me during several visits to the Library of Congress. Anne Syrcle patiently typed the manuscript.

Michael Davis

Coral Gables, Florida
April, 1971

1.

The South Discovers Lincoln: The Secession Crisis

Abraham Lincoln was unknown to the South when he was nominated for the presidency by the Republican party in May, 1860. A few Southerners might remember Lincoln as the opponent of Stephen A. Douglas in the important Illinois Senate race two years before. But the attention of the South and of the nation in 1858 had been focused upon Douglas and not upon the unknown prairie lawyer who forced his Democratic antagonist into the Freeport doctrine—the admission, obnoxious to the South, that territorial legislatures could exclude slavery indirectly by denying it protective legislation. When Douglas won, Lincoln dropped from view. Few Southerners noticed how Lincoln rose from the ashes of defeat, growing in stature in the eyes of his party, until, on the eve of the Chicago convention, he was a serious contender for the presidential nomination.[1]

Most Southerners expected the Republicans to name William Seward as their candidate. Seward, twice governor and now senator from New York, had been the leading Republican since his Rochester speech in

1. James Ford Rhodes, *History of the United States from the Compromise of 1850 to the Final Restoration of Home Rule at the South in 1877* (New York, 1907–1919), II, 340–43.

1858 declaring an "irrepressible conflict" between North and South. If Seward's many enemies could agree, perhaps Salmon P. Chase of Ohio or Edward Bates of Missouri would receive the nomination. But Southerners feared Seward. Two weeks before the Republicans met, the Democratic convention at Charleston adjourned, unable to agree upon candidate or platform. Southern delegates predicted, "William H. Seward will be the next President of the United States."[2]

Most Southerners reacted with relative indifference to Lincoln's nomination. Many Southern newspapers carried only the briefest news dispatches of the events in the Wigwam at Chicago. Their columns were crowded with news of the breakup of the Charleston convention, the nomination of John Bell by the hastily formed Constitutional Union party, and reports of debates in the Senate over Jefferson Davis' resolutions on the territories. Even gossip about the curious Japanese and their new mission to Washington frequently crowded out reports of the Republican convention, testifying to the relative insignificance which most Southerns placed on the Republican proceedings.

The *Southern Literary Messenger* viewed the Republican candidate and his running mate with contempt: "The Republicans have thrust up two of their weakest specimens in the persons of Lincoln and Hamlin."[3] Other Southern journals, more familiar with Lincoln, warned that the Democrats were facing a formidable adversary. "Lincoln is the strongest Black-Republican in the Northwest—a man of power," a correspondent told the *Memphis Daily Appeal*.[4] The same newspaper warned its readers, "It would be uncandid to deny that Mr. Lincoln is a man of fair ability, and that against any other man than Senator Douglas, . . . he possesses elements of strength which would be formidable in a campaign."[5]

In the eyes of the South it mattered little whom the Republicans chose as their candidate. Born in 1854 in opposition to the Kansas-Nebraska Act, the Republican party was the *bête noire* of the South, and its candidate, whoever he might be, would share the odium visited upon his

2. William B. Hesseltine, ed., *Three Against Lincoln: Murat Halstead Reports the Caucuses of 1860* (Baton Rouge, La., 1960), 100–101.

3. 30 (June, 1860), 472.

4. May 28, 1860.

5. May 22, 1860. Reprint of article originally appearing in *Cincinnati Enquirer* (n.d.).

party. Like all successful American political parties, the Republicans were a motley group of diverse personalities and interests, including men of the loftiest principles and cynical office-seekers using the party as the vehicle for their ambitions. But the least common denominator of Republicanism was opposition to the expansion of slavery into the territories; the party platform denied "the authority of Congress, of a territorial legislature, or of any individual, to give legal existence to slavery in any territory of the United States." This principle struck at the sanctity of the institution which most Southerners believed to define the correct relationship between white and black and to be the foundation of Southern prosperity and of civilization itself. The victory of a Black Republican—rarely in the South was the party called simply "Republican"—standing upon that principle meant the establishment in power of forces hostile to the equal treatment of property. Slave property was to be discriminated against by denying its protection in the territories. In Southern eyes, this was an attack upon the Constitution itself. As the North outstripped the South in wealth and numbers, the South looked to constitutional guarantees for protection, within the Union, of its peculiar institution. The South's interpretation of these guarantees had been endorsed by the Supreme Court in the Dred Scott decision of 1857. Now, an avowedly sectional party had arisen in the North challenging these solemn guarantees. The slavery debate, hitherto confined to intraparty and extrapolitical spheres, finally had become an issue of party politics, to the alarm of the South. The Republican candidate, by the very nature of the party banner he carried, was damned in the South from the day of his nomination.

Yet, so strong was the hatred in some quarters for Stephen A. Douglas, candidate of the Northern Democrats, that Lincoln seemed the lesser evil. This was especially true in the lower South, where the race was between Douglas and John C. Breckinridge and where Lincoln electors were not permitted on the ballot. A correspondent of Jefferson Davis, contrasting the positions of Lincoln and Douglas on slavery in the territories, told the Mississippi senator, "Lincoln is consistent & logical. Douglas the reverse."[6] Similarly, Senator Judah P. Benjamin of Louisiana

6. W. H. Winder to Jefferson Davis, June 7, 1860, in Dunbar Rowland, ed., *Jefferson Davis, Constitutionalist: His Letters, Papers, and Speeches* (Jackson, Miss., 1923), IV, 459.

found "the perfect candor and frankness" of Lincoln a refreshing contrast to the perfidy of Douglas.[7]

Conservatives pointed out that Lincoln's written and spoken record suggested that he was more moderate and careful of Southern rights than was the extreme wing of his party. Had not Lincoln expressed his disbelief in Negro equality and citizenship, his intention to uphold the fugitive slave law, his disinclination to interfere with slavery where it existed, and his willingness to admit new slave states, if their citizens wished slavery? The influential *New Orleans Bee* observed that Lincoln was chosen over Seward precisely because his moderate views on slavery would command more votes in the North: "In the choice of a Presidential candidate . . . the Black Republicans have furnished a signal manifestation of their determination to avoid extremism."[8] Prominent unionists like Alexander H. Stephens and Benjamin F. Perry believed Lincoln, fearing civil war, would follow a deliberate policy of friendship and respect for the South.[9] Even Judah Benjamin, no friend of the Republicans, was surprised, upon reading the newly published Lincoln-Douglas debates of 1858, "to find that Mr. Lincoln is a far more conservative man, unless he has since changed his opinions, than I had supposed him to be."[10]

These conservative voices were little heard amidst the fear and hysteria which gripped the lower South during the campaign of 1860.[11] Powerful emotions resounded whenever the sensitive chord of the Negro question was touched. Terrible visions of slave uprisings were rarely absent in Southern minds before the Civil War. The South's fear of servile revolt mounted after the John Brown raid in 1859. It was not so

7. *Congressional Globe*, 36th Cong., 1st sess., May 22, 1860, p. 2237.

8. May 21, 1860, in Dwight L. Dumond, ed., *Southern Editorials on Secession* (New York, 1931), 104.

9. A. H. Stephens to J. Henly Smith, July 10, 1860, in U. B. Phillips, ed., *The Correspondence of Robert Toombs, Alexander H. Stephens, and Howell Cobb.* Annual Report of the American Historical Association for the Year 1911 (Washington, D. C., 1913), II, 487. Perry's views were expressed in his article "Disunion" in *Charleston Courier*, Aug. 20, 1860, quoted by Lilian Adele Kibler, *Benjamin Perry: South Carolina Unionist* (Durham, N. C., 1946), 325–28. "You will find many here [Charleston] who endorse Major Perry's views," wrote Robert N. Gourdin to William Porcher Miles, Aug. 20, 1860, *ibid.*, 328.

10. *Congressional Globe*, 36th Cong., 1st sess., May 22, 1860, p. 2237.

11. See Ollinger Crenshaw, "The Psychological Background of the Election of 1860 in the South," *North Carolina Historical Review*, 19 (July, 1942), 260–79.

much the raid itself, ill conceived and poorly executed, that alarmed the South, as the widespread sympathy and support Brown enjoyed in the North. Southerners did not fail to note that most Brown sympathizers identified themselves with the Republican party. What would these fanatics, who made a martyr of a murdering madman, do when they attained power? Gentleman planters, small farmers, and town tradesmen talked darkly of Yankee-inspired slave insurrections and recalled the fate of Santo Domingo. Little seemed to stand, within the Union, between the South and the unspeakable horrors attending the election of a Black Republican President. The political balance of power had disappeared long ago. The Northern people had displayed their want of good will and moderation with personal liberty laws and by support of a party avowedly hostile to the South. Constitutional guarantees were inadequate, because the very *raison d'être* of Black Republicanism was the denial of the constitutional right of slavery in the territories. Lincoln's alleged conservatism was a delusion; why should a Black Republican cease to act like a Black Republican after he has tasted power? And was not Lincoln the author of the "house divided" doctrine, announced even before Seward's "irrepressible conflict," and was not Lincoln on record as saying that slavery must be put on the course of ultimate extinction? Democratic majorities in Congress could not protect the South against hostile legislation if Lincoln were elected. Who could trust the Northern Democrats—followers of the perfidious Douglas—to protect Southern interests? They abandoned the South by refusing to accept the Alabama Platform (which, in 1848, had called for Congressional protection of slavery in the territories), and would abandon the South again. Conservatives urged the South to accept a constitutionally elected Lincoln and await an overt act of hostility before considering secession. Radicals answered that Lincoln's election was itself an overt act of hostility against the South. When your enemy stands pointing a revolver at you, must you await the first shot before moving to protect yourself? Questions and answers thus began to take shape in Southern minds.

Throughout the campaign Southerners were warned constantly that more than the election of a President, more than the triumph of a section or a party were at issue—union or disunion, the fate of the white race, of civilization itself hung in the balance.[12] So warned, Southerners

12. For example, the *Charleston Mercury* declared "at the next Presidential election the question is not only a Democratic or Black Republican President, but

then were told that their archenemies were almost certain to win the election. Only a united Democratic party offered hope to check the Republican threat. That hope vanished when the sundered Democracy failed to reunite at Baltimore. A few wishful thinkers hoped no candidate would get a majority and that the election would be thrown into the Democrat-controlled House of Representatives.[13] But as the campaign wore on, the inevitability of Republican victory grew more apparent.[14] By October, when returns for local elections in key Northern states showed a Republican sweep, all in the South knew that the hated Lincoln would soon be seated in the chair of Washington and Jefferson.

Southerners had been told that extreme measures would be taken by the South to protect itself in the event of Lincoln's election. Secession talk was everywhere. Many Southern public men declared they would never accept Lincoln's election,[15] and state legislatures resolved that the

---

union or disunion." April 16, 1860, in Dumond, ed., *Southern Editorials on Secession*, 69. Jefferson Davis saw the election as "between the defenders of constitutional government and the votaries of mob rule, fanaticism and anarchy." Letter to L. P. Conner and others, Oct. 7, 1860, in Rowland, ed., *Jefferson Davis* IV, 541. The *New Orleans Daily True Delta*—a Douglas paper—saw in Lincoln's election "the death knell of the political and social prosperity of the South." Oct. 12, 1860, in Dumond, ed., *Southern Editorials on Secession*, 186. The *Daily Nashville Patriot*—a supporter of John Bell—declared "war to the knife" would ensue were Lincoln elected, and the chief issue in the canvass of 1860 was not slavery in the territories, "but whether this Union shall be preserved or destroyed." Oct. 13, 1860, in *ibid.*, 190. One Southern author summed up the fears of many when he wrote: "No people ever had more at stake. In the maintenance, in all its integrity, of the relation of master and slave between the white and black races of the South, it is our universal sentiment that property, liberty, honor, and civilization itself, are involved." James P. Holcombe, *The Election of a Black Republican President an Overt Act of Aggression on the Rights of Property in Slaves* (Richmond, Va., 1860), 5. It is a matter of conjecture the degree to which these and other opinions represented sincere fears or were scare tactics to enlist the Southern voter behind a particular candidate or plan of action as the sole alternative to disaster. In any event, free circulation of such views contributed to the climate of hysteria which characterized the canvass of 1860 in the South.

13. Stephens to J. Henly Smith, Sept. 12, 1860, in Phillips, ed., *Toombs-Stephens-Cobb Correspondence*, 496.

14. Columbia *Daily South Carolinian*, Aug. 3, 1860, in Dumond, ed., *Southern Editorials on Secession*, 153–57.

15. A number of secession threats by Southern senators and representatives are assembled in the remarks of Senator Clark of New Hampshire, in *Congressional Globe*, 36th Cong., 1st sess., 840–41.

election of a Black Republican would justify secession. Public money was appropriated for defense, and militia companies organized across the South. South Carolina surely would go out, and, although immediate secession sentiment was at a minority beyond the boundaries of that irascible state, once she seceded few doubted she again would be left to stand alone. The combustible climate of the lower South on the eve of the election is illustrated by a fiery editorial in the *Atlanta Southern Confederacy*:

> The South will never permit Abraham Lincoln to be inaugurated President of the United States . . . . It is the determination of all parties in the South. Let the consequences be what they may, whether the Potomac is crimsoned in human gore, and Pennsylvania Avenue is paved ten fathoms deep with mangled bodies, or whether the last vestige of liberty is swept from the face of the American continent, the South, the loyal South, the constitutional South, will never submit to such humiliation and degradation as the inauguration of Abraham Lincoln.[16]

Against this background—the sense of enormous consequences of the election, the specter of defeat at the polls, and the awareness that cataclysmic events would be set into motion at the moment of that defeat—the campaign of 1860 in the South was fought out in an atmosphere of fear, hysteria, and crisis. The South had a long "vigilante tradition"—the phrase is Clement Eaton's—in enforcing orthodoxy on the slave question.[17] Southerners ever were ready with the writ in one hand to defend their rights and with the rod in the other to chastise dissenters.[18] In Lincoln the South saw the Hun at the gate, and Southern mobs acted to stamp out "Lincolnism" within the borders of Dixie. Abolitionist agents were reported everywhere, spreading terror and encouraging Negroes to arson and murder. Rumors swept the South of a gigantic plot in Texas to unleash slaves, poison wells, burn cities, and deliver the state to the Yankees. Negroes were reported cheering for Lincoln; they thought "Black Republican" meant Lincoln was a Negro who had come to set them free. Dangerous books were gathered and destroyed; to be dis-

16. Quoted by *New York Times*, Aug. 7, 1860.

17. Clement Eaton, *The Freedom-of-Thought Struggle in the Old South* (New York, 1964), 376.

18. Clement Eaton, "Mob Violence in the Old South," *Mississippi Valley Historical Review*, 29 (Dec., 1942), 370.

covered in possession of Helper's *Impending Crisis* was to risk being incinerated with the book. Yankees were cold-shouldered, frequently asked to leave the state, and occasionally lynched for suspected abolitionist activities. A luckless vendor of campaign medals was nearly murdered by a mob because a Lincoln and Hamlin badge was discovered in his stock. "Resistance to Lincoln is obedience to God" was the proposed motto of a young men's club formed in Montgomery during the canvass. Lincoln's effigy was hung and burned in all quarters of the South.[19]

In this climate of hate and fear, the image of Lincoln as constructed by Southern propagandists was hardly benign. He was the archetypal Black Republican, a "low and vulgar partisan of John Brown," a believer in Negro equality, "the beau ideal of a relentless, dogged free-soil border ruffian . . . a vulgar mobocrat and a Southern hater in political opinions," an unbending abolitionist whom the Republicans chose because Seward lacked the resolve to subdue the South and whose fancied moderate views "are the most subtle and dangerous form of anti-slavery-ism." He championed the party of "free love, free lands and free negroes" and flaunted his contempt for the South by accepting a mulatto as a running mate.[20] Lincoln's awkward and melancholy form inspired Southern pens to added poison: he was "the leanest, lankest, most ungainly mass of legs and arms and hatchet face ever strung on a human frame," whose principles and appearance were as lean and crooked as

19. Crenshaw, "Psychological Background of the Election of 1860." Allan Nevins, *The Emergence of Lincoln* (New York, 1950), II, 287, 306–9. *New York Times*, Nov. 10, Dec. 10 and 15, 1860. *Montgomery Mail*, Oct. 18, 1860, quoted by *New York Tribune*, Oct. 26, 1860, and in Arthur C. Cole, "Lincoln's Election an Immediate Menace to Slavery in the States?" *American Historical Review*, 36 (July, 1931), 743. Ralph W. Steen, "Texas Newspapers and Lincoln," *Southwestern Historical Quarterly*, 51 (Jan., 1948), 199. The common practice of newspapers' printing each other's copy helped give local rumors wide circulation.

20. *DeBow's Review*, OS 29 (July, 1860), 100–101. *Charleston Mercury* and *Richmond Enquirer* (no dates), quoted by Bruce Catton, *The Coming Fury* (Garden City, N. Y., 1961), 94. *Louisville Daily Courier*, May 26, 1860, in Dumond, ed., *Southern Editorials on Secession*, 115. *DeBow's Review*, OS 29 (Aug., 1860), 178. Letters of Lawrence Keitt to William Porcher Miles (Oct. 3, 1860) and Mrs. Frederick Brown (March 4, 1861), quoted by Clement Eaton, *A History of the Southern Confederacy* (New York. 1961), 18, 294n. It was widely believed in the South that Hannibal Hamlin was a Negro or mulatto, reason enough, said the *Montgomery Mail*, to resist the Lincoln administration; quoted in *New York Times*, Nov. 2, 1860.

the rails he split, "a horrid looking wretch . . . sooty and scoundrelly in aspect, a cross between the nutmeg dealer, the horse swapper, and the night man . . . ."[21] In short, the very antithesis of the Cavalier ideal.

Lincoln did little to counter his Southern image as a straight-out Black Republican. Throughout the campaign, and in the weeks before his inauguration, he refused to speak out on the issues of the day. Instead of campaigning, he remained quietly in Springfield and let others take the stump for him. He made no speeches and granted no interviews with the press. When letters were received inquiring of the candidate's position on this or that issue, the candidate or his secretaries would reply that Mr. Lincoln adhered to the Republican platform and to his published, pre-campaign statements and pledged "justice and fairness to all."[22]

Southern unionists appealed to Lincoln to restate his intentions not to interfere with slavery in the states, thereby weakening the disunionists' argument. In replies marked "private" and "confidential" Lincoln declined to speak publicly on such matters. His views on slavery, he wrote Tennessee unionist William S. Speer, were "in print, and open to all who will read. Those who will not read, or heed, what I have already publicly said, would not read, or heed, a repetition of it."[23] In a similar vein he wrote to George D. Prentice, editor of the *Louisville Journal* and a Douglas man: "I could not express my conservative views and intentions more clearly and strongly than they are expressed in our plat-form, and in my many speeches already in print, and before the public." He added, perhaps with a trace of bitterness:

> And yet even you, who do occasionally speak of me in terms of personal kindness, give no prominence to these oft-repeated expressions of conservative views and intentions, but busy yourself with appeals to all conservative men, to vote for Douglas—to vote any way which can possibly defeat me—thus impressing your readers that you think, I am the very worst

21. [John Townsend], *The South Alone Should Govern the South* (Charleston, S.C., 1860), 30. *Houston Telegraph* (n.d.) and *Charleston Mercury*, June 9, 1860, quoted by Emerson D. Fite, *The Presidential Campaign of 1860* (New York, 1911), 210.

22. Abraham Lincoln, *Collected Works of Abraham Lincoln*, ed. Roy P. Basler (Brunswick, N. J., 1953), IV, 60, 83, 93, 94, 130, 138. David M. Potter, *Lincoln and His Party in the Secession Crisis* (New Haven, Conn., 1942), 135–36.

23. Oct. 23, 1860, in Lincoln, *Works* IV, 130.

> man living. If what I have already said has failed to convince you, no repetition of it would convince you.[24]

Lincoln's reply to Prentice suggests his despair of persuading even moderate Southern men of his willingness to tolerate slavery where it existed. He seemed confident, however, that events would convince the South of his conservatism and would discredit the secessionist argument. Moreover, Lincoln was following a calculated policy of public silence, one designed to deny to his enemies the opportunity to twist his words to their political advantage. "Bad men," both North and South, he wrote Prentice,

> are eager for something new upon which to base new misrepresentations—men who would like to frighten me, or, at least, to fix upon me the character of timidity and cowardice. They would seize upon almost any letter I could write, as being an "*awful coming down*." I intend keeping my eyes upon these gentlemen, and to not unnecessarily put any weapons in their hands.[25]

Lincoln once departed from his policy of silence, and the result confirmed his fears of being misrepresented. Shortly after the election, the President-elect, seeking to quiet rising discontent in the South, wrote a few paragraphs incorporated into a speech delivered by his friend, Senator Lyman Trumbull. Lincoln sat on the platform with Trumbull during the Springfield address, and it was widely assumed that the senator's words represented Lincoln's views. Through Trumbull, Lincoln sought to assure the South that every state would be left alone to control its affairs, especially as to the protection of property and the maintenance of peace and order within its boundaries. Trumbull added on his own that the Republicans in power would demonstrate they do not favor "negro equality or amalgamation," a course which ought to restore fraternal feeling.[26] The reaction to this gesture was immediate and widespread. Northern critics feared the abandonment of Republican principles, and the Southern press was silent or suspicious. "This is just as I expected," Lincoln wrote Henry J. Raymond, editor of the *New York Times*, "and just what would happen to any declaration I could

24. Oct. 29, 1860, in *ibid.* IV, 134–35.

25. *Ibid.* James G. Randall, *Lincoln the President: Springfield to Gettysburg* (New York, 1945–1955), I, 234.

26. Nov. 20, 1860, in Lincoln, *Works* IV, 141–42.

make."[27] Lincoln resumed his public silence until the day of his departure from Springfield to Washington.

However judicious Lincoln's policy of silence may have been in checking his Northern critics, it had no effect upon the tumble of events in the South. South Carolina seceded December 20, followed by six sister states which together formed the Confederate States of America on February 8. In fact, Lincoln's policy in respect to the South was based upon a misreading of the Southern temper. He overestimated unionist sentiment in the South and correspondingly underestimated potential secessionist strength—misconceptions which colored his judgment until rebel guns opened on Fort Sumter.[28]

In later years, when the passions of war had cooled, it became fashionable to point to Lincoln as a Southern man; indeed, Lincoln not infrequently referred to himself as such. He was born in Kentucky of Virginia parents and grew to manhood in those parts of Indiana and Illinois with a Southern flavor. His wife was of a Bluegrass slaveholding family, and many of his in-laws wore the gray against the Union. His law partners were Kentuckians, as was his best friend, Joshua Speed. His political hero was Henry Clay.[29] Lincoln's heart beat in sympathy with the border states, but neither he nor his party had many contacts in the Deep South. What few Lincoln supporters there were in the South were border state men. Republicans did not campaign deep in Dixie; of the eleven states that were to secede, only Virginia permitted Republican electors on the ballot.[30] Lincoln may have been empathic with the border state men, but he little understood the Yanceys, Rhetts, and Davises of the cotton states. Nor did he appreciate the full power of their appeal upon the excited minds of their section.

27. Nov. 28, 1860, in *ibid.*, 146. Potter, *Lincoln and His Party*, 140–42. "He [Lincoln] evidently entertains the conviction that he can do nothing that is likely to stem the tide of the times," observed correspondent Henry Villard. "What is asked of him in the way of public definitions of his policy, he would probably give if he could but persuade himself that it would do aught toward the adjustment of the present trouble. But he considers all such demonstrations futile, as the South, to use his own language, 'has eyes but does not see, and ears but does not hear.'" Henry Villard, *Lincoln on the Eve of '61: A Journalist's Story*, ed. Harold G. and Oswald Garrison Villard (New York, 1941), 34.

28. Potter, *Lincoln and His Party*, 374–75.

29. Randall, *Lincoln the President* I, 6.

30. W. Dean Burnham, *Presidential Ballots, 1836–1892* (Baltimore, Md., 1955), 78.

Lincoln also underestimated the bitterness and animosity which Southerners felt toward him as spokesman of Black Republicanism. When Samuel Haycraft, a Kentucky old Whig and Union man, suggested that Lincoln visit his birthplace during the campaign, Lincoln replied, half in jest, that such a visit would be pleasant, "but would it be safe? Would not the people Lynch me?"[31] Although assassination threats, indecent caricatures, and challenges to duels were received daily in the mails from the South, Lincoln appears to have shrugged them off as routine campaign excesses.[32] In December he chanced to confront a live secessionist. A gruff Mississippian, sporting a blue secession cockade, turned up in Lincoln's reception room in the Illinois state capitol, causing a "considerable sensation." He told Lincoln the South feared not him, but the extremists of his party. Lincoln turned away his visitor's wrath by assuring him that the Republicans, while being anti-extensionists and believing slavery wrong, would not interfere with slavery where it existed. The Mississippian, mollified, left with an inscribed copy of the Lincoln-Douglas debates.[33]

"Rest fully assured," Lincoln wrote to his Kentucky friend, Haycraft, "that the good people of the South who will put themselves in the same temper and mood towards me which you do, will find no cause to complain of me."[34] Lincoln apparently failed to grasp that there were pitiably few Southerners of such open temper. Nor would he be able to confront and persuade Southerners *en masse* as he did his single Mississippi visitor. Lincoln further failed to realize that secession, once forced, would act to discredit the position of the Southern unionist. For the secession of a single state would force Southerners to take sides on the issue of the legality of secession—a wholly different and more dangerous issue than that of the prudence of disunion. Few Southerners might have been straight-out secessionists in 1860, but hundreds of thousands more would chose disunion rather than lift their hands against a sister state exercising

31. June 4, 1860, in Lincoln, *Works* IV, 69–70.

32. Villard, *Lincoln on the Eve of '61*, 17, 28, 52–53. David Herriott, "Abraham Lincoln: Some Hitherto Unpublished Correspondence," The *Dearborn Independent*, Dec. 17, 1927, pp. 8–9, 26. David Hunter to Lincoln, Oct. 20, 1860, in Lincoln, *Works* IV, 132. James Petigru Carson, *Life, Letters, and Speeches of James Louis Petigru* (Washington, D. C., 1920), 370.

33. Villard, *Lincoln on the Eve of '61*, 41–43.

34. Nov. 13, 1860, in Lincoln, *Works* IV, 139.

what they believed to be her constitutional rights. Throughout the campaign Lincoln misread the many storm signals predicting secession in the event of his election. Like most members of his party, he believed secession threats were rhetorical bluster to coerce the North into accepting Southern demands. The South had cried "wolf" so many times that few Northerners were disposed to believe that a real danger existed in 1860.[35]

Lincoln, campaigning for Frémont in 1856, had dismissed secession mutterings as "humbug."[36] Four years later he wrote "of the many assurances I receive from the South that in no probable event will there be any very formidable effort to break up the Union." He believed most Southerners understood their best interests were in the Union. "The people of the South have too much of good sense, of good temper, to attempt the ruin of the government, rather than see it administered as it was administered by the men who made it. At least," he added, "so I hope and believe."[37] One week after the South Carolina legislature unanimously called a secession convention amidst the greatest excitement in the lower South, Lincoln, in remarks prepared for Trumbull's speech, claimed the disunionists "are now in hot haste to get out of the Union, precisely because they perceive that they can not, much longer, maintain apprehension among the Southern people that their homes, and firesides, and lives, are to be endangered by the action of the Federal Government."[38] Lincoln's optimism rested upon serious misreading of events and sentiments in the South.

35. Rhodes, *History of the United States* II, 488; Potter, *Lincoln and His Party,* ch. 1. Charles Francis Adams, Jr., recalled the campaign of 1860: "We all dwelt in a fool's Paradise. It is a source of excitement now to realize our short-sightedness. . . . We were, all around, of an average blindness. . . . We knew nothing of the South, had no realizing sense of the intensity of feeling which there prevailed; we fully believed it would all end in gasconade." Charles Francis Adams, Jr., *Charles Francis Adams, 1835–1915, An Autobiography* (Boston, 1916), 69–70.

36. July 23, 1856, at Galena, Ill., in Lincoln, *Works* II, 355.

37. Lincoln to John B. Fry, Aug. 15, 1860, in *ibid.* IV, 95.

38. *Ibid.*, 142. William Herndon, Lincoln's law partner, observed that Lincoln "apprehended no such grave danger to the Union as the mass of people supposed would result from the Southern threats, and said he could not in his heart believe that the South designed the overthrow of the Government." William H. Herndon, *Herndon's Life of Lincoln; The History and Personal Recollections of Abraham Lincoln as Originally Written by William H. Herndon and Jesse W. Weik* (Cleveland, Ohio, 1942), 382. As late as July 4, 1861, Lincoln told Congress, "There is

Even after secession was realized and the Confederacy established, Lincoln clung to the hope that the departed sisters would return of their own free will. There was some sentiment in both North and South that the cotton states had withdrawn merely to dramatize their grievances and that they would bargain their way back into the Union in return for stronger guarantees for the safety of their institutions.[39] Lincoln may have been responsive to this interpretation of events. His conduct suggests that he was prepared to rely upon the chimerical unionist forces in the South—strengthened by the loyalty of the border states and by the moderate course of his administration—to guide the seceded states back into the Union.

In order to impress his conservative intentions upon the South, Lincoln was willing to offer a cabinet post to a reputable, conservative Southerner, although he had doubts such a man would serve the Republicans. Leading Republicans such as Seward, Hamlin, and Thurlow Weed urged this gambit, and John J. Crittenden, John Bell, Alexander Stephens, William Cabell Rives, John Minor Botts, Sam Houston, and Winfield Scott were among those rumored under consideration.[40] Through his friend Joshua Speed, Lincoln sounded out James Guthrie for a cabinet portfolio. Guthrie, president of the Louisville & Nashville Railroad, was a conservative and respected Kentuckian who had been secretary of

---

much reason to believe that the Union men are the majority in many, if not in every other one [than South Carolina], of the so-called Seceded States." *Works* IV, 437. Lincoln's faith that latent Union strength in the South would assert itself once Confederate power were broken helped shape his generous reconstruction policy.

39. "We do not propose to go out of the Union for the purpose of breaking up this government . . . ," Mississippi Commissioner A. H. Handy told Marylanders in urging that border state to secede; "We will . . . say to the aggressive States of the North, when you can learn to respect this sacred instrument [the Constitution], and will mark your sincerity by conceding to us new and sufficient guarantees, we will gladly renew our fraternal relations with you." John A. Reagan, T. R. R. Cobb, and Stephen Mallory, among other Southern leaders, expressed similar sentiments. Potter, *Lincoln and His Party*, ch. 9. Reunion sentiment was sufficiently widespread in the South that Jefferson Davis, in his inaugural address as provisional Confederate president, saw fit to remind his countrymen of the permanency of their experiment in independence. "We have entered upon the course of independence, and it must be inflexibly pursued," he said. "A reunion with the States from which we have separated is neither practicable nor desirable." Feb. 18, 1861, in Rowland, ed., *Jefferson Davis* V, 51, 52.

40. Lincoln, *Works* IV, 150, 155, 164. *New York Times*, Nov. 12, 1860. Randall, *Lincoln the President* I, 267–68. Potter, *Lincoln and His Party*, 147, 148–50.

the treasury under Franklin Pierce. Guthrie declined the offer, pleading his advanced age.[41] Lincoln approached one more Southern Democrat for a cabinet position. If such a man were to serve, Lincoln wanted an active, respected public man—one who enjoyed "a living position" in the South.[42] Such a man was John A. Gilmer, a conservative North Carolina congressman. Gilmer had written Lincoln inquiring of his position on certain matters regarding slavery and patronage. Lincoln answered at some length, replying to most of Gilmer's questions, referring him to his published speeches, and declaring "I have never been, am not now, and probably never shall be, in a mood of harassing the people, either North or South."[43] Lincoln followed up this message with another letter and a telegram urging Gilmer to come to Springfield to talk about a cabinet post. Gilmer hesitated, promised to consider the offer, and finally declined to make the trip.[44] The South brushed away the proffered hand, and the idea of adopting a conservative Southerner into Lincoln's official family was abandoned.

Of all Southern men with "living positions" perhaps Alexander Hamilton Stephens knew best that Lincoln was neither a rabid abolitionist nor the tool of a wicked party. Stephens, soon to be elected vice president of the Confederacy, knew Lincoln in 1848 and 1849 during Lincoln's single term in the House of Representatives. The two men had labored together for Whig causes and had earned each other's respect and affection.

"I knew Mr. Lincoln, thought well of him personally, believed him to be a kind-hearted man . . . ," wrote Stephens, imprisoned in Boston's Fort Warren, in his diary after the war.[45] As congressmen both men opposed the Mexican War as unjustly forced upon the Mexicans by

41. Guthrie was sixty-nine, but he outlived Lincoln and after the war served as U. S. senator from Kentucky (1865–1868). *Dictionary of American Biography* VIII, 60–62. Herndon, *Herndon's Life of Lincoln*, 386. Potter, *Lincoln and His Party*, 150–51. Guthrie had been a minor contender for the Democratic presidential nomination; he had been a distant second to Douglas on most of the fifty-seven futile ballots at Charleston. Hesseltine, ed., *Three Against Lincoln*, 99–103.

42. Lincoln to Seward, Jan. 12, 1861, in Lincoln, *Works* IV, 173.

43. Dec. 15, 1860, in *ibid.*, 151–53.

44. Lincoln to Seward, Dec. 29, 1860, Jan. 3 and Jan. 12, 1861, in *ibid.*, 164, 170, 173. Gilmer later served in the Confederate Congress.

45. Myrta L. Avery, ed., *Recollections of Alexander H. Stephens: His Diary Kept When a Prisoner at Fort Warren, Boston Harbour, 1865* (New York, 1910), 276.

President Polk, although Lincoln, before taking his seat, had spoken at a Springfield war rally for vigorous action against the enemy.[46] It was a speech by Stephens against Polk which moved Lincoln to write his friend and law partner, Herndon: "I just take up my pen to say, that Mr. Stephens of Georgia, a little, slim, pale-faced, consumptive man, with a voice like Logan's has just concluded the very best speech, of an hours length, I ever heard. My old, withered, dry eyes, are full of tears yet."[47]

The two had their differences. Lincoln supported the Wilmot Proviso, which sought to bar slavery from the territories acquired from Mexico, while the Georgian believed the Constitution guaranteed the right of a man to carry his property—slave or not—throughout the Union. Lincoln supported a bill to abolish the slave trade in the District of Columbia and wished to offer a resolution for gradual, compensated emancipation there, with the consent of the inhabitants; Stephens, of course, opposed even these mild steps toward abolition.[48] But these policy differences did not stop Stephens and Lincoln from cooperating on matters of mutual interest. Stephens was instrumental in organizing an informal group of congressmen to boost Zachary Taylor for President. Lincoln counted himself among these "Young Indians"; when he realized his idol Henry Clay could not be elected, Lincoln stumped hard for Taylor—Southerner, slaveholder, and hero of the war which he opposed at the cost of his political popularity in Illinois.[49]

In later years Stephens would look back upon the intimate relations he remembered enjoying with Lincoln in Congress.[50] But it is difficult to estimate the depth of the friendship of these two Whig politicians. Lincoln suffered the usual anonymity of a first-term congressman—the more so because his colleagues knew that he was a lame-duck from the moment he was sworn in, the custom being among the Whigs of Illinois to rotate

46. Benjamin Thomas, *Abraham Lincoln, a Biography* (New York, 1952), 108.

47. Feb. 2, 1848, in Lincoln, *Works* I, 448. The Logan to whom Lincoln refers is Stephen T. Logan, his former law partner, who succeeded Lincoln as Whig candidate for Congress in 1848 and failed of election. Stephens' speech is in *Congressional Globe*, 30th Cong., 1st sess., Appendix, 159–63.

48. Thomas, *Lincoln*, 126–27, 163.

49. Avery, ed., *Recollections of Alexander Stephens*, 21. Thomas, *Lincoln*, 122–23.

50. Richard Malcolm Johnston and William Hand Browne, *Life of Alexander H. Stephens* (Philadelphia, 1884), 624.

congressional nominations.[51] Benjamin Thomas, Lincoln's biographer, noted that although Lincoln was diligent in his work and was popular with his fellow congressmen, "his colleagues generally appraised him as a droll Westerner of average talents."[52] Stephens probably shared this opinion. He spoke well of Lincoln as a person when Lincoln was a candidate for President, but probably he had taken little notice of his former colleague until Lincoln was thrust into the national limelight.[53] The two never corresponded until after Lincoln's election, and then but briefly.[54] Lincoln's respect for Stephens' eloquence is obvious in his Herndon letter, but he was not above invoking the name of his supposed friend for partisan political purposes. In an 1859 speech in Columbus, Ohio, in which Lincoln argued that the recognition of the right of slavery would lead inevitably to reopening the slave trade, Lincoln said: "They will be ready for Jeff Davis and Stephens and other leaders of that company, to sound the bugle for the revival of the slave trade, for the second Dred Scott decision, for the flood of slavery to be poured over the Free States, while we shall be here tied down and helpless and run over like sheep."[55]

It is improbable that an intimate friendship existed between these two who were destined to become mighty adversaries. They had a certain amount in common besides their political affinity. Both were lawyers and came from humble backgrounds. Perhaps the tall, gaunt Lincoln and the diminutive, sickly Stephens felt a spiritual kinship in their common melancholia. More likely there was between the two in Congress a cordial working agreement and some mutual respect, a routine political acquaintance which, had not the two men been elevated to leadership in their respective countries, probably would have been lost. As it was, Stephens provided Lincoln with a channel to Southern

51. Thomas, *Lincoln*, 123.

52. *Ibid.*, 121.

53. Stephens did take a lively interest in the Illinois Senate race of 1858. He spent part of that summer in Chicago on private business and, although he did not stump for his friend Douglas, he seldom failed to express his political opinions when asked. Johnston and Browne, *Life of Stephens*, 337–38.

54. An alleged exchange of letters between Stephens and Lincoln in Jan., 1860, was published in 1909. It has since been judged a forgery. See Worthington C. Ford, "Forged Lincoln Letters," *Massachusetts Historical Society Proceedings*, 61 (1928). Lincoln, *Works* VIII, 460.

55. Sept. 16, 1859, in Lincoln, *Works* III, 423.

thinking in 1848 and again in 1860. There were few such channels between the new President and the South.

Stephens was a strong Union man, so long as the Union held true to the principles of state sovereignty which, he believed, made the government "the best in the world."[56] But should the Union fail these principles, secession was the legitimate and necessary course for the South. "Whenever this Government is brought in hostile array against me and mine, I am for disunion—openly, boldly and fearlessly, for *revolution*," he asserted in 1850, adding, "I am for conciliation if it can be accomplished upon any reasonable and just principle."[57]

In the crisis of 1860 Stephens, quietly practicing law in Crawfordville, Georgia, spoke for many Southern conservatives who did not see in Lincoln's nomination an immediate threat to Southern institutions. He would not advocate secession in the mere event of Lincoln's election, he told a correspondent:

> In point of merit as a man I have no doubt that Lincoln is just as good, safe and sound a man as Mr. Buchanan, and would administer the Government so far as he is individually concerned just as safely for the South and as honestly and faithfully *in every particular*. I know the man well. He is not a bad man. He will make as good a President as Fillmore did and better too in my opinion. He has a great deal more practical common sense. Still his party may do mischief.[58]

A Douglas man, Stephens was bitter toward those fire-eaters who engineered the split in the Democratic party; if Lincoln wins, he wrote, it will be the result "of the folly and madness of our people."[59] Although ill and weak, he stumped his state for Douglas.[60] For a time he entertained the hope that no candidate would receive a majority and the election would be thrown into the House of Representatives, where Douglas might emerge victorious.[61] But after Republican victories in

56. Stephens to J. Henly Smith, July 10, 1860, in Phillips, ed., *Toombs-Stephens-Howell Correspondence*, 487.

57. *Congressional Globe*, 31st Cong., 1st sess., Appendix, 1083.

58. Stephens to J. Henly Smith, July 10, 1860, in Phillips, ed., *Toombs-Stephens-Cobb Correspondence*, 487.

59. *Ibid.*

60. Rudolph von Abele, *Alexander H. Stephens: A Biography* (New York, 1946), 185.

61. Stephens to J. Henly Smith, Sept. 12, 1860, in Phillips, ed., *Toombs-Stephens-Cobb Correspondence*, 496.

the Northern state elections in October, even this slender hope was gone. Stephens feared the results of a Republican triumph not for what Lincoln would do, but for how the South would react. "Should Mr. Breckinridge get the entire South and Lincoln the entire North no earthly power could prevent civil war," he wrote in despair. "I do not know that it can be anyhow should Lincoln be elected."[62]

Lincoln's election and the impending withdrawal of South Carolina pushed Georgia closer to secession. Stephens aroused his frail body for one last effort to save the state he loved for the Union he cherished. On November 14, 1860, before the Georgia legislature and in reply to Robert Toombs' plea for secession, Stephens rose to address "the good sense" and "good judgment" of the assembled lawmakers:

> Shall the people of the South secede from the Union in consequence of the election of Mr. Lincoln to the Presidency of the United States? My countrymen, I tell you frankly, candidly, and earnestly, that I do not think that they ought. In my judgment, the election of no man, constitutionally chosen to that high office, is sufficient cause for any State to separate from the Union.

What about the Black Republican Lincoln, one, as Stephens admits, "whose opinions and avowed principles are in antagonism to our interests and rights, and we believe, if carried out, would subvert the Constitution under which we now live"? Stephens urged that the South accept Lincoln but not his principles and programs. Whatever his intentions Lincoln has little power to injure the South, for he is bound by constitutional checks and a conservative Congress. "Why," asked Stephens, "should we disrupt the ties of this Union when his hands are tied—when he can do nothing against us?" Should "the fanatics of the North" attempt to carry out their program, then it will be time for the South to take counsel together and act. If the Republicans force the issue, concluded Stephens, "no man in Georgia will be more willing or ready than myself to defend our rights, interests, and honor at every hazard and to the last extremity."[63]

When Stephens finished, his political opponent and personal friend Toombs, who shared the platform with him, sprang to his feet and called

62. Stephens to J. Henly Smith, Oct. 13, 1860, in *ibid.*, 501.

63. Henry Cleveland, *Alexander H. Stephens, In Public and Private, With Letters and Speeches, Before, During, and Since the War* (Philadelphia, 1866), 694–713.

for three cheers from the assemblage for "one of the brightest intellects and purest patriots that now lives."[64]

Stephens' union speech was widely reported in the Northern press and caught the attention of the President-elect in Springfield. Amidst the assassination threats and vituperations reported from Dixie, it no doubt was comforting to hear a note of moderation from the lips of a prominent Southerner. Besides, Stephens may have been on Lincoln's mind, as his name had been suggested for inclusion in the cabinet.[65] Lincoln wrote his old political colleague for a revised copy of the speech. Stephens replied that the newspaper account was pretty much as he had given it; he had made no revisions. He warned Lincoln of the great peril the country was in and reminded him of the heavy responsibility he bore in the crisis.

In a private letter marked "For your eye only," Lincoln replied that he fully appreciated the present perils of the country and the weight of responsibility upon him. He then asked Stephens, with an innocence that suggests an unsophisticated appreciation of Southern views:

> Do the people of the South really entertain fears that a Republican administration would, *directly* or *indirectly*, interfere with their slaves, or with them, about their slaves? If they do, I wish to assure you, as once a friend, and still, I hope, not an enemy, that there is no cause for such fears.
>
> The South would be in no more danger in this respect than it was in the days of Washington. I suppose, however, this does not meet the case. You think slavery is *right* and ought to be extended, while we think it is *wrong* and ought to be restricted. That I suppose is the rub. It is certainly the only substantial difference between us.

Stephens, in reply, tried to educate Lincoln as to Southern fears. The South does not expect direct or immediate interference with the slaves;

64. Johnston and Browne, *Life of Stephens*, 367n.

65. John D. Defrees, chairman of the Indiana State Republican Committee, wrote Lincoln on Dec. 15, 1860, that a number of Republicans would accept Stephens as, of all things, secretary of the navy. Lincoln replied three days later: "Would Scott or Stephens go into the cabinet? And if yea, on what terms? Do they come to me? or I go to them? or are we to lead off in open hostility to each other?" Lincoln, *Works* IV, 155. Lincoln's reply suggests sarcasm; in any event, he never offered Stephens a cabinet portfolio. A. H. Stephens, *A Constitutional View of the Late War Between the States* (Philadelphia, 1868, 1870), II, 265. Note that this exchange between Lincoln and Defrees occurred at the same time Lincoln and Stephens were corresponding.

it does object to antislavery being made a party principle, the object being "to put the Institutions of nearly half the States under the ban of public opinion and national condemnation." This alone was enough to rouse a spirit of revolt. Such a party could arise only from fanaticism, asserted Stephens, "and when men come under the influence of fanaticism, there is no telling where their impulses or passions may drive them. This is what creates our discontent and apprehensions." Personal liberty laws and public approval of the John Brown raid suggest how far the disease of fanaticism has spread in the North. Speaking to Lincoln as "not a personal enemy, but as one who would have you to do what you can to save our common country," Stephens advised that "a word 'fitly spoken' by you now, would indeed be 'like apples of gold, in pictures of silver.' " Finally, Stephens intimated that the South would resist federal attempts to coerce South Carolina back into the Union. In a Union of consenting sovereign states, "conciliation and harmony . . . can never be established by force." "Under our system, as I view it, there is no rightful power in the General Government to coerce a State, in case one of them should throw herself upon her reserved rights, and resume the full exercise of her Sovereign Powers."[66]

Lincoln did not answer, and this delicate link between Northern and Southern opinion was severed. Events were moving too swiftly for a rational exchange of views. On December 16, 1860, Georgia seceded from the Union. Alexander Stephens, true to his principles, went with his state.

Lincoln left Springfield by rail on February 11, 1861—the day before his fifty-second birthday—for the long trip to Washington and his inauguration. His route had been planned carefully and announced in advance so that as many citizens as possible might get a glimpse of their President-elect. Lincoln apparently contemplated traveling a southerly route via Cincinnati, Wheeling, and Baltimore, to assure personally the border states of his peaceful intentions and to demonstrate he had no fears for his safety from his Southern brethren.[67] But political considerations weighed heavily for a northern circuit—the states of Indiana, Ohio, Pennsylvania, and New York delivered big majorities for the Repub-

66. Lincoln's letters to Stephens, Nov. 30 and Dec. 22, 1860, are in Lincoln, *Works* IV, 146, 160. Stephens' letters to Lincoln are in Stephens, *Constitutional View* II, 266–70.

67. Villard, *Lincoln on the Eve of '61*, 49.

licans and deserved to see the man whom their votes were putting into the presidential chair. Even so, Lincoln planned a side trip into his birth state of Kentucky from Cincinnati, the nearest point on his scheduled itinerary, and he prepared remarks for the occasion.[68]

Lincoln spoke frequently on his eleven-day journey, from major addresses before state legislatures to brief, impromptu remarks in country villages delivered from his railway carriage.[69] In the seceded states and in those slave states still loyal to the Union, Southern men sought to hear in Lincoln's words the promise of peace or the drum taps of war. Hitherto silent, save for the Trumbull speech, Lincoln was pretty much of an unknown quantity, and the South, with the rest of the nation, held its breath, waiting to hear what course he would take. Although Lincoln occasionally touched eloquence, as in his address in Independence Hall, Philadelphia, his remarks were generally uninspired and did not suggest that the President-elect had a clear vision of the desperate situation of the nation. With due allowance for the terrible fatigue of the journey, the brutal speaking schedule—at least seventy speeches have been recorded—and his understandable reluctance to announce his commitment to policies before he assayed events from the perspective of Washington, Lincoln did little to reassure his anxious countrymen of the safety of the republic.[70]

Most Southern observers were alarmed at Lincoln's words and conduct, and the more extreme Southrons found their worst fears confirmed. The President-elect, trying to enhearten his troubled listeners, frequently alluded to his brief tenure of office and to his slight capacity to do evil; in Cincinnati, he told the South, "We mean to leave you alone, and in no way to interfere with your institution; to abide by all and every compromise of the constitution. . . ."[71] Southern commentators generally chose to overlook these peaceful overtures, concentrating instead upon what they deemed foolish or malicious in Lincoln's remarks. "It is evident that

68. Lincoln, *Works* IV, 200–201.

69. The recorded speeches of Lincoln during this journey are in *ibid.*, 190–245.

70. Villard, who traveled with Lincoln from Springfield to New York, reported the growing weariness of the President-elect. By the time Lincoln reached New York, nine days out of Springfield, he was "so unwell and fatigued that he seemed to take very little interest in the political conversation." *Lincoln on the Eve of '61*, 91. For a more favorable estimate of Lincoln's conduct, see Victor Searcher, *Lincoln's Journey to Greatness* (New York, 1960).

71. Feb. 12, 1861, in Lincoln, *Works* IV, 199.

the South has been quite as much deceived in its estimate of Lincoln as the North and his own party have been," opined the *New Orleans Daily Delta*:

> His bearing in the debate with Douglas produced a general impression that he was a man of some ability, as a politician and a polemic. This estimate . . . was confirmed by his silence during the campaign. But he is no sooner compelled to break that silence, and to exhibit himself in public, than this delusion vanishes, and the Hoosier lawyer dwindles into far smaller proportions than his bitterest enemies have ever assigned to him. . . . [H]e never opens his mouth but he puts his foot into it. In supreme silliness—in profound ignorance of the institutions of the Republic of which he has been chosen chief—in dishonest and cowardly efforts to dodge responsibility and play a double part—in disgusting levity on the most serious subjects, the speeches of Lincoln, on his way to the capital, have no equals in the history of any people, civilized or semi-civilized.[72]

In Indianapolis, Lincoln hinted that his administration would collect the customs, hold the federal forts, and might insist on "retaking those forts which belong to it"; such action, in his opinion, would not constitute coercion or invasion of a state.[73] In these words, many in the South saw civil war—"Heaven alone can avert war," despaired the *Louisville Courier*—and the triumph of the radical wing of the Republican party within Lincoln's councils.[74] These fears were heightened with reports that Lincoln told a wildly cheering New Jersey legislature that "it might be necessary to put the foot down firmly."[75]

Other remarks by Lincoln were singled out for attention by Southern critics. When Lincoln suggested that a state had no more "original right" to break up the Union than did a county, he was accused of overthrowing the doctrine of state sovereignty, demonstrating ignorance of the founding ideals of the Republic, and propagating an absolutist central government to be headed by a king or dictator.[76] Lincoln frequently assured his

72. Feb. 26, 1861, in Dumond, ed., *Southern Editorials on Secession*, 470.

73. Feb. 11, 1861, in Lincoln, *Works* IV, 195.

74. *Louisville Courier*, Feb. 13, 1861; St Louis *Daily Missouri Republican*, Feb. 15, 1861; *New Orleans Bee*, Feb. 20, 1861. All quoted in Dumond, ed., *Southern Editorials on Secession*, 453, 460, 464.

75. Feb. 21, 1861, in Lincoln, *Works* IV, 237.

76. *Louisville Courier*, Feb. 13, 1861, and *New Orleans Crescent*, Feb. 21, 1861, in Dumond, ed., *Southern Editorials on Secession*, 454, 466. Rowland, ed., *Jefferson Davis* V, 70.

audiences that the secession emergency was an "artificial crisis," one that will resolve itself if left alone (he continued this theme even after Jefferson Davis was sworn in as provisional Confederate president on February 18); he told the Ohio legislature that, in spite of public anxiety, "there is nothing going wrong"—"there is nothing that really hurts anybody"—"nobody is suffering anything"—and "all we want is time, patience and a reliance on that God who has never forsaken this people."[77] These remarks, thought incredulous Southerners, betrayed a profound ignorance of the wretched state of the country. How can Lincoln voice such halcyon sentiments, asked one amazed border state newspaper, with the Union sundered, federal treasury bankrupt, and economic depression abroad in the land? "Politically and socially, did the United States ever present such an aspect of complete wreck and abandonment, and yet Mr. Lincoln tells us 'nobody is hurt' and 'nobody is suffering'!"[78]

Few details of Lincoln's journey escaped hostile Southern pens. Condemned as vulgar buffoonery was Lincoln's habit of exchanging quips with his audiences and his kissing the little New York girl who solemnly had advised him by letter to grow whiskers ("your face is so thin"). Those who professed to love the Union but who would deny the federal government the right to assert its authority, Lincoln had characterized as viewing the Union "as a family relation, . . . not . . . like a regular marriage at all, but as a sort of free-love arrangement, to be maintained on what that sect calls passionate attraction."[79] This mildly risqué simile offended sensitive Southern Victorians, who were given to idealizing their (white) women and who no doubt recalled Lincoln as the champion of the "free love" party. "Who would have supposed," huffed the *New Orleans Crescent*, "that a man elevated to the Presidency of a nation would indulge in comparisons of this sort? Imagine George Washington or James Madison, on their way to the capital, making public speeches, destined to be read by the whole world, in which illustrations were drawn from such sources as these!"[80]

77. Lincoln, *Works* IV, 204, 211, 215–16, 238.

78. St. Louis *Daily Missouri Republican*, Feb. 15, 1861, in Dumond, ed., *Southern Editorials on Secession*, 460–61. See also verse in Frank Moore, ed., *Rebel Rhymes and Rhapsodies* (New York, 1864), 44–45.

79. Lincoln, *Works* IV, 195.

80. Feb. 21, 1861, in Dumond, ed., *Southern Editorials on Secession*, 466.

Upon hearing of an alleged assassination plot in rebel-sympathizing Baltimore, Lincoln was persuaded to alter his schedule and pass through the hostile city in the dead of night. His train reached Washington without incident the next morning. An imaginative *New York Times* reporter wrote that Lincoln had been disguised in a "Scotch plaid cap and a very long military cloak."[81] This erroneous account, widely published in the South and across the country, added another element to the Southern image of Lincoln—the Black Republican was a coward as well as a fool. The Scotch cap and cloak became a familiar feature of the Lincoln caricatured in Confederate cartoon and verse.

Not long after Lincoln arrived in Washington, a Tennessee newspaper began a series of articles purporting to tell the real story of the President-elect's journey through Baltimore to the capital. The articles came from the pen of George Washington Harris, a Knoxville humorist, entrepreneur, and minor Democratic politician. Harris' protagonist in the stories is Sut Lovingood, an archetypal illiterate Tennessee cracker, who describes his fictional adventures escorting Lincoln through the dangers of Baltimore to the safety of Washington.

Harris, who created Sut Lovingood as a medium through which he might express his own social and political views, was born in Pennsylvania of Southern parents and settled in Knoxville as a boy.[82] His life was a failure by most standards: at various times he captained a steamboat (in which capacity he assisted in removing Cherokee Indians from their ancestral lands), jockeyed quarter horses, farmed, operated a metal-working shop, surveyed copper mines, helped organize a sawmill, was connected in some way with a glass works, and was a conductor and freight agent on the Louisville & Nashville Railroad.

Sut's creator was a staunch Democrat of some reputation in Tennessee. He wrote political propaganda, and his name turns up in a number of minor civic and party posts: member of this or that committee, delegate to a Southern commercial convention, alderman and, briefly, post-

81. Feb. 21, 1861, quoted by Robert S. Harper, *Lincoln and the Press* (New York, 1951), 89.

82. Biographical details on Harris have been drawn from Milton Rickels, *George Washington Harris* (New York, 1965), and Donald Day, "The Life of George Washington Harris," *Tennessee Historical Quarterly*, 6 (March, 1947), 3–38.

master of Knoxville. As a leading secessionist in strongly unionist East Tennessee, he found it prudent to remove himself and his family from Knoxville, probably soon after Lincoln's election.

Harris and his family maintained a shabby gentility, owning slaves, books, and property, despite his financial uncertainty. But he lost his farm in payment of debts and never realized his ambition of becoming a landed gentleman. A note of frustration runs through his life and, according to one critic, through his works, which feature a frustrated Sut indulging himself in malevolent and cruel fantasies.[83]

Harris published his first writings—a series of political articles—in a Knoxville newspaper in 1839. Under several pseudonyms he later wrote a number of stories on rural Tennessee life for a New York sporting magazine. Sut Lovingood made his appearance in 1854, and Sut pieces were printed from time to time, with the exception of the war years, until Harris' death in 1869. Harris based his creation on a real local character named Sut Miller. The fictional Sut was a coarse mountaineer, equally fast with a bottle or a devastating quip, whose rough, cruel wit assailed the gentry, frontier preachers, and Yankees. Sut is a rather disagreeable character—Edmund Wilson called him a "peasant squatting in his own filth"—whose species of fun seems often merely brutal and sadistic.[84] But he represents a certain Southern type, and Harris, whose politics ran along the lines of the Southern poor white, used Sut to amplify his own opinions.

Lincoln was Sut's target in three stories printed February 28, March 2 and 5, 1861, in the *Nashville Union & American*, a secessionist newspaper which had called Lincoln a "half-witted village politician."[85] In "Sut Lovingood travels with Old Abe as his confidential friend and adviser," Sut overhears the plot of the Baltimore secessionists to murder

83. Edmund Wilson, *Patriotic Gore: Studies in the Literature of the American Civil War* (New York, 1962), 516.

84. *Ibid.*, 510. Wilson finds Sut a brutal, sordid lout with few redeeming virtues. Harris' 1867 edition of Sut Lovingood, Wilson deems "by far the most repellent book of any real literary merit in American literature." *Ibid.*, 509.

85. Rickels, *Harris*, 60. The three Lincoln stories were omitted from the 1867 edition of *Sut Lovingood*, Harris' only book. They were published in *Sut Lovingood Travels with Ole Abe Lincoln*, ed. Edd Winfield Parks (Chicago, 1937); in *High Times and Hard Times: Sketches and Tales by George Washington Harris*, ed. M. Thomas Inge (Nashville, Tenn., 1967); and, with Sut's frontier dialect considerably altered, in *Sut Lovingood*, ed. Brom Weber (New York, 1954). I have quoted from the Parks edition below.

Lincoln as he passes through the city. Sut journeys to Harrisburg, Pennsylvania, to warn Lincoln and offer his services in helping Lincoln through the dangers ahead. Lincoln hears and agrees, and the two retire to bed, drunk. Sut—who calls Lincoln "ole Windin Blades," perhaps because his long arms and legs suggest long blades used in winding yarn—then offers a vivid physical description of Lincoln:

> if he aint a long wun an a narrow wun, I'm durned. His mouf, his paw, an his footsez am the principil feeters, an his strikin pint is the way them ar laigs ove lizen gets inter his body. They goes in at each aidge sorter like the prongs goes intu a pitch fork. Ove all the durned skeery lookin ole cusses fur a president ever I seed, he am decidely the durndest. He looks like a yaller ladder with half the rungs knocked out.
>
> I kotch a ole bull frog once a druv a nail thru his lips inter a post, tied two rocks tu his hine toes an stuck a darnin needil inter his tail tu let out the misture, an lef him there tu dry. I seed him two weeks arter wurds, an when I seed ole Abe I thot hit were an orful retribution cum ontu me, an that hit were the same frog, only stretched a little longer, an had tuck tu waring ove close tu keep me from knowin him, an ketchin him an nailin him up agin; an natral born durn'd fool es I is, I swar I seed the same watry skeery look in the eyes, an the same sorter knots on the "back-bone." I'm feard, George, sumthin's tu cum ove my nailin up that ar frog. I swar I am, ever since I seed ole Abe, same shape same color same feel (cold as ice) an I'm d—— ef hit aint the same smell.

In the second installment, "Sut Lovingood with Old Abe on his journey," Harris concentrates on making Lincoln play the fool. Sut's favorite way of emphasizing the foolishness of his antagonists was to compare them with himself, "a natral born durn'd fool." Winfield Scott and Horace Greeley suffer by comparison, and so does Lincoln. When Lincoln, well attended by fleas, announces that he has heard that Alexander Stephens is waiting for him in Baltimore with a twelve-pounder loaded with round shot strapped to his back, Sut exclaims:

> I felt that I wer a standin fur the fust time afore a man I warnt feared ove, an tu, I knowed wer scaser ove sence then I wer, an I wer glad I had found him, fur you know, George, that I thot I wer the king fool ove the world, and aller felt ashamed an onder cow about hit. *Aleck Stephens totin a twelve pounder*. I stood stonished, fust et him an then et old Scott, two bigger fools in the world than me, and boff ov em able tu read an rite an a holdin high places in the naseun. Sut's got a chance yet, thinks I.

Sut then tells Lincoln of the "fool-killers," elected county officials in the South whose duty is to kill off fools wherever found. He implies that Lincoln had better not come South, else he will run afoul of these public-spirited officials.

Sut's caricature of Lincoln reaches the height of grotesqueness in the final chapter, "Sut Lovingood lands Old Abe safe at last." Sut disguises Lincoln as an idiot giant, padding his costume with whisky bottles and hay bales and painting Abe's face red, until "when I wer dun with him he looked like he'd been on a big drunk fur three weeks." Sut tells a curious railway agent that his giant companion is stupid; Lincoln takes exception, but then relents, saying, "on thinkin over hit you wer right tu tell him that I warn't smart, ur I woudent be here in sich imedjut danger, just fir my party an a pack ove durned niggers." When Lincoln sees the hostile crowds in Baltimore he flees the train, is caught, and, unable to control his fear, fouls himself. A disgusted Sut observes: "now jist tu think ove this cross-barr'd gnat beastes bein ole Abe, President ove the United States ove North Ameriky. I swar, natral born durn'd fool es I no's I is, I felt shamed, an sorter humbled, an I sorter felt like cuttin ove his throat an a sellin the hay tu pay fur my shame, an drink all the whisky on his carcuss tu make miself feel good agin." The two escape Baltimore in a shower of rotten eggs.

Harris' burlesque of Lincoln—which one modern critic has compared in intent and execution to Charlie Chaplin's film *The Great Dictator*—is an attempt to reinforce certain impressions of Lincoln which already existed in the imagination of many Southerners.[86] Lincoln is represented as a pitiable fool, rather than as a formidable antagonist: drunk, afflicted with fleas, cowardly, a tool of his party, and pretty much regretting the whole business—altogether a rather disgusting and grotesque figure. Harris' was a savage caricature, but one which appealed to anti-Lincolnites on both sides of the Mason-Dixon line.

Sut Lovingood spoke for many in the South when he concluded that Lincoln, on the eve of his inauguration, was a complete fool and simpleton. Lincoln was dismissed as a mere "stump orator" whose vulgar petti-

86. Walter Blair, *Horse Sense in American Humor, From Benjamin Franklin to Ogden Nash* (Chicago, 1942), 51. For a study of the Lincoln pieces in the broader context of Harris' political satires, see Donald Day, "The Political Satires of George W. Harris," *Tennessee Historical Quarterly*, 4 (Dec., 1945), 320–28.

foggery aroused a "feeling of intense disgust"; the nation was "shamed and debased before the world by the ridiculous, vulgar and pusillanimous antics of the coarse and cowardly demagogue"; his words were "the ignorant conceits of a low Western politician, and the flimsy jests of a harlequin."[87] The *Montgomery Post* concluded Lincoln lacked even the most ordinary capacities. "We may readily anticipate," said the *Post*, voicing a commonly held opinion, "that such a man will be the pliant tool of ambitious demagogues, and that his administration will be used to subserve their wicked purposes."[88]

Southerners contrasted this prairie buffoon with Jefferson Davis, the veteran Mississippi statesman who had assumed leadership of Confederate affairs. Like Lincoln, Davis had taken a circuitous railway route from his home to his seat of government at Montgomery and had made numerous speeches to the thousands of his countrymen who had turned out to see him.[89] Davis' dignity and candor seemed a refreshing contrast to Lincoln's conduct. "Davis has immediate and urgent business in Montgomery," remarked the *Nashville Patriot*, "and he goes like an earnest man to attend to it. Lincoln is tedious—Davis as swift as steam."[90] "Ah, would that Jefferson Davis were our President," lamented a young North Carolina girl to her diary. "He is a man to whom a gentleman could look, without mortification, as chief of the Nation."[91]

Lincoln's inauguration as sixteenth President of the United States on March 4, 1861, climaxed his long journey to Washington. The capital city had always been a Southern town, but few Southerners came to see the Black Republican sworn in.[92] One who was there, seventeen-year-old Constance Cary, a Virginia girl who was to marry Jefferson Davis' secretary and become one of the South's leading novelists, years later recalled meeting Lincoln at a White House levee:

87. *New Orleans Daily Crescent*, Feb. 21, 1861, and *New Orleans Daily Delta*, Feb. 26, 1861, in Dumond, ed., *Southern Editorials on Secession*, 465, 469–70. E. A. Pollard, *Southern History of the War* (New York, 1866), I, 48. *Southern Literary Messenger*, 34 (June, 1862), 349.

88. Feb. 22, 1861, quoted in Catton, *Coming Fury*, 222.

89. E. Merton Coulter, *The Confederate States of America, 1861–1865* (Baton Rouge, La., 1950), 26.

90. Feb. 16, 1861, in Dumond, ed., *Southern Editorials on Secession*, 463.

91. Catherine Devereux Edmondston, *The Journal of Catherine Devereux Edmondston, 1860–1866*, ed. Margaret Mackey Jones (privately published, 1954), 23.

92. Randall, *Lincoln the President* I, 294.

> Budding secessionist although I was, I can distinctly remember that the power of Abraham Lincoln's personality then impressed itself upon me for a lifetime. Everything faded out of sight beside the apparition of the new President, towering at the entrance of the Blue Room. He held back the crowd a minute, while my hand had a curious feeling of being engulfed in his enormous palm, clad in an ill-fitting white kid glove. He said something kind to his youthful visitor, and over his rugged face played a summer lightening smile.[93]

Less sanguine was the dark presence of Senator Lewis T. Wigfall, duelist, dipsomaniac, and fire-eater extraordinary. The Texan had stayed on in Washington after his state seceded to take the measure of the new administration. He stationed himself beside a capitol doorway as a harbinger of war and contemptuously viewed the inauguration scene spread below.[94]

In his inaugural address the new President repeated his purpose not to interfere with slavery in the states, gave guarded acceptance to the enforcement of the fugitive slave law, and expressed "no objection" to the proposed constitutional amendment guaranteeing slavery in the states against federal interference. Although Lincoln maintained that duty demanded he "hold, occupy, and possess" federal property, collect duties, and deliver the mails ("unless repelled") in the seceded states, he eliminated from his final draft the overt intention to "reclaim the public property and places which have fallen." Nor would "obnoxious strangers" be forced upon the South as federal office-holders. But Lincoln denied that the South had real grievances; the sectional conflict, he held, grew out of honest differences in interpreting the Constitution. At the same time, he abjured the legality of secession, stating unequivocally that "the Union of these states is perpetual" and is older than the Constitution or the states themselves. "The central idea of secession, is the essence of anarchy."[95]

Southerners read their own hopes and fears for the Union into Lincoln's inaugural message. Conservatives, especially in the border states, found promise for peace and reunion; Confederates, and those longing to join them, scorned the address as foolish or menacing. William W.

93. Mrs. Burton Harrison, *Recollections Grave and Gay* (New York, 1911), 43.

94. Herndon, *Herndon's Life of Lincoln*, 401.

95. The text of the inaugural address, with first draft and corrections, is in Lincoln, *Works* IV, 249–71.

Holden's *North Carolina Standard*, fighting to keep its state in the Union and hoping for peaceful reconstruction, said that Lincoln held the same ground as Buchanan. "*It is not a war message*. . . . It is not unfriendly to the South. It deprecates war, and bloodshed, and it pleads for the Union."[96] The South's indefatigable diarist, Mary Boykin Chesnut, was less sure of Lincoln's intentions. "I read Lincoln's inaugural," she recorded the day after the event. "Comes he in Peace, or comes he in War?"[97] For the fiery Senator Wigfall, "Inaugural means war," a sentiment shared by many Southern newspapers and public men.[98] The daughter of a wealthy North Carolina planter, appalled to learn her father and sister approved of Lincoln's sentiments, confided to her diary, "Could I have believed that any Southern person could have liked Lincoln's message?"[99] It was too late for soft words to stay the flood-tide of events. The Union was sundered, and millions had cast their fortunes with the new Confederacy. "We are receiving Lincoln's inaugural by telegraph," wrote T. R. R. Cobb from Montgomery; "it will not affect one man here, it matters not what it contains."[100]

Neither offers of compromise nor recitation of conservative views by Lincoln during the campaign, after his election, or at his inauguration was likely to counter the rising secessionist sentiment in the South. Conservatives like Stephens and Prentice might believe that "a word 'fitly spoken' " by Lincoln would strengthen the anti-secessionist forces in the South, but the *Charleston Mercury* more nearly spoke the truth of the matter when it declared: "If Mr. Lincoln was to come out and declare that he held sacred every right of the South, with respect to African slavery, no one should believe him; and, if he was believed, his professions should not have the least influence on the course of the South."[101]

Lincoln had little power to influence events in the South because

96. March 9, 1861, in Dumond, ed., *Southern Editorials on Secession*, 476–79.

97. Mary Boykin Chesnut, *A Dairy from Dixie*, ed. Ben Ames Williams (Boston, 1949), 12.

98. *War of the Rebellion: A Compilation of the Official Records of the Union and Confederate Armies* (Washington, D.C., 1880–1901), Ser. I, Vol. I, 261. Dumond, ed., *Southern Editorials on Secession*, 474–75. Catton, *Coming Fury*, 268.

99. Edmondston, *Journal*, 23.

100. Quoted by Catton, *Coming Fury*, 268.

101. Oct. 13, 1860, quoted in Cole, "Lincoln's Election an Immediate Menace to Slavery in the States?" 744. Such sentiments did not prevent the *Mercury* from printing on Jan. 30, 1861, a forged Lincoln letter in which Lincoln is made to say that, had he the power, he would have dealt more mercifully with John Brown, and

most Southerners saw him not as a source of authority and influence but rather as a symbol of hostile forces immeasurably more powerful than the man himself. For years the South had watched with apprehension the growing strength of a sectional party opposed to its institutions. Now the Republicans, having gained ascendancy in the North and standing at the threshold of national power, placed at their head a silent and unknown candidate. Many Southerners assumed Lincoln was a mere cipher, a figurehead for Seward or William Lloyd Garrison or other evil spirits identified with Black Republicanism—a conviction strengthened by Lincoln's ambiguous conduct after the election.[102]

Many Southerners conceded Lincoln's excellent personal character, his intention not to interfere with slavery where it existed, and even his desire to conciliate the South. But these personal qualities and proposed policies were dismissed as of little moment. The great power of the North seemed set upon a course hostile to the South, regardless of the character or purposes of the new President.[103] Other critics believed Lincoln's professed good intentions a mask. The *New Orleans Crescent* was convinced that Lincoln's alleged conservatism was an abolitionist plot to disarm the South, the easier to carry out antislavery schemes; the *Crescent* reviewed Lincoln's record and was convinced it proved him "a thorough radical Abolitionist, without exception or qualification."[104] The *Southern Literary Messenger* saw an even greater and more subtle danger in Lincoln's conservatism. Declaring "unreservedly in favor of a Southern Confederacy," the journal granted that Lincoln would be just and fair in his dealings with the South, would repudiate much of his party's platform, and might even "make the best President we ever had. Precisely for this reason are we opposed to remaining in the Union during his

---

that he did not consider the Dred Scott decision binding upon the people of the North. Harper, *Lincoln and the Press*, 71–73.

102. Cole, "Lincoln's Election an Immediate Menace to Slavery in the States?" 749. *New Orleans Bee*, Jan. 15, 1861, in Dumond, ed., *Southern Editorials on Secession*, 393. *New Orleans Picayune*, Jan. 20, 1861, in *Extracts from the Editorial Columns of the New Orleans Picayune. Read and Circulate* (New York, 1861). William Henry Holcombe, "The Alternative: A Separate Nationality, or the Africanization of the South," *Southern Literary Messenger*, 32 (Feb., 1861).

103. Thomas, *Lincoln*, 228. *New York Times*, Dec. 15, 1861. *Springfield Republican*, Jan. 1, 1861. Dr. J. H. Thornwall, "The State of the Country," *DeBow's Review* OS 30 (April, 1861), 414.

104. Nov. 12, 1861, in Dumond, ed., *Southern Editorials on Secession*, 228–31.

administration. The danger to the South will be in exact proportion to his 'goodness.' " He "will mix so sweetly the poisons of Republican principles," seduce the South with cheap lands and federal bounties, and set slaveholder against nonslaveholder. To accept a friendly Lincoln administration would be tantamount to embracing the antislavery, antiplanter views of the apostate North Carolinian, Hinton Rowan Helper.[105]

It mattered little, then, whether Southerners considered Lincoln the real head of his party or the mere instrument of powers behind the scenes. If leader, his professed conservatism was suspect; if instrument, his conservative intentions might be genuine, but inconsequential. These attitudes toward Lincoln were grounded in the conviction that Lincoln's election meant little in itself but signaled the triumph in the North of attitudes unfriendly to the South and its institutions. Republican victory was a declaration by the North of its determination to impose its will upon the South; it was, wrote Confederate apologist T. W. MacMahon, "the consummation—the capital crime—and the final victory—of an historical and persistent conspiracy."[106] Lincoln, the man, "was nothing," explained Jefferson Davis the day after his state seceded, "save as he was the representative of opinions, of a policy, of purpose, of power, to inflict upon us those wrongs to which freemen never tamely submit."[107]

Men rarely undertake great deeds unless they are convinced they are acting in behalf of great causes. Southerners in 1861 did not advocate, or accept, the destruction of the Union of their fathers because of the mere election of an obnoxious individual as President. They believed, or were willing to be convinced, that Republican victory represented a fundamental reordering of the terms of Union by men determined to extend their new order into the South. Southerners saw themselves defending the principles of 1776; it was the North which had broken the pact of Union, which had, in fact, "seceded." Only separation and the establishment of a new confederacy rededicated to those principles could protect and preserve Southern institutions and the "Southern way of life" from Yankee civilization.

The secessionists in part correctly assessed the situation. The rise of the Republicans did represent historical forces fundamentally opposed

105. *Southern Literary Messenger*, 31 (Dec., 1860), 468–74.

106. *Cause and Contrast: An Essay on the American Crisis* (Richmond, Va., 1862), 120.

107. Jan. 10, 1860, in Rowland, ed., *Jefferson Davis* V, 31.

to a Southern civilization based upon agriculture, slavery, localism, and state sovereignty. For all of Lincoln's disposition to reassure the South, he and his party were pledged to the ultimate extinction of slavery. The necessity of slavery had become the point of departure of Southern thinking. Slavery had become "the foundation of all property in the South"; faith in the inequality of races was the "corner-stone" of Southern institutions.[108] Given the belief in the legality of secession as an alternative to accepting Republican rule, the secessionists merely acted with the logic of their principles in withdrawing from the Union to protect what they deemed the best interests of their state and section. Only a minority of Southerners in every slave state outside South Carolina favored immediate secession, yet millions of Southerners shared South Carolina's views to the extent that ten other states seceded rather than see her stand alone or suffer coercion. One cannot condemn the secessionists for moving boldly and decisively to protect themselves. The great tragedy—for which the nation paid a full price in blood—was the South's permitting slavery to become absolutely identified with its great interests. Southerners were quick to see great changes in the North; they were slow to realize that they could not immunize themselves against history.

The image of Lincoln in the secession crisis was formed from a mixed set of impressions. Unknown to the South before the campaign of 1860, he was considered a figurehead of his party. He was generally pictured as rude and awkward, vulgar in his humor, probably insensitive to the great issues of the day, and certainly not big enough for his great office—impressions shared by some Northerners. The South saw Lincoln as one might see an unpleasant neighbor, the better tolerated if a fence were thrown up between you—which is what the South tried to do. It was the coming of war that significantly altered the image of Lincoln in the South. In Southern eyes Lincoln never lost completely the cap and bells of the fool, but when hopes of peaceful separation vanished and the guns began to sound at Sumter, he also assumed the grim visage of the captain of the invading hosts and, ultimately, the destroyer of the Southern dream. The reflex hostility of the campaign deepened to the bitterness of a defeated and demoralized people. It was in the theater of war that Lincoln ascended to greatness in the North. But in the South his image changed from that of fool to monster.

108. *Charleston Mercury,* Oct. 11, 1860. Alexander Stephens, speech at Savannah, Ga., March 21, 1861, in Cleveland, *Alexander H. Stephens,* 717–29.

2. Lincoln and the South on the Eve of War

During the campaign of 1860, Southerners saw Lincoln as merely the symbol of the deeply rooted causes of Southern discontent. But in the opening months of 1861, the image of Lincoln in the South changed into something more personal and sinister. Peace or war hung in the balance. Would the North agree to a compromise that might retain the loyalty of the border slave states? Would the North attempt to coerce the seceded states back into the Union? The decisions, Southerners believed, lay with the Republican party and its leadership. The events of January to April, 1861, have an important place in this narrative, because Lincoln's conduct, or what Southerners believed that conduct to be, helped shape the image of Lincoln in the minds and hearts of thousands of Southern men.

Border statesmen in Congress took the lead in seeking avenues of compromise. Crises over slavery expansion thrice had been quieted by compromises hammered out in Congress. On December 18, 1860, John J. Crittenden, venerable senator from Kentucky who aspired to the mantle of Henry Clay, offered a series of proposed constitutional amendments to the Senate. Crittenden's proposals—an amalgam of Missouri Compromise ideas of 1820 and popular sovereignty principles of 1854—bespoke a long tradition of territorial concessions and sectional pledges of good conduct. The most important provisions of the Crittenden Compromise would guarantee that slavery would be recognized and protected from federal interference in territories "now held or hereafter acquired" south of 36°30′ (the old Missouri Compromise line); north of that line slavery would be prohibited. Any territory might become a state with or without slavery, as its constitution stipulated. Other provisions would prohibit or restrict congressional interference with the domestic slave trade and with slavery where it existed, would make the federal government liable for losses of slave property in violation of the fugitive slave clause of the Constitution, and would prohibit future constitutional changes from affecting these guarantees.[1]

Crittenden's proposals were referred to special committees in the two houses of Congress. The more distinguished was the Senate Committee of Thirteen, in which sat some of the nation's most eminent leaders, including Davis, Toombs, Douglas, Crittenden, and Seward. This august body was unable to agree on the key provision regarding slavery in the territories, and on New Year's Eve, it confessed to the Senate its failure to concur on a plan of compromise.[2]

The failure of the Senate Committee of Thirteen did not end efforts to find means of adjustment. Congress continued to debate and vote. In mid-January, the Virginia General Assembly called upon the states to send delegates to a peace convention "to adjust the present unhappy controversies." Commissioners from twenty-one states—the seven seceded states were among those not represented—assembled in Washington on February 4. Former President John Tyler was chosen to preside. Among the 132 delegates were six former cabinet members, fourteen former senators, and fifty former congressmen; only seven delegates were under forty years of age, and more than half were over fifty.[3] These distinguished elder statesmen, whom Horace Greeley unkindly called "political fossils," were of a border state cast of mind; they hoped to extract concessions from both Republicans and secessionists in order to save the Union which had given them honors and offices.[4] After three weeks of

1. *Congressional Globe*, 36th Cong., 2nd sess., 114. Jesse L. Keene, *The Peace Convention of 1861*, Confederate Centennial Studies, No. 18 (Tuscaloosa, Ala., 1961), Appendix A.

2. Randall, *Lincoln the President* I, 222–23.

3. Robert Gray Gunderson, *Old Gentlemen's Convention. The Washington Peace Conference of 1861* (Madison, Wis., 1961), 10.

4. *Ibid.*, 13–14.

sometimes bitter and impassioned debate, the Washington Peace Conference reported to Congress a proposed thirteenth amendment to the Constitution, which incorporated most of Crittenden's original proposals together with a guarantee that new territories open to slavery would be annexed only with consent of Northern senators.[5] But two days before Lincoln's inauguration, the Senate decisively rejected the compromise plan; the House did not deign even to consider it.

Probably a majority of Americans at the end of 1860 favored some kind of compromise to keep the Union together. If the November vote meant anything, it meant that most Americans rejected both the Republican platform and immediate secession in the event of Lincoln's victory.[6] If the Crittenden compromise proposals had been submitted to a national referendum, as some of its partisans wished, it might well have had a majority.[7] Why, then, did compromise fail?

No compromise would be acceptable to the South unless the Republicans abandoned their campaign pledge against slavery expansion in the territories. Willingness to accept and abide by an agreement whereby Southerners could take their slave property into at least some of the territories would be a test of faith to Southerners in measuring Republican sincerity. Lincoln sought to make his position clear. "On the territorial question, I am inflexible," he wrote John Gilmer of North Carolina. "You think slavery is right and ought to be extended; we think it is wrong and ought to be restricted."[8] As Congress debated compromise, Lincoln warned his followers to stand firm. "Let there be no compromise on the question of *extending* slavery," he instructed Senator Lyman Trumbull. "If there be, all our labor is lost, and, ere long, must be done again."[9] Lincoln was reported to have remarked that he would prefer death to buying or bargaining his way into the presidency after being constitutionally elected; such compromise, he felt, would put American

5. Keene, *Peace Convention of 1861*, Appendix C.
6. Potter, *Lincoln and His Party*, 189–95.
7. Rhodes, *History of the United States* III, 261.
8. Dec. 15, 1860, in Lincoln, *Works* IV, 152. Note that he repeated this analysis of the situation to Alexander Stephens and again in his inaugural address, adding that the question of slavery expansion was the only "substantial" difference between North and South and ought not to be the cause of war. *Ibid.*, 160, 258. One wonders if Lincoln ever fully appreciated the deeply rooted Southern fear of the Republican threat to the permanency of slavery. Agitation over slavery in the territories was but a symptom of this fear.
9. Dec. 10, 1860, in *ibid.*, 149.

politics on a level with Mexico's.[10] Moreover, to submit on the territorial issue would ruin the Republican party in the North and only postpone the inevitable confrontation with slavery. Lincoln feared that a settlement along the lines of the Crittenden Compromise would open the entire hemisphere south of 36°30′ to aggressive slavery expansion. Vast territories had been wrested from Mexico only twelve years before. Rumored conspiracies of the expansionist Knights of the Golden Circle and memories of the Ostend Manifesto, of William Walker and other filibusters were fresh in Northern minds. "A year will not pass," Lincoln wrote James T. Hale, "till we shall have to take Cuba as a condition upon which they [secessionists] will stay in the Union. . . . There is in my judgment, but one compromise which would really settle the slavery question, and that would be a prohibition against acquiring any more territory."[11]

On slavery expansion in the territory, then, Lincoln urged his followers to "hold firm, as with a chain of steel."[12] But he was willing to pledge his administration's good faith in enforcing the fugitive slave law. On December 20—the day South Carolina seceded—he drew up three suggested resolutions which he sent by Thurlow Weed to the Republican members of the Committee of Thirteen. These called for the preservation of the Union, stronger congressional legislation to enforce the fugitive slave clause of the Constitution, and repeal of any state laws which might conflict with a congressional fugitive slave law.[13] By February, he intimated to Seward that he was willing to go further in placating Southern fears: "As to fugitive slaves, District of Columbia, slave trade among the slave states, and whatever springs of necessity from the fact that the institution is among us, I care but little, so that what is done be comely,

10. *New York Herald*, Jan. 28, 1861, quoted in *ibid.*, 176.

11. Jan. 11, 1861, in *ibid.*, 172. That Lincoln's fears about aggressive slavery expansion were not misplaced may be suggested by the remarks of Senator Albert G. Brown, of Mississippi: "*I want Cuba*; I want Tamaulipas, Potosi, and one or two other Mexican states; and *I want them all for the same reason*: *for the planting and the spreading of slavery.* And a footing in Central America will powerfully aid us in acquiring those other States. Yes, *I want these countries for the spread of slavery.* I would spread the blessings of slavery, *like the religion of our Divine Master*, to the uttermost ends of the earth; and rebellious and wicked as the Yankees have been, *I would even extend* it to them." *Congressional Globe*, 36th Cong., 1st sess., Vol. I, 571.

12. Lincoln to Elihu Washburne, Dec. 13, 1860, in *Works* IV, 151.

13. *Ibid.*, 156–57.

and not altogether outrageous. Nor do I care about New-Mexico, if further extension were hedged against."[14] "New-Mexico" referred to that territory which now constitutes the states of New Mexico and Arizona. Lincoln was willing to take the very slight risk that slavery might establish itself in these existing United States territories south of 36° 30′. The proposal by the Washington Peace Conference that no new territory be acquired without consent of a majority of senators from nonslave states seemed to be a sufficient guarantee against further slavery expansion. In his inaugural address, Lincoln said he would not oppose a constitutional amendment prohibiting the federal government from interfering with slavery in the states; he was confident that slavery, if contained, would become unprofitable and wither away.

When the original Crittenden Compromise was under consideration in the Senate, Lincoln had opposed any concessions to slavery expansion. By the time he assumed office two months later, he had taken a position on compromise which was nearly identical to the proposals offered by the border statesmen of the Washington Peace Conference. The terrible dilemma of balancing the demands of Republican radicals with the necessity of holding the border states had driven Lincoln to accepting a qualified popular sovereignty program.

Historians disagree in weighing Lincoln's responsibility for defeating compromise attempts.[15] Compromise sentiment was rising in the North in December, 1860, but it is doubtful that a majority of Republicans were willing to abandon the territorial plank of the Chicago platform.[16] Moreover, it takes two to compromise, and whatever the position of Lincoln and his fellow Republicans, the states of the Deep South seemed little disposed to accept concessions. Secession sentiment, catalyzed by the action of South Carolina, prevailed in the Gulf states. South Carolina had seceded on the very day the Senate Committee of Thirteen was organized, and while that body deliberated, four more states elected secessionist-minded conventions. Although Davis and Toombs an-

14. Lincoln to Seward, Feb. 1, 1861. *Ibid.*, 183.

15. James Ford Rhodes, for example, thought Lincoln's views were decisive in persuading Republican senators on the Committee of Thirteen to defeat the Crittenden Compromise. Rhodes, *History of the United States* III, 164, 167. Potter suggests that a majority of Republican senators would have voted against the Crittenden proposals if Lincoln had remained silent. Potter, *Lincoln and His Party*, 176–86.

16. Kenneth M. Stampp, *And the War Came. The North and the Secession Crisis, 1860–1861* (Baton Rouge, La., 1950), 141.

nounced they would accept the Crittenden Compromise if the Republicans did, most of their Southern colleagues refused to follow their lead. On December 13, thirty Southern senators and congressmen declared there was no hope of compromise within the Union and that "the honor, safety, and independence of the Southern people are to be found in a Southern Confederacy."[17] Ten days later, Toombs called upon his fellow Georgians to vote unanimously for secession before Lincoln's inauguration.[18]

The compromisers of 1860–1861 were overwhelmed by events. By the time the Washington Peace Conference gathered, seven states were out of the Union and Southern statesmen were sitting down to write the constitution of the Confederate States of America. The day ex-President Tyler brought his peace convention to order, his granddaughter raised the stars and bars over the new Confederate capitol at Montgomery.[19] The Washington Peace Conference never had a chance to mend the Union; if the Crittenden proposals failed to deter states from secession in December and January, a slightly revised Crittenden plan could hardly succeed in bringing them back in February.

The border statesmen failed in the efforts to roll back secession and save the Union. Those who were Southerners and Democrats blamed Lincoln and the Republicans. Because Lincoln set his face against compromise on slavery in territories, they reasoned, there was no hope of persuading the North to agree to guarantees acceptable to the South. James Guthrie, the Kentucky unionist whom Lincoln had approached for his cabinet and who played a leading role in the Washington conference, summed up the sentiments of many border men when he wrote:

> Mr. Lincoln might have prevented all the States but South Carolina from going out by advising his friends in the Senate & the House to go for the Crittenden Constitutional Amendments and he might have saved the border states by saying to his friends in Congress & the Peace Convention to go for the Franklin and Guthrie Constitutional amendments. He might have done it by declaring for such in his inaugural.[20]

17. Nevins, *Emergence of Lincoln* II, 385, 387.
18. Phillips, ed., *Toombs-Stephens-Cobb Correspondence*, 525.
19. Gunderson, *Old Gentlemen's Convention*, 10.
20. Guthrie to Paul Washington, March 13, 1861, quoted in *ibid.*, 99–100. See also Rhodes, *History of the United States* III, 154–55.

In truth, neither a majority of Republicans nor a majority of secessionists were willing to accept compromise as an alternative to disunion. Republicans preferred to force the issue rather than destroy their party and abandon their idea of Union; the secessionists who controlled the Gulf states chose disunion rather than gamble on another round of Yankee promises of good behavior. The compromises offered by Crittenden and the men of the Washington Peace Conference had an old and honorable tradition dating back to 1820, but forty years later such proposals were too little and too late. The actual, rather than the threatened, secession of South Carolina made the traditional framework of compromise obsolete. Even if a compromise could have been forged which would keep the other states from withdrawing, Lincoln would have faced the problem of dealing with proud, contumacious South Carolina, out of the Union and determined not to return. Would he coerce her, or would he permit her to remain a symbol of successful defiance to federal authority—a symbol around which the Southern states could rally in some future crisis? Either way, the dilemmas facing both Lincoln and the South would have been basically the same whether one or seven states had seceded by the time he entered office.

Northern and Southern men sensed that immense issues touching the very foundation of the Union were at hand, issues of which the agitation over slavery in territories was only a symptom. That statesmen of good will could only offer up the old framework of compromise suggests the bankruptcy of moderate views in a period of revolution. Leafing through the futile debates of the compromises, one cannot escape a sense of almost inevitable tragedy in seeing these old men and old ideas overtaken by events and swept into the maelstrom of war.

"The Union is Dissolved!" This towering reality, as announced by the fiery *Charleston Mercury*, greeted Lincoln as he arrived in Washington on February 23. The seven seceded states had united into a new federation and declared their determination to maintain their independence. United States authority had been swept from the area of the Confederacy, save in four tiny offshore forts. The eight remaining slave states clung tenuously to the Union; any attempt to coerce their departed sisters might transform their conditional unionism into secession. Border statesmen, failing in their attempt to construct a grand compromise, implored the new administration to take all steps necessary to avoid war. They urged Lincoln to evacuate the forts, especially Fort Sumter, whose flag and garrison deeply offended the proud Charlestonians. Withdraw the troops and erase all pretext for an armed clash, they counseled; the border states would remain loyal, and the seceded states, realizing the futility of their isolated independence, would return to the Union. But, at the first cannon shot, these gentlemen warned, the border states would withdraw rather than acquiesce in the unconstitutional coercion of a state.

On the evening after Lincoln's clandestine arrival in Washington, a delegation from the peace conference called upon the President-elect in his suite at the Willard Hotel. Lincoln turned aside queries as to his course of action on Sumter. "My course is as plain as a turnpike road," he told William C. Rives, of Virginia. "It is marked out by the Constitution. I am in no doubt which way to go." When William E. Dodge, a New York business leader, melodramatically warned Lincoln that a wrong policy would bankrupt the Union and cause grass to grow in the streets of the cities, Lincoln retorted that he would enforce the Constitution and "let the grass grow where it may." Are not concessions necessary to avoid war, the President-elect was asked? "In a choice of evils, war may not always be the worse," Lincoln answered, adding that he would try to avert war if possible within his constitutional duties.

Lincoln's answers impressed his curious and skeptical Southern callers. Lucius Chittenden, a Vermont delegate present at the interview, remembered Rives as saying afterward that Lincoln had been misrepresented to the South, that he was neither fool nor an abolitionist creature. "He will be the head of his Administration, and will do his own thinking," Rives had concluded. Judge Thomas Ruffin, of North Carolina, respected Lincoln's constitutional position but wished Lincoln had been less determined against compromise.[21]

Actually, Lincoln had not decided yet upon a course regarding Sumter. He had talked bravely of holding the forts and of retaking them if Buchanan evacuated before the Republicans took power; in his inaugural address he said he would execute the laws and hold federal property.[22] It was all very well to stand upon the Constitution, but the trouble was that all parties stood upon the Constitution as they saw it. Here might be an excellent point of departure for a policy, but it did not trans-

21. Lucius E. Chittenden, *Recollections of President Lincoln and His Administration* (New York, 1891), 67–68.

22. Lincoln, *Works* IV, 159, 162, 265–66.

late into a specific plan for dealing with hard and immediate problems like that of Sumter.

In a subsequent conversation with border statesmen, Lincoln casually tossed out a proposition which suggests that the President-elect had not fully come to grips with the Sumter dilemma. A group including Rives and Charles S. Morehead, former governor of Kentucky, called upon Lincoln on February 27. Morehead began on familiar ground: withdraw the Sumter garrison, he urged, and assure the eight border slave states of their safety within the Union, and the seven seceded states would "by the mere force of gravitation, come back, and we should have a safer and firmer bond of union than ever." Lincoln replied that he would approve a constitutional amendment guaranteeing slavery in the states against federal interference but would not yield on the matter of slavery in the territories. Morehead pointed out that slavery could never establish itself in the hostile climate and soils of New Mexico or the territories north of it. Lincoln said that he feared the acquisition of new lands to the south favorable for slavery. At least, Morehead entreated, to avoid bloodshed Lincoln ought to make no effort to collect tariff duties off Southern ports or to retake the lost forts. Lincoln replied obliquely, saying that he was reminded of Aesop's fable about the lion who wished to enter polite society, but was refused because the others feared his claws and teeth. The lion had his claws cut and his teeth pulled and presented himself to society, whereupon he was attacked with clubs and killed. Morehead was not amused.

At this point Rives broke in and told Lincoln that, much as he loved the Union, he would urge Virginia to secede should the federal government attempt coercion. Lincoln reputedly offered a bargain: he would withdraw the Sumter garrison if Virginia would stay in the Union. "I took the occasion to write down the entire conversation soon after it occurred," Morehead recalled later. "The impression undoubtedly left upon my mind was, that the new administration would not resort to coercion." As Lincoln remembered the incident, "a state for a fort is no bad business." The border state men at this informal gathering were not authorized to make a deal, and the meeting broke up.[23]

23. Morehead to John J. Crittenden, Feb. 23, 1862, in Mrs. Chapman Coleman, *The Life of John J. Crittenden, with Selections from His Correspondence and Speeches* (Philadelphia, 1871), II, 337–38. Morehead expanded on the incident in a speech in Liverpool, England, Oct. 2, 1862, which is reproduced in David Rankin

The terrible urgency of the fate of Sumter was made clear to Lincoln the day after his inauguration, when he received intelligence that Major Robert Anderson's garrison had only limited provisions and must either be supplied or evacuated within a few weeks.[24] For the next month Lincoln wrestled with the problem of Sumter. The course of his thinking was marked by divided counsel within his cabinet and military advisers, growing intransigent opinion in the North, uncertainty of the reaction of the vital border states, Anderson's diminishing stores, and the ever-increasing Confederate strength ringing Charleston harbor.[25]

The Sumter problem was compounded when three commissioners

Barbee and Milledge L. Bonham, Jr., eds., "Fort Sumter Again," *Mississippi Valley Historical Review*, 28 (June, 1941), 63–78. Baringer says Lincoln offered to evacuate Sumter if the Virginia secession convention, then sitting in Richmond, would disband. William E. Baringer, *A House Dividing: Lincoln as President-Elect* (Springfield, Ill., 1945), 315–18. John Hay, Lincoln's secretary, recorded in his diary on Oct. 22, 1861, that Lincoln had mused over the incident that evening: "He promised to evacuate Sumter if they would break up their convention, without any row or nonsense. They demurred." Tyler Dennett, ed., *Lincoln and the Civil War in the Diaries and Letters of John Hay* (New York, 1939), 211. Morehead's account does not mention any specific reference to the Virginia convention. When Lincoln recounted the incident a few days later to Rudolf Schleiden, minister of the Republic of Bremen, he apparently said nothing about a desire to adjourn the convention. Ralph Harwell Lutz, "Rudolf Schleiden and the Visit to Richmond, April 25, 1861," *Annual Report of the American Historical Association for the Year 1915* (Washington, D.C., 1917), 211. Schleiden gave a dinner for Lincoln on March 1, 1861, where Lincoln told him of his meeting with the border statesmen. According to Lutz, Schleiden included an account of this incident in his dispatches to Bremen "to illustrate the President's humor even in the face of the disruption of the Union." What does this comment mean? Did Lincoln suggest to Schleiden that his offer to the border statesmen was made in jest? Morehead certainly did not think so. Did Schleiden misunderstand Lincoln? Did Lutz misunderstand Schleiden? Lutz plumbed the Bremen state archives for Schleiden's dispatches, but, sadly, he chose to reprint only excerpts taken out of context and without dates. Incidentally, James G. Randall misuses the Schleiden testimony. He strongly implies that Lincoln was referring to a conversation he had with John B. Baldwin, of Virginia, on April 4, wherein Lincoln did discuss the possibility of adjourning the Virginia secession convention. Randall says Schleiden's record "is both impartial and close to the event." Randall, *Lincoln the President* I, 326. Correct, but the event it describes occurred a month before the Baldwin interview.

24. Potter, *Lincoln and His Party*, 332–35. Lincoln to Winfield Scott, March 9, 1861, in Lincoln, *Works* IV, 279.

25. The whole of Lincoln's correspondence during this period is illuminating, but see especially cabinet memoranda of March 15, 1861, and memorandum of Fort Sumter, March 18 [?], 1861, in Lincoln, *Works* IV, 284–85, 288–90.

from Montgomery turned up in Washington determined to secure recognition for the Confederacy. Secretary of State Seward refused their request for an interview. On March 12, Commissioners John Forsyth and Martin J. Crawford, soon to be joined by A. B. Roman, addressed a note to Seward declaring the independence of the Confederacy, expressing their desire for "a speedy adjustment of all questions growing out of this political separation," and requesting that they present their credentials to the President.[26] It would have been impolitic for the secretary of state to communicate directly with these rebel commissioners, thereby tendering some degree of recognition to their mission and their government. Seward did consent, however, to exchange views with them through various third parties, the most important of whom was Justice John A. Campbell, an Alabamian who had opposed secession and who had not yet resigned his seat on the United States Supreme Court. The result of these informal exchanges, in which Seward promised the South that Sumter would be peacefully evacuated, was a conviction in the hearts of many Southerners that Lincoln and his government deliberately practiced deceit upon the South to mask their preparations for war—a conviction which persisted long after the guns were silenced at Appomattox.

In the latter half of March, when Justice Campbell was acting as intermediary between Seward and the Confederate commissioners, it was widely believed that Sumter soon would be abandoned. Newspapers announced that the cabinet had agreed to evacuate the garrison. Seward, whose opinions many believed were decisive in the administration, talked freely of his desire to give up Sumter to create a favorable climate for peaceful reunion. Lincoln's friend, Ward Hill Lamon, turned up in Charleston and assured both Governor Pickens and Major Anderson that the troops soon would be removed. Lincoln himself, by mid-March, may have agreed tentatively with General Scott and the cabinet that Sumter would have to be evacuated because of its military vulnerability, if at the same time Fort Pickens in Pensacola harbor could be reinforced as a sign of federal determination to hold its property where possible.[27]

With rumors of evacuation at every hand, Campbell saw no reason to doubt Seward's integrity or authority when the secretary of state told him that Major Anderson's men would be withdrawn in a few days and

26. Rowland, ed., *Jefferson Davis* V, 86–87.

27. Rhodes, *History of the United States* III, 332–34. Potter, *Lincoln and His Party*, 339–42, 359.

that no action was contemplated for reinforcing Pickens.[28] Campbell wanted to effect a detente between the embattled sections, and he asked Seward if he might inform the Confederate commissioners unofficially of the decision to evacuate. Seward agreed. Campbell told Martin Crawford on his own authority—although Crawford recognized his source of information—that Sumter would be abandoned in five days. The word was telegraphed to Montgomery. When several days passed without a sign of evacuation, Seward sought to reassure Campbell. A cabinet decision to withdraw had been made, he said; he did not know why Lincoln hesitated, "but there was nothing in the delay that affected the integrity of that promise or denoted any intention not to comply."

Campbell next visited Seward on March 30. Governor Pickens of South Carolina had informed the commissioners of Lamon's visit to Charleston and his promise to remove the garrison. What, Campbell asked, was causing the delay? Seward promised an answer the next day. On April 1, he told Campbell that the President was disturbed; Lamon had no authority to make such a promise. The President might desire to reinforce Sumter, Seward went on, but would not do so without first notifying Governor Pickens. Campbell immediately noticed Seward's shift of position. "Does the President design to attempt to supply Sumter?" he asked. Seward said he believed Lincoln would resist pressure to maintain the garrison. Crawford warned that Charleston's mind was closed and its temper quick; even the suggestion of a desire to relieve the fort might touch off a bombardment. At this point Seward excused himself to confer with Lincoln. Returning a few minutes later he wrote out a note for Campbell to give the commissioners: "I am satisfied the Government will not undertake to supply Fort Sumter without giving notice to Governor Pickens." Campbell later recalled, "It was understood between us that the import of the conversations previously had were not affected by what had taken place."

The stars and stripes still waved over Sumter, and rumors of supply expeditions and troop movements filled Washington in the first week of

28. Campbell's account of his conversations with Seward, together with documents, are in "Papers of Hon. John A. Campbell—1861–1865," *Southern Historical Society Papers*, NS, 4 (Oct., 1917), 30–43. Excerpts of the correspondence between the Confederate commissioners and their government are in John G. Nicolay and John Hay, *Abraham Lincoln: A History* (New York, 1890), III, 396–414. See also Rowland, ed., *Jefferson Davis* V, 85–99. Henry G. Connor, *John Archibald Campbell* (Boston, 1920), is a pious biography.

April. Crawford again asked Campbell to inquire into the situation. Campbell penned a note to Seward, informing him of the anxiety of the commissioners and suggesting that the status quo be maintained in "any existing garrison." Seward replied on April 8 with an unsigned assurance: "Faith as to Sumter fully kept. Wait & see." The Confederate commissioners construed this as meaning that Fort Pickens, not Sumter, was the object of a relief expedition.[29] The reinforcing of one fort was as obnoxious as of the other, and the commissioners demanded an answer to their formal note of March 12. Seward's answer was delivered immediately: the United States declined to recognize the "so-called Confederate States" as an independent power, and the secretary of state was without authority to recognize or correspond with its agents. The commissioners replied with an angry note declaring that history would absolve the Confederacy of guilt for the blood which would follow, and they left Washington.

Faith as to Sumter had been kept, at least within the spirit of Seward's note of April 1. In the closing days of March and the first week of April Lincoln moved toward a decision on the Sumter garrison. On March 29 he ordered the preparation of an expedition to Charleston "to be ultimately used, or not, according to circumstances."[30] It was this outfitting of ships and gathering of supplies and men in New York and Washington which alerted the Confederate commissioners.[31] Lincoln was determined to reinforce federal authority at either Fort Pickens or Fort Sumter. On March 11 he had ordered reinforcements to land at Pickens, and it wasn't until April 6 that he learned a confusion of orders had caused this plan to miscarry.[32] On that day Lincoln ordered the Sumter expedition forward. At the same time he dispatched a messenger to Governor Pickens, informing him that Sumter would be resupplied with provisions only; no troops or munitions would be thrown in without further notice.[33] Confederate authorities interpreted this move as an overt challenge. General P. G. T. Beauregard, commanding Confederate forces

29. Nicolay and Hay, *Lincoln* IV, 3.

30. Lincoln, speech to Congress on July 4, 1861, in Lincoln, *Works* IV, 425.

31. Lincoln to Gideon Welles and Simon Cameron, March 29, 1861, in *ibid.*, 301.

32. *Ibid.*, 424–25. Nicolay and Hay, *Lincoln* III, 393. *Official Records, Army*, Ser. I, Vol. 1, 260. *Official Records of the Union and Confederate Navies in the War of the Rebellion* (Washington, D. C., 1894–1922), Ser. I, Vol. 4, 109–10.

33. Lincoln to Robert S. Chew, April 6, 1861, in Lincoln, *Works* IV, 323–24.

surrounding Sumter, demanded the surrender of the garrison. Anderson's reply was considered unacceptable, and at 4:30 A.M. on April 12, civil war began.[34]

Anxious to avoid a shooting crisis which would prevent peaceful reunion, Seward far exceeded his authority and the limits of diplomatic prudence in assuring the Confederate commissioners that Sumter would be evacuated.[35] As secretary of state his words carried official weight, even in indirect and informal conversations. Campbell assumed Seward was the spokesman of Lincoln's policy. Actually, Seward proceeded on his own and without close consultation with his chief. As Lincoln debated the wisdom of evacuation, Seward announced it to Campbell as a decided policy; as Lincoln moved to assert control over his divided cabinet, Seward still acted as if he were prime minister. The matter came to a head on April 1, when Seward submitted his muddled memorandum, "Some thoughts for the President's consideration," wherein he proposed evacuating Sumter and holding the Gulf forts, provoking a war with European powers as a means of rallying national sentiment North and South, and suggested that he, Seward, should direct these policies.[36] Lincoln quickly let his secretary of state know who was boss, and in short order Seward saw his advice on foreign wars set aside, his ambitions to leadership frustrated, and his Sumter policy rejected. Seward's next conversation with Campbell, in which he hinted that Sumter might be resupplied but not without notifying Governor Pickens, reflected Lincoln's true thoughts on the problem.

The rupture of negotiations and the rush toward war bewildered and dismayed Justice Campbell, who had acted as an honest intermediary between Seward and the commissioners and who soon found himself under attack in the South as a Yankee agent.[37] After he learned of

34. Randall, *Lincoln the President* I, 339–42.

35. Glyndon G. Van Deusen, *William Henry Seward* (New York, 1967), 277–87. Rhodes, *History of the United States* III, 338–49. Potter, *Lincoln and His Party*, 348–49.

36. Lincoln, *Works* IV, 316–18.

37. "Campbell Papers," 36–41. President Davis, in part to exonerate Campbell from unjust criticism, presented to Congress the correspondence of the commissioners with Seward and of Campbell with Seward and Davis. He referred to Campbell as one "who made earnest efforts to promote the successful issue of the mission intrusted to our commissioners, and by whom I was kept advised, in confidential communication, of the measures taken by him to secure so desirable a result." Rowland, ed., *Jefferson Davis* V, 85.

Beauregard's demand for Sumter's surrender, Campbell wrote Seward, reviewing their exchange of communications and asking for an explanation. "I think no candid man, who will read over what I have written and consider for a moment what is going on at Sumter," he wrote, "but will agree that the equivocating conduct of the administration, as measured and interpreted in connection with these promises, is the proximate cause of this great calamity." Receiving no answer, Campbell wrote a final letter to Seward demanding an explanation but assuring Seward that he had reached no conclusion "unfavorable to your integrity in the whole transaction."[38]

Other Southern critics were less generous with Lincoln and his secretary of state. It was widely believed in the South that Lincoln had followed a calculated course of deception in his negotiations with the commissioners, buying time with lies while he prepared for war. The *New Orleans Daily Delta* protested the "duplicity and treachery of Lincoln and Seward"; such perfidious conduct well illustrated "the disgusting baseness of the pitiable creature, this burlesque of a President."[39] A writer in *Southern Literary Messenger* declared that Lincoln probably had no intention of giving up the fort, but, lulling the South to sleep with sweet promises of peace, had determined to let the Sumter garrison perish "in order to rouse the North to a war of extermination against slavery and slave owners! ! The annals of the world in its blackest and bloodiest periods, do not furnish an instance of more inhuman and fiend like policy."[40]

Edward A. Pollard, pleonastic Confederate chronicler and outspoken editor of the *Richmond Examiner*, concluded that Lincoln and his cabinet had "resolved on a policy of perfidy." They had sought a way by which to unite the North and put the onus of blame for war on the South. Thus, reasoned Pollard, the Confederate commissioners were deceived, war preparations went forward, and a gesture was made to relieve the fort.

> The fact was [wrote Pollard] that the President had long ago calculated the result and effect . . . of hostile movements which he had directed against the sovereignty of South Carolina. He had procured the battle of

38. April 13 and 20, 1861, "Campbell Papers," 41–42.

39. April 18, 1861, in Dumond, ed., *Southern Editorials on Secession*, 498.

40. Robert R. Howison, "A History of the War," *Southern Literary Messenger*, 34 (July and Aug., 1862), 403–404.

> Sumter; he had no desire or hope to retain the fort: the circumstances of the battle and the non-participation of his fleet in it, were sufficient evidences, to every honest and reflecting mind, that it was not a contest for victory, and that "the sending provisions to a starving garrison" was an ingenious artifice to commence the war that the Federal Government had fully resolved upon, under the specious but shallow appearance of that government being involved by the force of circumstances, rather by its own volition, in the terrible consequence of civil war.[41]

In a message to the Confederate Congress on April 29, Jefferson Davis condemned Lincoln and Seward: "the crooked paths of diplomacy can scarcely furnish an example so wanting in courtesy, in candor, and directness as was the course of the United States Government toward our commissioners in Washington."[42] Davis refused to believe that Lincoln was ignorant of Seward's machinations. As President, Davis reasoned, Lincoln bore full moral and legal responsibility for the actions of his cabinet ministers.[43] Even Campbell, after reviewing his negotiations with Seward, sadly concluded that he had been the victim of fraud and treachery.[44]

Some Southerners, however, believed that Lincoln preferred peace but was weak and vacillating and had surrendered to the will of Republican radicals who were determined to force war over Sumter. The widely told story of Lincoln's interview with Virginia unionist John B. Baldwin seemed to confirm this appraisal of events. According to Baldwin, Lincoln and Seward dispatched Allan B. Magruder, a Virginian practicing law in Washington, to Richmond on the night of April 3, 1861. Magruder was to return with Judge George W. Summers, a promi-

41. Pollard, *Southern History of the War* I, 53–61. For a modern amplification by two Southerners of the thesis that Lincoln maneuvered the South into firing the first shot at Sumter, see Charles W. Ramsdell, "Lincoln and Fort Sumter," *Journal of Southern History*, 3 (Aug., 1937), 259–88, and, less judiciously presented, John Shipley Tilley, *Lincoln Takes Command* (Chapel Hill, N. C., 1941). A good review of the historiographical controversy concerning Lincoln's conduct at Sumter is Ch. 7 of Richard N. Current, *Lincoln and the First Shot* (Philadelphia, 1963). According to Current, Lincoln had determined by April 4 to reinforce Sumter.

42. April 29, 1861, in Rowland, ed., *Jefferson Davis* V, 75.

43. Jefferson Davis, *The Rise and Fall of the Confederate Government* (New York, 1881), I, 269–76.

44. Robert Garlick Hill Kean, *Inside the Confederate Government. The Diary of Robert Garlick Hill Kean, Head of the Bureau of War*, ed. Edward Younger (New York, 1957), 112–13. Diary entry of Oct. 22, 1863.

nent unionist in the Virginia secession convention then sitting, for consultations in the White House. As a delegate to the Washington peace convention, Summers had talked freely with the President-elect. If the judge found it inconvenient to leave Richmond, Magruder was to return with another prominent unionist in the Virginia convention in whom Summers had confidence. Summers could not leave, and Baldwin was selected in his stead.

Baldwin arrived in Washington in the early morning of April 4, and soon was taken to the President for a private audience. "I am afraid you have come too late," Baldwin recalled Lincoln as saying as soon as they were seated behind locked doors. "I wish you could have been here three or four days ago." Baldwin replied that Lincoln's summons had arrived only yesterday, and he had come as quickly as possible. What did Mr. Lincoln mean? Ignoring the question, Lincoln asked Baldwin why the Virginia convention did not adjourn *sine die*; it was an embarrassment, a "standing menace" to the President. Baldwin told Lincoln that the convention was controlled by Union men and would remain so if they were supported by conservative policies from Washington. If the convention adjourned in the midst of the national crisis, Baldwin warned, the unionists would be discredited, and a new convention would be elected with a secessionist majority. Baldwin asked Lincoln to support the unionists with "the force of constitutional protection." He urged the President to call a national convention to settle outstanding issues and to withdraw the troops from the forts in the interest of peace. Such a course, Baldwin believed, would rally nationalist feeling across the country and in the seceded states. What about the national revenue lost through the closing of Southern ports? Lincoln asked. Baldwin assured him that civil war would cost far more than would a temporary interruption of tariff revenue. He told a skeptical Lincoln that Virginia would secede in twenty-four hours if a cannon were fired at Sumter and implored him to act quickly. The conversation then broke off, and Baldwin returned to Richmond. Two days later the Sumter expedition sailed.[45]

45. Testimony of John B. Baldwin relating to this interview with Lincoln is in *Report of the Joint Committee on Reconstruction at the First Session, Thirty-Ninth Congress* (Washington, D.C., 1866), Part II, 102–109. A conflicting account of that interview is given by John Minor Botts in *ibid.*, 114–23. See also Allan B. Magruder, "A Piece of Secret History: President Lincoln and the Virginia Convention of 1861," *Atlantic*, 35 (April, 1875), 438–45; R. L. Dabney, "Memoir of a Narrative Received of Colonel John B. Baldwin, of Staunton, Touching the Origin of the

What did Lincoln mean when he said Baldwin was too late? "Too late for what?" Baldwin had asked and so did many others who heard the story.[46] After Sumter, the mystery seemed clearer to Baldwin. He concluded that Lincoln had been undecided about Sumter's fate, but "immense outside pressure [was] brought to bear upon the President" to force war and save his party. Baldwin remembered seeing seven or eight Republican governors in the White House during his brief visit.[47] These governors, according to some versions of the story, became the central villains in the Sumter drama. They were the principals in a partisan conspiracy—this "Seven-headed Monster" Alexander Stephens later called it—which, just before Baldwin arrived, forced the irenic and hesitant Lincoln to commit himself to sending the Sumter expedition.

Had Lincoln, so the story goes, been able to confront the Republican radicals with the information Baldwin provided—that Virginia would certainly go out if the Confederates were forced to fire on Sumter—they would have been subdued, the garrison would have been withdrawn, there would have been no secession of the upper South, no war, and peaceful reunion probably would have followed.[48] Hence, Lincoln's lament, "You have come too late." This "conspiracy" interpretation of the events of April 3–4, 1861, was popular in the South after the war when some ex-rebels were more kindly disposed to the late Lincoln. It placed the blame for war upon the North, yet it relieved Lincoln of sins

---

War," *Southern Historical Society Papers*, 1 (June, 1876), 443–55; Wilmer Hall, "Lincoln's Interview with John B. Baldwin," *South Atlantic Quarterly*, 13 (July, 1914), 260–69; Thomas, *Lincoln*, 540.

46. The story spread quickly among Baldwin's acquaintances in Richmond and beyond. "It was a subject of more interest to me than anything that ever happened to me," Baldwin remarked years later, "and when I returned I repeated it over and over again to the gentlemen who had concurred in sending me, and it impressed itself deeply on my mind." *Report of the Joint Committee*, 106.

47. *Ibid.*, 105. Dabney, "Memoir of a Narrative." The account of the good Reverend Dabney, who claimed to have heard the story from Baldwin himself in 1865, must be used with discretion. There are a number of errors and exaggerations in Dabney's memoir; for example, he has Lincoln casually spitting on the White House carpets, and, at one point, Lincoln supposedly stalks about the room wailing and tearing out his hair. One suspects that between the time of Baldwin's visit with Lincoln and Dabney's writing of that visit, someone's memory had gone awry or some embellishments were added to the story to further discredit Lincoln's claim to statesmanship.

48. Stephens, *Constitutional View* II, 84, 354–55. Dabney, "Memoir of a Narrative." Magruder, "A Piece of Secret History," 445.

greater than those of weakness and indecision, leaving the way open for him to grow into a wise and magnanimous foe.

According to Baldwin, Lincoln at one point in their conversation had asked, "What about the revenue? What about the collection of duties?" This anecdote, and variations upon it, was repeated all over the South during the war.[49] It seemed to confirm what many Southerners believed was the North's real motive in waging war: to protect Yankee profits from an independent South with low tariffs. Robert Lewis Dabney, Stonewall Jackson's brigade chaplain and later biographer, was not alone in concluding: "When Virginia offered him [Lincoln] a safe way to preserve the Union, he preferred to destroy the Union and preserve his tariffs. The war was conceived in duplicity, and brought forth in iniquity."[50]

Two days after Major Anderson marched his garrison out of embattled Sumter, Lincoln proclaimed that the laws were being resisted in seven states "by combinations too powerful to be suppressed by the ordinary course of judicial proceedings" and called for 75,000 militia from the loyal states "in order to suppress said combinations and to cause the laws to be duly executed." He appealed to loyal citizens to aid the Union and ordered rebels to disperse and return home within twenty days.[51] On April 19, Lincoln proclaimed a blockade of the coasts of the seceded states.[52]

The reaction of the southern tier of border states was swift and sure. Virginia, Tennessee, North Carolina, and Arkansas quickly seceded. The other four border states remained loyal although bitterly divided within themselves. Lincoln's call for troops was condemned everywhere in the South as a despotic, unconstitutional assumption of power. The President, it was believed, had no right to coerce sovereign states exercising their constitutional right to secede. Many Southerners were amazed that Lincoln chose war. "We find it difficult to believe," said the *Charlottesville* (Va.) *Review*, formerly a strong Union paper, "that Abraham Lincoln, speaking the same language, professing the same religion, belonging to the same advanced race—born even upon southern soil—really contemplates serious war." Yet, the *Review*'s editors accepted

49. Howison, "A History of the War," 420–21.
50. Dabney, "Memoir of a Narrative," 455.
51. April 15, 1861, in Lincoln, *Works* IV, 331–33.
52. *Ibid.*, 338–39.

war as imposed upon the South and warned Lincoln he faced a united South: "there are no divisions here now. . . ."[53] Alexander Stephens thought "preposterous" the idea that Lincoln urged a war of subjugation. He feared Lincoln had no design, no policy, "that he is, like the fool, scattering fire without any definite purpose."[54] Jefferson Davis had no such doubts. He called Lincoln's proclamation "a declaration of war," and he hurried his nation to arms.[55]

Lincoln's proclamation caused Charles Henry Smith, a Georgia lawyer, to take up his pen in the Confederacy's cause. Smith, a Union man until Lincoln's call for troops, sought a literary medium through which he could express his opinions on the affairs of the day. He created a fictitious Georgia cracker, Bill Arp, who, like George W. Harris' Sut Lovingood, probably was modeled after a real local character. Bill Arp, rustic wit and dispenser of folk homilies, became a familiar literary character in the New South, but Arp first appeared in the *Rome* (Ga.) *Confederacy* in April, 1861. In this letter, "Bill Arp to Abe Linkhorn," Smith represents Arp as a Union man finding it mighty hard to obey the President's proclamation to disperse. "I tried my darndest yisterday to disperse and retire," Arp lamented, "but it was no go. . . ."

> The fact is, the boys round here want watchin, or they'll take sumthin. . . . Most of em are so hot that they fairly siz when you pour water on em, and that the way they make up their military companies here now—when a man applies to jine the volunteers, they sprinkle him, and if he sizzes they take him, and if he don't they don't.[56]

Most Southerners reacted to Lincoln's proclamation with the kind of enthusiasm Bill Arp described. Lincoln's act—so palpably unconstitutional and tyrannical to almost every Southerner—seemed to elevate the Confederate cause to a new and higher moral plane. Suspected of being merely a political gambit to save slavery, secession now could be defended as an honest and necessary popular revolution to preserve American

53. April 19, 1861, in Dumond, ed., *Southern Editorials on Secession*, 503–504.

54. Stephens to Richard Malcolm Johnston, April 19, 1861, in Johnston and Browne, *Life of Stephens*, 397.

55. Davis to Congress, April 29, 1861, in Rowland, ed., *Jefferson Davis* V, 67–84.

56. [Charles H. Smith], *Bill Arp's Peace Papers* (New York, 1873), 19–22. C. H. Smith, *Bill Arp, from the Uncivil War to Date, 1861–1903* (Atlanta, Ga., 1903), 58–60.

liberties from a usurping despot.[57] One suspects that, beyond the turgid rhetoric and finely spun constitutional arguments, Lincoln's proclamation touched many in the border states in a more simple and elemental way. "We cannot become parties to the subjugation of our Southern brethren," resolved the *North Carolina Standard*, once a strong Union paper.[58] Perhaps William W. Blackford, a Virginian who rode with Jeb Stuart, best expressed the simple, tragic course of thinking shared by many border state men: "I was opposed to secession. . . . I thought that Lincoln, though a sectional candidate, was constitutionally elected and that we ought to have waited to see what he would do. But when he called for troops from Virginia and we had to take one side or the other, then of course I was for going with the South in her mad scheme, right or wrong."[59]

As the nation descended into war in spring of 1861, Southern men increasingly looked upon Abraham Lincoln as the cause of their woes. During the campaign of 1860 and in the first wave of secession, Lincoln was viewed merely as the symbol of the ills of the Union—the man, as Jefferson Davis said, was "nothing." But during Lincoln's first weeks in office, the man emerged to influence events decisively. As Southerners saw it, Lincoln ordered, or permitted, deceit to be practiced upon the Confederate commissioners, promising them quick evacuation of the forts while surreptitiously plotting their relief. He forced the Confederates to fire upon Sumter. Finally, he unconstitutionally called out troops to suppress the seceded states and to impose his despotism upon the South. He was held responsible, by weakness or design, for killing the peace. Thus he incurred the enmity of those Southerners who desired peaceful secession and, at the same time, of those border statesmen who hoped to maintain a climate of peace in which reunion could be worked out. The South began secession with little personal animosity toward Lincoln, the symbol of Black Republicanism. It entered war with a deepening hatred of Lincoln, the destroyer of peace.

57. E. A. Pollard, *Life of Jefferson Davis, With a Secret History of the Confederacy. . . .* (Philadelphia, 1869), 113. Pollard, *Southern History of the War* I, 65. Rhodes, *History of the United States* III, 401–402.

58. April 20, 1861, in Dumond, ed., *Southern Editorials on Secession*, 505–506.

59. William Wallis Blackford, *War Years with Jeb Stuart* (New York, 1945), 13–14.

3.

The Confederates' Lincoln

A people at war tend to personify their enemy and his nature, selecting individual foemen to stand as symbols of what they are fighting against. Propagandists know that it is easier for a people to fix their enmity upon men than upon abstract ideas or upon foreign populations *en masse*. Thus, George III, to his rebellious colonists, became the "Royal Brute," the personification of all the evils of an oppressive empire. Nearly a century and a half later, the kaiser became the symbol of Hunnish, arrogant German imperialism. Frequently it is the task of historians to rescue such unfortunate men from the odium where the passions of war have placed them.

Southerners at war saw certain Yankees as especially deserving of their rancor. William Tecumseh Sherman was hated not merely for his excesses on the march to the sea, but because he represented a cruel, ruthlessly efficient war machine before which Southerners were helpless. Ben Butler was never feared as a warrior, but he inspired Southern hatred because his conduct and very countenance insulted Southern values. Butler's treatment of the women of occupied New Orleans, expropriation of private property, and execution of Confederate prisoners caused the Confederacy to brand him a felon liable to execution if captured.

Abraham Lincoln was the Confederates' chief villain. As President and commander-in-chief of an enemy nation, he generally was held responsible for the cruel wages of war. Southerners believed that Lincoln's policies inaugurated the war and that he ordered, or permitted, many atrocities and excesses upon Confederate civilians and property.

During the war Lincoln frequently was the object of Confederate propaganda. The lanky Westerner with his rough frontier ways was the delight of Confederate caricaturists. Lincoln was represented in the press and in private anecdote as the very opposite of the Cavalier ideal: crude, boorish, cowardly, demagogic, and cruel. He was portrayed variously as the architect of Yankee policy and as the simple tool of others, as a real threat to the South and as a contemptible buffoon.

> My name it is Abe Lincoln,
> I lead a wretched life.
> I come from Springfield, Illinois,
> Me and my dear wife.
> We brought with us our dear son Bob,
> To let the people know,
> That the country I would plunder and rob,
> Where ever I would go.[1]

Fanciful descriptions of Lincoln's "wretched life" (the above doggerel is from a piece of Confederate broadside verse) engaged Confederate propagandists and titillated Southern readers throughout the war. An early attempt at such caricature came from the pen of young Samuel Clemens. Clemens, under the pseudonym Quintus Curtius Snodgrass, wrote a series of ten humorous pieces for the *New Orleans Crescent* in the first three months of 1861. These letters described the bloodless Confederate expedition to capture Baton Rouge and offered "hints to young campaigners" about the ins and outs of army life. The seventh letter, which appeared on March 14, was entitled "Snodgrass dines with Old Abe." It featured Snodgrass' breaking bread with Lincoln, Mrs. Lincoln, their son Robert, and a coven of Yankee villains including Simon Cameron, Owen Lovejoy, Charles Sumner, Norman Judd, and Andrew

1. "My Name It is Abe Lincoln," n.p., 1861 [?]. Confederate Collection, Rare Book Division, Library of Congress, Washington, D. C.

Johnson. Frontier delicacies of boiled beef, cabbage, and pork and beans comprised the fare; the entire dinner reflected "the patriarchal simplicity that characterized H. O. A. [Honest Old Abe] and marks him as a genuine Sucker and A1 Rail splitter." Lincoln's speech was distinguished by frontier slang and informality. Mrs. Lincoln was dismissed as "a thrifty, notable housewife" who set her own table. Robert Lincoln was roughly dealt with. He was portrayed as vain, boorish, a drunkard, and a wastrel who shamed his parents. The Lincolnian wit did not escape Clemens' satire: "His Excellency, the President, then got off in rapid succession several jokes, which we are unable to give you now, having not yet seen the several points. . . ." Lincoln, however, is permitted one good joke at the expense of Andy Johnson, who failed to appreciate it. Finally, Snodgrass takes leave of the banquet: "In the hall, I had some conversation with the servant who opens the door, and in whose judgment Mr. Lincoln is said to have much confidence, to whom I presented all my loose change, and who in return has faithfully promised to get me an office."[2]

Clemens' pasquinade contained many elements which were to become familiar fare in Confederate caricatures of Lincoln: the literary device of seeing the President through the incredulous eyes of a visiting Southerner, the jibes at Lincoln's rough ways, his family, his style of humor, and at the doings of the new administration. George W. Harris (Sut Lovingood) already had exploited some of these possibilities. But Clemens' burlesque of Lincoln exhibited a good-natured innocence which was absent in Harris' Sut and in many later lampoons by war-hardened Southerners.

A staple feature of Lincoln's image in the South was that Lincoln was a drunk. The Yankee President was reported to spend much of the time in his cups. William Russell, the English war correspondent, observed that rebel newspapers fanned the flames of sectional discord by telling their readers that Lincoln was always drunk.[3] A young rebel wrote his wife that visitors from Washington had said "that Abe Lincoln had been

2. Ernest E. Leisy, ed., *Mark Twain: The Letters of Quintus Curtius Snodgrass* (Dallas, Texas, 1946), 45–48. Leisy says that Clemens never acknowledged the authorship of these letters, but he believes Clemens was the writer because the pieces are in the style of the early Twain, Clemens was in New Orleans at the time, and Clemens was fond of the *nom de plume* Snodgrass and used it frequently.

3. William Howard Russell, *My Diary, North and South* (Boston, 1863), 171.

drunk for thirty six hours & was still drunk when he left."[4] "It is rumored that LINCOLN has been drunk *for three days* . . . ," shouted the *Norfolk* (Va.) *Herald*.[5] The nature of Lincoln's drinking habits later became a subject of fierce debate in the Lincoln hagiography, but there is no reliable evidence to show that Lincoln took more than an occasional drink. Lincoln was a Westerner, and Westerners were known as formidable drinkers. It was easy for Confederate propagandists to stigmatize Lincoln as a drunkard by association with his section if by no other evidence. One wonders if this reputation for inebriety really discredited Lincoln with Southerners, who were, after all, a hard-drinking people themselves.

Lincoln was represented in Confederate prose and verse as a physical coward. The story of Lincoln's secret, nocturnal journey to the capital to escape possible assassination in Baltimore was reported widely in the South. In cartoon and verse the President was dressed in his supposed disguise of Scotch cap and cloak to remind Southerners of the cowardice of their archenemy.[6] Lincoln's conduct at his inauguration, where he was closely guarded by General Scott's soldiery, drew Southern contempt. "Then was seen, for the first time in the history of this Country," wrote one scornful Confederate, the "Chief Magistrate, in abject terror of his life, inaugurated into his high office under the countenance and protection of shining bayonets, gleaming swords and loaded cannon."[7] Lincoln's fearfulness was born of prudence, Southerners were told, since Jefferson Davis' army and Lincoln's Northern enemies were poised to

4. Robert M. Gill to Bettie Gill, April 29, 1861, quoted in Bell I. Wiley, *The Common Soldier of the Civil War* (New York, 1958), II, 169.

5. April 22, 1861, quoted in Frank Moore, ed., *The Rebellion Record: A Diary of American Events. . . .* (New York, 1861–1868), I (Poetry), 57.

6. For examples of these themes, see "Abe-iad," a popular song written in 1861, in Pearl Brown Brands, "Music Written About Abraham Lincoln," *Étude*, Feb., 1938, p. 77. "The M. F. Savage Collection of Lincoln Sheet Music," *Lincoln Herald*, 53 (Fall, 1951), 38–40. "Song of the Exile," in A Member of the GAR, *The Picket Line and Camp Fire Stories* (New York, [1864]). "The Last Face of the Rail-Splitter" (poem), n.p., 1861 [?]. "Uncle Abe, or a Hit at the Times" (song), n.p., 1861 [?]. "Old Virginia's Knocking Around" (song) (Baltimore, Md., 1862). Moore, ed., *Rebellion Record* I (Poetry), 73–74. "Imaginary Conversations," in *Bugle Horn of Liberty*, I (Sept., 1863), 13. A South Carolinian, *The Confederate* (Mobile, Ala., 1863), 77.

7. "Confederate No. 10," in A South Carolinian, *The Confederate*, 77.

capture the wretched railsplitter. Stories circulated that Lincoln slept in the White House guarded by a praetorian guard of Kansas border ruffians who, according to one version, dictated policy and held the President a virtual prisoner.[8] "He has not passed a night in the White House for two weeks," ran another tale, "but goes into the barracks to sleep with his armed hirelings all around him. He does not so much as take off his boots, that he may be ready to run on a second's warning."[9] In Louisiana, it was said that Lincoln locked himself up in an iron cage in fear of assassination.[10] Mississippians were told that Lincoln woke up every night screaming, "Jeff Davis is after me! Jeff Davis is after me!"[11]

Lincoln's craven conduct was contrasted with that of Jefferson Davis, who slept serenely in the Confederate White House, safe in the bosom of his loving nation. Mused *DeBow's Review*:

> While looking at his [Davis'] house, one cannot help thinking of the contrast between the conditions of the two Presidents. The chief of the great and invincible United States is continually surrounded by a chosen body guard, and trembles for his safety at every creak of his door, while the rebel leader lives as modestly and securely as the humblest citizen. Not even a policeman hovers around the nearest street corner, and the great rebel walks about the city as unconcernedly as if he was on his own plantation and gathering cotton instead of "concocting treason." The differences are these: Lincoln knows he is a despot, and that thousands of men around his home hate him, while Jeff. Davis feels that he lives in the hearts of his countrymen, and that his security is in their love. Were it not that Lincoln is so securely guarded, I have reason to know that he would have been brought a captive to Richmond ere this.[12]

The cowardly Yankee President also was represented in the South as a near-illiterate. His speeches were dismissed as "beastly and idiotic" and not to be compared with the lofty, statesman-like addresses of Jefferson

8. *New Orleans Sunday Delta*, April 28, 1861, in Moore, ed., *Rebellion Record* I (Poetry), 54. See also *ibid.* I (Diary), 39.

9. *Petersburg* (Va.) *Express*, May 4, 1861, in *ibid.* I (Poetry), 9.

10. *Ibid.* VI (Poetry), 9.

11. Daniel Perrin Bestor to his brother, June 27, 1861, in Arthur E. Bestor, Jr., "Letters from a Southern Opponent of Secession, September, 1860, to June, 1861," *Journal of Southern History*, 12 (Feb., 1946), 120.

12. *DeBow's Review*, OS 31 (Oct.–Dec., 1861), 470. See also "The Shadow and the Substance," in *Natchez Courier*, May 21, 1861, in Moore, ed., *Rebellion Record* I (Poetry), 128–29.

Davis.[13] When it was rumored that Lincoln himself had written the poem he called his favorite—William Knox's "Mortality"—the *Southern Illustrated News* denied that Lincoln possibly could be the author. "Of all living men, he is the very least to whom the gift of poesy could ever be ascribed voluntarily. We can hardly fancy the lantern-jawed, lank, gaunt, jocular rail-splitter wooing the coy and reluctant muse."[14]

Lincoln's family did not escape censure. The sins of the father oft were visited upon the son, Robert Todd Lincoln. Robert Lincoln was the subject of much gossip about his alleged drinking and dissipations. Frequently he was called a coward because he spent most of the war as a student at Harvard College. Mrs. Lincoln generally was depicted as a simple, dowdy housewife and busybody who made life difficult for her husband. In one Lincoln family joke which circulated about the South, Mrs. Lincoln was so taken with the White House gardener that she desired to make him a major general. "Well," said the resigned Lincoln, "the little woman must have her way sometimes."[15]

Lincoln's tall, awkward form inspired such commonly used metaphors as "the Illinois Ape," "Gorilla," and "Baboon." The bestial Lincoln usually took simian form, but a Virginia congressman described him as "a cross between a sandhill crane and an Andalusian jackass."[16] Other reports conceded Lincoln's membership in the human race but claimed he was a bastard or a Negro.[17]

Many Lincoln stories current in the South represented the President as an oaf and buffoon. Mary Boykin Chesnut heard that Lincoln's habit was to dress slowly and deliberately before a White House window. "Picturing Lincoln adonizing!" she confided to her journal, adding, "They say Lincoln is frightfully uncouth and ugly, with the keenest sense

13. *Southern Literary Messenger*, 32 (March, 1862), 244. Cleland J. Huger, Jr., to D. E. Huger Smith, Jan. 20, 1863, in Daniel E. Huger Smith, Alice R. Huger Smith, and Arney R. Childs, eds., *Mason Smith Family Letters, 1860–1868* (Columbia, S. C., 1950), 32–33.

14. *Southern Illustrated News*, Feb. 14, 1863, p. 2.

15. Chesnut, *Diary*, Jan. 1, 1864, p. 344.

16. Sherrad Clemens, letter to unnamed correspondent, March 1, 1861, quoted in Catton, *Coming Fury*, 247.

17. *New Orleans Picayune*, reprinted in *Spartanburg* (S. C.) *Press*, Oct. 2, 1861, quoted in Martin Abbott, "President Lincoln in Confederate Caricature," *Journal of the Illinois State Historical Society*, 51 (Autumn, 1958), 309. *Southern Field and Fireside*, NS 2 (March 12, 1864), 4. *Bugle Horn of Liberty*, 1 (Aug., 1863), cover engraving.

of vulgar humor."[18] That vulgar humor was the subject of much idle gossip. According to one story Lincoln ordered up a gay minstrel air while touring the bloody Antietam battlefield, testifying to the coarseness and insensitivity of the man.[19] Lincoln was accused of indulging in tasteless frivolities—frequenting the theater, giving opulent balls and White House levees—instead of tending to the grim and austere business of war.[20] In contrast to the dignified Republican simplicity of his presidential predecessors and of his counterpart in Richmond, Lincoln surrounded himself with obscene luxury, including, according to the *Wilmington* (N. C.) *Daily Journal*, an elegant private railway carriage: "Now a vulgar buffoon, who grins ghastly jokes over the grave of the Union, rides in a sumptuous sixteen-wheeled car . . . such as no King, Emperor, Czar, Kaiser, or even despotic Caesar himself ever indulged in."[21]

Confederates delighted in telling each other of Lincoln's rumored want of social graces and many *faux pas*. A brigade commander in Jeb Stuart's cavalry told this representative story to a visiting English officer during Lee's retreat from Gettysburg: a delegation of Virginians visited Lincoln just after the fall of Sumter and implored him to do something to allay the public excitement. "I would beg you to lend me your finger and thumb for five minutes," one of the delegation asked Lincoln, meaning he wished the President to draft an appeasing public manifesto. "My finger and thumb," Mr. Lincoln was said to have replied; "What would you do with them? Blow your nose?"[22]

18. Chesnut, *Diary*, Aug. 18, 1861, p. 114.

19. [Felix G. Fontaine], *Marginalia; or, Gleanings from an Army Note-Book. By "Personne"* (Columbia, S. C., 1864), 240–41. Like many Lincoln stories popular in the South, this one circulated widely in the North as well and apparently was gleaned from Northern newspapers.

20. Pollard, *Southern History of the War* II, 214.

21. Jan. 4, 1865, quoted in Richard Bardolph, "Malice Toward One: Lincoln in the North Carolina Press," *Lincoln Herald*, 53 (Winter, 1952), 36.

22. Fitzgerald Ross, *Cities and Camps of the Confederacy*, ed. Richard B. Harwell (Urbana, Ill., 1958), 78–79. Ross wrote up his experiences in *Blackwood's Edinburgh Magazine* in 1864 and 1865 and published *A Visit to the Cities and Camps of the Confederate States* (Edinburgh, 1865). This incident was described as occurring during the visit of three Virginia delegates—William Ballard Preston, Alexander H. H. Stuart, and George W. Randolph—to Abraham Lincoln on April 13, 1861. Yet John B. Baldwin testified that he used the same thumb-and-finger

Southerners damned and ridiculed Lincoln through almost every medium known to the age—in books and broadsides, in the press and on the stage, in the pulpit and legislative halls, in casual gossip. Some of these attempts at caricature showed talent and an imaginative flair, such as the cartoons of Dr. Adalbert J. Volck, a German-born Baltimore dentist of Southern sympathies.[23] But most were simply bad art, remembered only as social documents illustrating certain Southern attitudes toward Lincoln.

The most ambitious attempts to caricature Lincoln came in the form of long dramatic poems and in dramas designed for the Richmond stage. None of these pieces reveals much in the way of literary talent; at best, they demonstrate some satirical cleverness and at worst, tasteless scurrility. In a long poem by E. P. Birch, "The Devil's Visit to Old Abe," Lincoln is represented as having sold his soul to the Devil in return for political success, but Confederate courage and federal ineptness in battle have combined to frustrate Lucifer's ambitions for protracted war.[24] In the pseudo-classical "Abram, a Military Poem," written by a veteran of Longstreet's corps, Lincoln is gibbeted for his crimes and usurpations by Jefferson Davis.[25]

John D. McCabe's *The Aid-de-Camp*, a bad melodrama whose prose imitates Sir Walter Scott, contrasts Southern chivalry and Yankee perfidy in early 1861. There is a standard triangle of characters: a pure and

---

figure of speech in his conversation with Lincoln on April 4. *Report of the Joint Committee on Reconstruction*, Part II, 103. For another story of Lincoln's alleged social ineptitude, see Chesnut, *Diary*, 413.

23. The author examined a set of Volck etchings in the Illinois State Historical Library, Springfield, Ill. Volck etchings have been reproduced in *The Magazine of History With Notes and Queries. Extra Number—No. 16* (Tarrytown, N. Y., 1917); *Cosmopolitan* (Aug., 1890); Van Dyke MacBride, "The Lincoln Caricatures. Eight Etchings by Dr. Adalbert Volck," *Lincoln Herald*, 56 (Fall, 1954), 23–43. See also William Murrell, *A History of American Graphic Humor* (New York, 1933), I, 201–206. In 1905, Volck wrote, "I feel the greatest regret ever to have aimed ridicule at that great and good Lincoln,—outside of that the pictures represent events as truthfully as my close connections with the South enabled me to get at them." Quoted in MacBride, "The Lincoln Caricatures."

24. Rev. E. P. Birch, *The Devil's Visit to "Old Abe." Written on the Occasion of Lincoln's Proclamation for Prayer and Fasting after the Battle of Manassas. Revised and Improved Expressly for LaGrange Republic by the Author* (n.p., [1862]).

25. *Abram. A Military Poem, by a Young Rebelle, Esq. of the Army* (Richmond, Va., 1863).

beautiful Southern heroine, a blackguardly Yankee villain, and a heroic young Confederate officer. This officer-hero, Marshall, is one of those remarkably peripatetic creatures of fiction who is forever turning up in the right place at the right time—in Washington for Lincoln's inaugural, in Charleston as an aide to Beauregard during the bombardment of Sumter, at Manassas where he is promoted by Jefferson Davis for valor in battle, and so on. At one point, Marshall finds himself in a secret passageway within the walls of the White House. He eavesdrops on a cabinet meeting in which plans are laid to force the South to fire upon Sumter. The cabinet is dominated by Seward, a man of great wickedness and power, "the true ruler of the Union." Marshall spies Lincoln:

> Seated in one of these chairs, with his feet thrown carelessly upon the table, with a cigar thrust between his lips, was a tall, dark-complexioned man with heavy black whiskers. He was dressed in a plain suit of black, which but imperfectly hid the natural ungainliness of form. His whole appearance was expressive of great awkwardness, and there was about him an air of restraint, which impressed the gazer painfully. There was a dejected and careworn look upon his countenance, an eager, uneasy gleam in his dark eyes. He was Abraham Lincoln, President of the United States. [Marshall] could hardly believe that the awkward and ungainly man before him, whose appearance was at once suggestive of fraud and ignorance, could indeed be the Ruler of the American Republic. He searched his features closely, but nowhere could he discover the evidences of the genius, intellect or wisdom necessary to enable him to conduct the Ship of State safely through the dark waters which were swelling about her. The more he looked at the man before him the more he became satisfied that he had been chosen only that he might be a weak tool in the hands of the wicked rulers of his party.[26]

One of the few plays actually staged in the war-time South was *King Linkum the First*, a musical satire. Its author, John Hill Hewitt, a composer, poet, and dramatist who never permitted his slight talents to restrain his self-esteem, portrayed Lincoln as many Southerners imagined him to be: a wretched figure plagued by a wastrel son and indulging wife, Democratic election gains, rebellion in the North against the Emancipation Proclamation, failing national credit, Southern victories,

26. John D. McCabe, Jr., *The Aid-de-Camp: A Romance of the War* (Richmond, Va., 1863).

and incompetent Yankee generals. Hewitt's Lincoln finds solace in the bottle and foolish revelries, and, finally, in death.[27]

Not all Confederate versification was unsympathetic to Lincoln. A few pieces, despite their general defamatory theme, suggest an appreciation of the terrible dilemmas which confronted the Northern President. A case in point is William Russell Smith's closet drama, *The Royal Ape*. The usual themes are present: Lincoln's cowardice and despotism, family troubles, drinking, and suggestions of his madness. Lincoln is made to lust after one of the White House maids—a bit much even for Southern critics, one of whom pronounced the play "grossly indecent."[28] Yet *The Royal Ape* occasionally touches eloquence. Smith's Lincoln rises above the usual standard of Confederate caricature when he is permitted to feel something of the great burdens of his office and when he generously forgives a pompous and jealous old General Scott for the disaster at Manassas. Smith is not unkind to his foe when the play's Lincoln, gathering up his personal letters and papers before fleeing Washington and an invading rebel army, soliloquizes:

> If history should damn me as a failure,
> And write me down as a tyrant on its pages,
> So that the curses of posterity
> Shall animate all coming generations,
> On seeing the name of Lincoln, these soft lines
> May link me with some gentler memories:
> And plead, that, Lincoln, being out of place,
> Was not himself; as Cicero in war,
> And grand Demosthenes, in errant spheres,
> Left not such blotches as to blink their glories.[29]

Even more sympathetic is Stephen Franks Miller's verse drama, *Ahab Lincoln*. Miller's Lincoln is a reluctant President—"By nature harmless and of gentle mood / Neither craving nor deserving honor"—

27. John Hill Hewitt, *King Linkum the First; a Musical Burletta, as Performed at the Concert Hall, Augusta, Georgia, February 23, 1863*, ed. Richard Barksdale Harwell. Emory University Publications, Sources & Reprints, Series IV (Atlanta, Ga., 1947).

28. Richard Barksdale Harwell, "Confederate Anti-Lincoln Literature," *Lincoln Herald*, 53 (Fall, 1951), 23.

29. William Russell Smith, *The Royal Ape: A Dramatic Poem* (Richmond, Va., 1863).

pushed by radicals into the role of abolitionist champion. Overwhelmed by the war, Lincoln, before killing himself, says to Jefferson Davis:

> I am the guilty cause of all the blood
> Spilt on either side in this unnatural war,
> And terrible shall be my expiation.
> . . . Having my country ruined,
> I yield up my life in honest retribution,
> Hoping that my sins will be forgiven,
> As all men freely I forgive—Farewell!

Davis forgives his fallen foe, and Alexander Stephens muses, "Lincoln was better in his heart / Than the rabid crew who to frenzy drove him," anticipating a distinction widely held in the South after the war.[30]

The treatment of Lincoln by Confederate journalists and jurists, poetasters and playwrights, reflected and reinforced the identity of the symbolic Lincoln in Southern minds with the Yankee enemy. In the popular idiom, the North was "Lincolndom," the Republican party "Abolitionists" or "Lincolnites," the Union army "Lincoln mercenaries" or "Lincolnpoops."[31] Southern boys marched off to war promising their sweethearts a lock of Lincoln's hair.[32] A company of volunteers from the Southwest carried with them a coffin in which they vowed to bring home Lincoln's body.[33] The crew of the Confederate raider *Alabama*, hove-to by an island in the Gulf of Mexico, carried out a mock funeral of the Yankee President.[34] Even in defeat, rebel soldiers could find amusement in Old Abe. After the bloody repulse at Gettysburg, a column of Longstreet's men passed around colored prints of Lincoln, accompanied by lively remarks on his singular personal beauty.[35]

30. Stephen Franks Miller, *Ahab Lincoln; A Tragedy of the Potomac*, introduction by Richard B. Harwell (Chicago, 1958). The piece was written in 1861.

31. Such references are so common in the literature of the Confederacy that even a partial list would weary the reader. A casual perusal of almost any war-time Southern newspaper would document the point. For an English visitor's observations of the subject, see Russell, *My Diary*, 163, 302.

32. Pollard, *Life of Jefferson Davis*, 193.

33. Russell, *My Diary*, 303.

34. "The Cruise of the Alabama, Narrated by Her Officers," in *The Grayjackets: And How They Lived, Fought, and Died For Dixie. By a Confederate* (Richmond, Va., 1867), 417.

35. Walter Lord, ed., *The Fremantle Diary. Being the Journal of Lieutenant Colonel Arthur James Lyon Fremantle, Coldstream Guards, On His Three Months in the Confederate States* (Boston, 1954), 223. Originally published in 1863.

Hatred for Lincoln among civilians often ran deep and strong. Colonel Arthur J. L. Fremantle, an English officer traveling in the Confederacy, recalled driving from Brownsville to San Antonio with a crew of colorful Texas characters. Fremantle's driver had lost his business—a halfway house on the overland route to California—because of the war, and he damned the man he believed responsible for his fall in fortune. Flogging his reluctant mules, the driver yelled, "I wish you was Uncle Abe, I'd make you move, you G—d d——n son of a ———." Fremantle observed: "His idea of a perfect happiness seems to be to have Messrs. Lincoln and Seward in the shafts."[36] Another English visitor, the journalist William Russell, found himself on a Gulf coastal steamer with a group of ardent rebels as fellow passengers. "The fiercest of them all was a thin, fiery-eyed little woman, who at dinner expressed a fervid desire for bits of 'Old Abe'—his ear, his hair." Russell added dryly, "whether for the purpose of eating or as curious relics, she did not enlighten the company."[37]

Dixie's children were not isolated from the prejudices of their elders. They were inculcated with a hatred of Lincoln along with all things Yankee. Confederate school texts set the tone. An exercise in a Confederate speller ran thus: "A despotism is a tyrannical, oppressive government. The administration of Abraham Lincoln is a despotism."[38] A popular reader sought to set Lincoln in historical perspective for young rebels:

> 4. In the year 1860 the Ablitionists [*sic*] became strong enough to elect one of their men for President. Abraham Lincoln was a weak man, and the South believed he would allow laws to be made, which would deprive them of their rights. So the Southern States seceded, and elected Jefferson Davis for their President. This so enraged President Lincoln that He declared war and has exhausted nearly all the strength of the nation, in a vain attempt to whip the South back into the Union. Thousands of lives have been lost, and the earth has been drenched with blood; but still Abraham is unable to conquer the "Rebels" as he calls the South. The South

36. *Ibid.*, 30, 38–39.

37. Russell, *My Diary*, 229.

38. Rev. Robert Fleming, *The Elementary Spelling Book, Revised and Adapted to the Youth of the Southern Confederacy, Interspersed with Readings on Domestic Slavery* (Atlanta, 1863), 97. The good Reverend Fleming felt that Webster's speller needed revising in light of events caused by "protracted, unjust, and oppressive Federal legislation" (Preface).

> only asked to be left alone, and to divide the public property equally. It would have been wise in the North to have said to her Southern sisters, "If you are not content to dwell with us longer, depart in peace. We will divide the inheritance with you, and may you be a great nation."[39]

The lessons of school, street, and home were not lost upon young rebels, many of whom were among the most zealous of Confederate patriots. Lizzie Hardin, an ardent Kentucky secessionist, watched a gang of young boys seize an unfortunate lad who had cheered for Lincoln, carry him into a livery stable, and dunk him in the horse trough.[40] Mrs. Chesnut once gave the little son of poet Paul Hayne an album of photographs to look over. The fiery young rebel exclaimed, "You have Lincoln in your book! I hate him!" and pounded Old Abe's photograph with his fists.[41]

Responsibility for the atrocities of war was laid at the door of the Northern commander-in-chief. Lincoln was accused of authorizing acts contrary to all the rules of war as Southerners understood them: destroying private property, mistreating civilians and prisoners of war, encouraging slave revolts, waging war on world commerce by his blockade and thus causing mass starvation in Britain, and hiring vast armies of mercenaries and Negroes to ravish the South.[42] Confederate commanders, like their counterparts in every war in every age, issued bombastic manifestoes detailing these alleged atrocities to exhort their people to greater resistance. A fair sample was issued over the name of P. G. T. Beauregard:

> A reckless and unprincipled tyrant has invaded your soil. ABRAHAM LINCOLN, regardless of all moral, legal and constitutional restraints, has thrown his abolition hosts among you, who are murdering and imprisoning your citizens, confiscating and destroying your property, and

39. Mrs. Marinda Brandon Moore, *The Geographic Reader for the Dixie Children* (Raleigh, N. C., 1863), 13–14.

40. Elizabeth Pendleton Hardin, *The Private War of Lizzie Hardin; A Kentucky Confederate Girl's Diary of the Civil War in Kentucky, Virginia, Tennessee, Alabama, and Georgia*, ed. G. Glenn Clift (Frankfort, Ky., 1963), 64. Lizzie Hardin was first cousin to Ben Hardin Helm, husband of Mary Todd Lincoln's sister.

41. Chesnut, *Diary*, July 12, 1862, p. 268.

42. Jefferson Davis to Abraham Lincoln, July 2, 1863, in Rowland, ed., *Jefferson Davis* V, 517–18.

committing other acts of violence and outrage too shocking and revolting to humanity to be enumerated. All rules of civilized warfare are abandoned, and they proclaim by their acts, if not on their banners, that their war cry is "Beauty and Booty." All that is dear to man—your home and that of your wives and daughters—your fortunes and your lives are involved in this momentous contest.[43]

The good clergy of the South were not far behind the military in pointing out the barbarities of the invader and calling the people to arms. The Reverend Thomas Smyth, for example, damned

> The usurpations of Lincoln, Scott & Co.—the arbitrary, unconstitutional, tyrannous, unnatural, inhuman, and diabolical course pursued by them—the barbarities perpetrated, the blood of patriot martyrs murdered, the curses of outraged women, the ailings of widows, the tears of orphans, houses burned, cities subjugated, fields devastated, *all decency and civilization set at defiance by unlicensed lynx-eyed generals and soldiers. . . .*[44]

Southerners condemned the Union blockade as inhumane and barbaric since it caused a severe shortage of medicines to treat wounded soldiers. One North Carolina captain of infantry reported six out of seven men in his regiment were ill. Lincoln was responsible for this, he wrote his wife angrily, and "ought to be burnt in a hell ten thousand times hotter than fier [*sic*]."[45] According to rumor, Lincoln and his followers were prepared to go beyond the mere denial of medicines. One Confederate newspaper reported "a most diabolical attempt by the enemy to poison our army" at Corinth, Mississippi, by smuggling contaminated medical supplies within Confederate lines to be used upon the unsuspecting sick and wounded.[46]

The attitude of the Lincoln government toward the exchange of prisoners of war stirred deep anger and resentment in the South. "It may be truly and emphatically said," Edward A. Pollard wrote bitterly, "that

43. "A Proclamation to the Good People of the Counties of Alexandria, Loudoun, Fairfax & Prince William" (broadside, 1861).

44. Reverend Thomas Smyth, "The Battle of Fort Sumter: Its Mystery and Miracle—God's Mystery and Mercy," *Southern Presbyterian Review*, 14 (Oct., 1861), 399.

45. Alfred Bell to his wife, April 25, 1862, quoted in Wiley, *Common Soldier of the Civil War* II, 244.

46. April 19, 1862, quoted in Bardolph, "Malice Toward One," 41.

on no subject had the enemy shown such bad faith as on that of the exchange of prisoners."[47] Southerners expected that their captured prisoners would be paroled and exchanged promptly. For a number of reasons—the uncertain status of rebels, threats of retaliation upon prisoners, difficulty of enforcing paroles—a satisfactory policy was never worked out, and exchanges, especially after 1863, were effected only sporadically.[48] The result was overcrowded, inadequate military prisons on both sides, attended with much suffering and death. After Appomattox, when the terrible conditions in Southern prisons had become a matter of public record and after the ritual sacrifice of the unfortunate Major Henry Wirz, commandant at Andersonville, much Southern ink and oratory were spent attempting to prove that (1) Southern prisons were not as bad as the Yankees said; (2) such bad conditions as did exist were the result of Union policies such as the refusal to trade prisoners, the blockade of medicines, and the destruction of food by invading armies; and (3) Yankee prisons were at least as bad if not worse.

During the war many Southerners who witnessed the wretched conditions endured by Union prisoners blamed Lincoln for insensitivity to the suffering of his own soldiers. A young Virginia lady wrote in her diary just after the first battle of Manassas:

> Abraham Lincoln professes to conduct this war on the most humane and merciful principles yet he had declared all medicines and surgical instruments contraband of war, a thing never before heard of among civilized people. And now having deprived us as far as in his power, of all means of attending to our own sick and wounded, he leaves his poor soldiers to our care.[49]

Kate Cumming was a well-brought-up Southern girl, who, as an army nurse, discovered that war is not always fought by tournament rules. She shared with many of her countrymen the not unreasonable belief that the Union government deliberately impeded prisoner ex-

47. Pollard, *Southern History of the War* II, 433.

48. A dispassionate account of the problem of prisoner exchanges is to be found in James G. Randall and David Donald, *The Civil War and Reconstruction*, 2nd ed. (Boston, 1961), 333–39.

49. Betty Herndon Maury, diary entry of July 28, 1861, in Katherine M. Jones, ed., *Heroines of Dixie, Confederate Women Tell Their Story of the War* (Indianapolis, 1955), 54.

changes in order to deny the Confederacy manpower in the form of returning prisoners and to tie down Southern men and resources needed to guard and feed large numbers of captured Yankees. While attending the sick and wounded in a Georgia hospital, Kate reflected:

> Lincoln has again refused to exchange prisoners. I do think that this is the cruelist act of which he has been guilty, not only to us, but to his own men. . . . Human lives are nothing to him; all the prisoners we have might die of starvation, and I do not expect it would cost him a thought, as all he has to do is issue a call for so many more thousand to be offered up on his altar of sacrifice. How long will the people of the North submit to this Moloch. He knows that every one of our men is of value to us, for we have not the dregs of the earth to draw from; but our every man is a patriot, battling for all that is dear to him.[50]

Some months later, Kate's train paused at Andersonville and she caught a glimpse of the suffering in that terrible place. The heart of this good woman hardened further against the man whom she believed responsible for so much death and pain. "O, how I thought of him who is the cause of all this woe on his fellow countrymen—Abraham Lincoln," she confided to her diary. "What kind of heart can he have, to leave these poor wretches here?" adding grimly, "But as sure as there is a just God, his day of reckoning will come for the crimes of which he has been guilty against his own countrymen alone."[51]

In Southern eyes the most monstrous of Lincoln's atrocities was, of course, the war itself. Confederate propagandists never relented in their attack upon Lincoln as the author of the war. "Did not the Confederate government earnestly desire peace, and do its utmost to secure it?" asked the *Wilmington* (N. C.) *Daily Journal* rhetorically. "Did not Lincoln select his own blood-besmeared Cabinet and agents, and is he not therefore legally and morally responsible for the lives of the men who have been slain?"[52] The pages of the journals of the Confederate Congress breathed defiance of Lincoln and were filled with pledges to fight until

50. *Kate: the Journal of a Confederate Nurse*, ed. Richard Barksdale Harwell (Baton Rouge, La., 1959), 183. Diary entry of Dec. 30, 1863. See also p. 237.

51. *Ibid.*, 228–29. Diary entry of Aug. 19, 1864. When Kate Cumming heard of Lincoln's assassination months later, she recorded the news matter-of-factly in her journal, without speculations on God's will being done (p. 275).

52. Sept. 3, 1861, in Bardolph, "Malice Toward One," 40.

the end. Lincoln's offers of amnesty to repentant Confederates and his plans for reconstruction were dismissed with anger and contempt.[53] "He offers us pardon!" wrote Catherine Devereaux Edmondston in her diary.

> Pardon for what? Forgiveness for what? Forgive us for having himself invaded our lands, ravaged our homes and deluged our country with the blood of our brothers and sons. Pardon to us for having incited slaves to revolt. Forgive us for Butler's outrages and for the atrocities he, himself, has countenanced in his satraps.[54]

Confederate defiance of Lincoln could take brutal and powerful literary form, as in this piece of verse, an answer to the patriotic Union song, "We're Coming Father Abraham," which evokes the specter of corpses, cripples, widows, and orphans left in the wake of Lincoln's war:

> There is a long, long procession, of
> hearses at the gate,
> And they're coming, coming, coming—
> I see no end as yet,
> There's a wailing in the air, there's a
> trembling in the ground!
> The distant whirlwind roars! I hear
> the warning sound,
> But amid the lightening flash, and
> the earthquake's wild uproar,
> We are coming, Father Abr'am with three
> hundred thousand more.[55]

In a similar piece of broadside verse, a dying Union soldier on the battlefield at Manassas asks the meaning of this terrible fratricide:

> "Ah, how many, like this soldier,
> Have been duped by Lincoln's call;
> Left behind their wives and children,
> On the bloody field to fall.

53. See, for example, Pollard, *Southern History of the War* II, 192–95; *Journal of the Congress of the Confederate States of America, 1861–1865* (Washington, D.C., 1904–1905) VI, 536–38; *Weekly Register*, Jan. 16, 1864, p. 10; Kean, *Inside the Confederate Government*, 127.

54. Edmondston, *Journal*, Dec. 1, 1863, pp. 78–79.

55. "The Serenade of 300,000 Federal Ghosts, Respectfully Dedicated to Old Black Abe," n.p., n.d. Confederate Collection, Rare Book Division, Library of Congress, Washington, D.C.

What is all this for? You ask me,
The answer's plain and will be told,
'Twas to tread on Southern honors,
And to rob the South of gold.

Lincoln, Seward, Sumner, Beecher,
Greeley, Banks and Butler, too,
With John Brown and Hinton Helper,
Wretches that have caused our woe."[56]

Confederate recalcitrance was not without its lighter side. Southerners delighted in lampooning Lincoln's vain attempts to capture Richmond; at the same time they ignored Union victories in the West. Southern humor in this vein usually ran along the lines of the rather good-natured popular song which warned the railsplitter not to come South, else he would be whipped and sent "to the Happy Land of Canaan."[57] The reverses of the Army of the Potomac were grist for the mills of Southern humorists. In one punnish poem, Lincoln is made to dwell upon his troubles in subjugating the stubborn rebels and to conclude, "We've got an armed fleet on the sea, / And a *fleet army* on the shore."[58] Southern cartoonists sketched a schoolmaster Lincoln scolding his class of boy generals, all unfortunate victims of Lee and Jackson. In another caricature, "Master Abraham Lincoln Gets a New Toy," a boyish, buffoonish Lincoln plays with a stick puppet labeled "Fighting Joe" [Hooker]; on a shelf behind him are discarded several puppet-generals who had come to grief in Virginia.[59] Bill Arp had something to say about Lincoln's generals and the formidable topography they encountered on the road to Richmond: "The way they hav been tryin to cum is through a mity Longstreet, over two powerful Hills, and across a tremendious Stonewall," Arp observed. "It would be safer and cheaper for em to go round by the Rocky Mountings, if spendin time in military xcursions is their

56. "My God! What is All This For?" n.p., n.d. *Ibid.*

57. "Happy Land of Canaan" appeared in several versions throughout the South, which fact testifies to its popularity. For examples, see *Hopkins' New Orleans 5-Cent Song Book* (New Orleans, 1861), 7, 14; *Jack Morgan Songster* (Raleigh, N. C., 1864), 39; *Songs of the South* (Richmond, Va., 1863), 18–19; "The Happy Land of Canaan: An Unpublished Civil War Song," *Civil War History*, 11 (March, 1965), 44.

58. *Songs of the South*, 38.

59. *Southern Illustrated News*, Jan. 31 and Feb. 28, 1863.

objek."[60] One joke making the rounds in the South—one which Lincoln himself might have appreciated—featured a gentleman calling upon the President to solicit a pass to Richmond. "Well," said Lincoln, "I would be very happy to oblige you, if my passes were respected; but the fact is, sir, I have, within the past two years, given passes to two hundred and fifty thousand men to go to Richmond, and not one has got there yet."[61] Of course, such humor could be nourished only by Confederate victories. After Gettysburg and Vicksburg, Southern humor lost much of its good-naturedness. Mrs. Chesnut remarked, on New Year's Day, 1864, that one no longer heard of the drinking and clowning of Grant and Lincoln but only of their wisdom.[62]

Almost every Southerner believed Lincoln to be a terrible dictator and despot. Tyrant, Czar, Caesar, King, "American Nebuchadnezzar," Nero, Cambyses, Charles IX, Philip II, Cromwell, King John, and George II were among the imperial epithets synonymous with Lincoln's name. For Southerners, Lincoln's presidency had been a series of despotic acts: his election violated the spirit of the Constitution, and Lincoln's illegal attempts to coerce the South forced four border states out. Having themselves withdrawn from the protection of the Constitution, Confederates watched with dismay the abrogation of liberties in the North: Lincoln's usurpation of congressional powers, dismemberment of Virginia, federal interference with state legislatures and elections, the Emancipation Proclamation, seizure of private property, suppression of newspapers, arbitrary arrests, and the suspension of habeas corpus. The situation, many Southerners thought, was not without irony; the man whom the North elected to subjugate the South became instead the agent for imposing a dictatorship upon the North.[63]

Southerners wondered how a once proud and free people could surrender their liberties with so little protest, especially to a man so vulgar

60. "Another Letter From Bill Arp to Mr. Lincoln," in Smith, *Bill Arp's Peace Papers*, 34. There is no date on this letter, but it is apparently *c.* late 1862.

61. Fontaine, ed., *Marginalia*, 170.

62. Chesnut, *Diary*, 344.

63. Howison, "History of the War," *Southern Literary Messenger*, 34 (Nov. and Dec., 1862). MacMahon, *Cause and Conflict*, 1–2, 172. A Gentleman of Mississippi, *Secession: Considered as a Right in the States Composing the Late American Union of States, and as to the Grounds of Justification of the Southern States in Exercising the Right* (Jackson, Miss., 1863), 37–43. "To Brother Jonathan" (poem) in *Southern Literary Messenger*, 35 (April, 1863), 252–53.

and inept as Abraham Lincoln.[64] Some observers saw Lincoln's despotism as the natural result of Northern political democracy. "We see nothing inconsistent in the establishment of a usurped tyranny, following a triumph of Democracy," wrote a champion of the "aristocratic republic" ideal in the South. "History teaches that the one is the entirely legitimate, if not inevitable sequel of the other. . . . Lincoln's election was a complete triumph of Democracy. . . . Democracy triumphed, and despotism has followed."[65] Alexander Stephens saw no good coming out of the North, now that the conservative counterweight of the South had left the Union. The North, he speculated darkly, had lost its liberties and was heading for anarchy and collapse; perhaps Seward might emerge as a Robespierre.[66] The Confederacy could wish good riddance to the North, whose submission to Lincoln's tyranny seemed proof of its moral bankruptcy and of its unworthiness to be politically associated with the South. Said Jefferson Davis to his Congress: "We may well rejoice that we have forever severed our connection with a government that thus tramples on all the principles of constitutional liberty, and with a people in whose presence such avowals could be hazarded."[67]

64. Kean, *Inside the Confederate Government*, 41–42. Pollard, *Southern History of the War* I, 651–52.

65. Frank H. Alfriend, "A Southern Republic and a Northern Democracy," *Southern Literary Messenger*, 35 (May, 1863), 286–87. Pollard, *Southern History of the War* I, 650.

66. Johnston and Browne, *Life of Stephens*, 404–405.

67. July 20, 1861, in Rowland, ed., *Jefferson Davis* V, 116. See also *ibid.*, 170. Edward A. Pollard bore down hard in his many books on Lincoln's supposed despotism. See, for example, his *Southern History of the War* II, 370–76, and *The Southern Spy; Letters on the Policy and Inauguration of the Lincoln War. . . .*, 2nd ed. (Richmond, Va., 1861). Of course, he was called upon to explain away the growing concentration of power in the hands of the Confederate executive: "To compare the falsehoods and crimes of the Washington record with that rigor of measures in the Confederacy, which was really nothing more than the logical incident and the proper expression of resolute patriotism, is an outrage upon history. The noble memorials of self-sacrificing patriotism are very different from the scarlet record of ruthless despotism." *Southern History of the War* II, 376. Pollard, no friend of Davis, soon changed his tune. He later wrote: "There was exhibited in Richmond a military tyranny that outdid the 'strong government' at Washington, that committed outrages . . . unexcelled in the history of sudden and violent usurpations." *Life of Jefferson Davis*, 214. Eventually, the Confederate war president was the victim of many of the same charges that were hurled at his Northern counterpart. However, Davis was never censured for making vulgar jokes. No one ever accused Jefferson Davis of having a sense of humor.

The Emancipation Proclamation, in Southern minds, was Lincoln's crowning act of tyranny. On September 22, 1862, Lincoln proclaimed that on January 1, "all persons held as slaves within any State or designated part of a State the people whereof shall then be in rebellion against the United States, shall be then, thenceforward, and forever free."[68] Although Congress, in its several Confiscation Acts, already had gone as far as the President in declaring free the slaves of persons supporting the rebellion, Lincoln's announcement dramatized to the South that the war had taken a new turn.[69] The proclamation was a pregnant document. Lincoln expressed his wish for a program of voluntary, gradual, and compensated emancipation in loyal slave states, and he encouraged the voluntary colonization of freed slaves outside the United States. The wording of the document suggested that if the people of any seceded state ceased to be in rebellion before January 1—that is, would quit the Confederacy and return to the Union—the emancipation provisions would not apply to them.

The subtleties of Lincoln's message—this "supreme act of outrage"—generally were lost upon the South.[70] Lincoln, thought Southerners, had dropped the mask at last and revealed the true nature of his party's war aims. All of Lincoln's disclaimers against meddling with slavery in the states now seemed exposed as calculated lies. Lincoln's government, said the *Fayetteville* (N. C.) *Semi-Weekly Observer*, "tried to keep us in the Union, by telling us that they had no design to interfere with the peculiar institution of the South. That lie is now confirmed by Lincoln's Proclamation."[71]

In his final proclamation of emancipation, on January 1, 1863, Lincoln called his action "a fit and necessary war measure."[72] Southerners believed the proclamation was a desperate attempt to win the war by destroying the Confederacy from within after the utter failure to sup-

68. Lincoln, *Works* V, 433–36.

69. Randall and Donald, *Civil War and Reconstruction*, 372–73.

70. Pollard, *Life of Jefferson Davis*, 253.

71. Oct. 27, 1862, quoted in Bardolph, "Malice Toward One," 43. For other reactions, see Pollard, *Southern History of the War* I, 529–32; *Southern Illustrated News*, Nov. 8, 1862 (cartoon: "Masks and Faces"); A Gentleman of Mississippi, *Secession*, 42; Rowland, ed., *Jefferson Davis* V, 409–11; *Journal of the House of Delegates of the State of Virginia, for the Called Secession of 1863. Document No. I: Message of the Governor of Virginia, and Accompanying Documents* (Richmond, Va., 1863).

72. Lincoln, *Works* VI, 28–30.

press it by force of arms.[73] Southerners were convinced that Lincoln hoped to raise a servile insurrection behind Southern lines and, by declaring the war an antislavery crusade, set slaveholder against nonslaveholder in the Confederacy. Lincoln was charged with willing the extermination of both races in the South. "It would consign the whites and blacks of the North American continent to one common ruin," exclaimed the *Raleigh Semi-Weekly Standard*. "It would extinguish the black race in less than ten years."[74] Lincoln seeks to do the work of Nat Turner, charged the *Confederate Monitor*, referring to the leader of the 1831 slave revolt in Virginia, and is a worse villain than Ben Butler. "In addition to all that Butler authorized, Lincoln adds butchery—even the butchery of *babes*!" Because servile war would result in mass killings of both races, the journal branded "the Fiend" Lincoln as "the common enemy of white and black."[75] "I wonder what will be the result of this diabolical move," a young Louisiana girl speculated to her diary,

> Surely not as bad for us as they intended it to be. I think that there is little chance for a happy hereafter for President Lincoln. A thousand years of repentance would be but brief time to wipe out his sins against the South. How can he even sleep with the shades of thousands he has consigned to a bloody death darkening his soul?[76]

The Emancipation Proclamation struck the South's most sensitive chord, and official reaction was quick and heated. Legislatures debated the wisdom of retaliatory moves to check Lincoln's terrible gambit. The Virginia Senate was asked to consider simply executing all United States citizens found within her borders.[77] President Davis ordered all Union

73. Pollard, *Southern History of the War* I, 531–32. *Journal of the Senate of the Commonwealth of Virginia . . . Extra Session. Document No. X. Communication of the Governor of Virginia Relative to Abraham Lincoln's Proclamation of Emancipation. January 20, 1863* (Richmond, Va., 1863).

74. Oct. 3, 1862, in Bardolph, "Malice Toward One," 44. See also *Southern Literary Messenger*, 35 (May, 1863), 313; and "Address of Congress to the People of the Confederate States (Adopted in December, 1863)," *Southern Historical Society Papers*, 1 (Jan., 1876), 32–33.

75. H. W. R. Jackson, *Confederate Monitor and Patriot's Friend, Containing Numerous Important and Thrilling Events of the Present Revolution. . . .* (Atlanta, 1862), 84–86.

76. John Q. Anderson, ed., *Brokenburn: A Diary of Kate Stone, 1861–1865* (Baton Rouge, La., 1955), 145–46. Diary entry of Oct. 1, 1862.

77. *Journal of the Senate of the Commonwealth of Virginia . . . 1862 . . . Extra Session* (Richmond, Va., 1862), 184.

officers captured in the company of rebellious slaves to be turned over to state authorities and dealt with in accordance with state laws concerning the incitement of slave insurrections (which laws provided almost certain death).[78] A few weeks later Davis declared his intention to turn over all Union officers captured within the Confederacy to the tender mercies of state authorities.[79] Many congressmen endorsed this proposal. Others demanded that no quarter be given the enemy, that no prisoners be taken. In the end cooler heads prevailed, and Congress declared that captured United States officers ought to be dealt with by the Confederate government, not by the states, but the president was authorized to make retaliations "to such extent as he may think proper."[80] Fear of federal reprisals upon Confederate prisoners counseled prudence, and no Union officer was executed for enforcing Lincoln's Emancipation Proclamation.

Confederate reaction to Lincoln's Emancipation Proclamation illustrated the tension and ambivalence in Southern minds regarding their peculiar institution. Slavery was believed to be the only institution able to hold in check a savage and barbarous people. Yet it was necessary for Southerners to believe—as they were not a wicked people—that the slaves were docile and happy with their condition and appreciative of the occasional crumbs of Christian civilization which chanced to drop from their master's table. Southerners lived simultaneously in states of fear and grace. When emancipation was promulgated, Southerners, suffering awful visions of slaves unleashed and running amok, damned Lincoln to hell and called down "the execrations of the civilized world against the monster."[81] At the same time, many Southerners tried to ignore the message or reassure themselves of its ineffectiveness. The *Southern Literary Messenger* dismissed the proclamation as "a silly Message. . . . A farce written and played by an illiterate buffoon, is not worth discussion."[82] For Josiah Gorgas, a Pennsylvanian who had cast his lot with his

78. General Orders No. 111, Dec. 24, 1862, in James D. Richardson, comp., *A Compilation of the Messages and Papers of the Confederacy Including the Diplomatic Correspondence, 1861–1865* (Nashville, Tenn., 1905) I, 273–74.

79. Jan. 12, 1863, in Rowland, ed., *Jefferson Davis* V, 409.

80. *Proceedings of the Confederate Congresses*, in *Southern Historical Society Papers*, NS (Richmond, Va., 1923–1959) IX (Dec., 1930), 7–8, 25–31. *Journal of the Congress of the Confederate States* III, 386; V, 469; VI, 486–87.

81. A Gentleman from Mississippi, *Secession*, 42. See also the song "John Brown's Entrance into Hell" (Baltimore, Md., 1862).

82. 34 (Nov.–Dec., 1862), 689.

adopted South and become head of the Confederate Ordnance Bureau, Lincoln's proclamation was worth noting only as it showed the drift of Northern opinion.[83] Other Southerners professed to see positive good in the document: it would close ranks in the South, sow confusion and dissension among her enemies, raise the price of slaves, and, according to Edward Pollard, attract "the interest of a candid world to the virtues and benefits of Southern slavery."[84]

Southerners did not fail to notice that Lincoln's ukase "emancipated" only those slaves in areas still in rebellion—that is, behind Confederate lines where Lincoln had no immediate power. Loyal slave states and parts of the Confederacy occupied by Union troops specifically were exempted from the provisions of the January 1 decree. This strengthened Southern convictions that Lincoln's motives were not humanitarian, but sinister and diabolical. As one rebel rhymer explained:

> The slaves now under Lincoln's will
> Continue in their bondage still;
> He only means—the tricky wretch,
> To set those free, he cannot catch.[85]

But whatever Lincoln's motives, Southerners knew that their ultimate security lay in the loyalty of the slaves to the system. Southerners told the North and each other that their slaves would turn a deaf ear to Lincoln's temptations of freedom. Once again, Bill Arp addressed himself to the President. The Negroes don't want to be free, he informed Lincoln; "If they won't aksept your freedom, why let em alone. Its useless to call em if they wont cum. . . ."[86]

83. Frank E. Vandiver, ed., *The Civil War Diary of General Josiah Gorgas* (University, Ala., 1947), Oct. 4, 1862, p. 16.

84. *Ibid.*, Oct. 17, 1862, p. 22. John Beauchamp Jones, *A Rebel War Clerk's Diary at the Confederate States Capital*, ed. Howard Swiggett (New York, 1935) I, 157, 159, 164. *Southern Literary Messenger*, 35 (Jan., 1863), 58. Pollard, *Southern History of the War* I, 532.

85. "Rhymes for the Times," in *Southern Literary Messenger*, 35 (March, 1863), 161.

86. "Another Letter from Bill Arp to Mr. Lincoln," in Smith, *Bill Arp's Peace Papers*, 31–34. Since the Emancipation Proclamation, Smith's humor had lost some of its good-naturedness. See *ibid.*, 27–34. In 1865, after Congress passed the Thirteenth Amendment abolishing slavery, Arp wrote that freeing the Negro would make no difference: "What does all it amount to? I want to by a nigger, and I had jist lief by a chunk of *free* nigger as eny other. I don't keer a darn about his bein free, I can subjergate him; and if he gits above his natur, I'll put 39 whelks rite

Means were employed to reinforce the slaves' loyalty. Slave patrols were strengthened. Masters told their slaves that they would be murdered or sold if they fell into Yankee hands. Although slaves often became unruly and ran away when a Union army appeared in the vicinity, the faith of the slaveholders in the loyalty and ignorance of their chattels was not misplaced. Most slaves worked docilely and steadfastly for the cause which fought to keep them in bondage.[87]

The tide of war ran strongly against the South in the summer of 1864. Grant hammered away at the gates of Richmond, and Sherman's army invested Atlanta. Mobile had been closed by Admiral Farragut. The Mississippi was a Union river, and the Confederacy was cut in twain. The dream of foreign recognition had vanished. Manpower and material resources diminished as more and more of the Confederacy came under Yankee occupation. Confederate logistics, always inadequate, threatened to break down altogether. Confederate prospects in this desperate year of 1864 centered on the hope that the North would weary of the bloody and seemingly futile war before the Confederate armies were overwhelmed.

It was hoped that Northerners would grow impatient with Lincoln's destruction of their liberties as he was killing their sons and husbands. Just as Lincoln overestimated unconditional unionist sentiment in the South, Southerners overestimated Yankee sympathy with their ideas of the proper relation of state and federal government. Peace movements in the North, Democratic electoral victories, rumors of troop mutinies, draft riots, and other disaffections were publicized widely in the South as evidence of growing resistance to the Lincoln despotism. Robert G. H. Kean, head of the Confederate Bureau of War, read the newspapers and noted in his diary in the spring of 1864: "Many hopeful indications of a general breaking up in the United States, political as well as financial."[88]

---

under his shirt, and make him wish that old Linkhorn stood in his shoes." *Ibid.*, 105.

87. James M. McPherson, *The Negro's Civil War. How American Negroes Felt and Acted During the War for the Union* (New York, 1965), 58. Benjamin Quarles, *The Negro in the Civil War* (Boston, 1953), 165. Coulter, *Confederate States of America*, 266.

88. Kean, *Inside the Confederate Government*, May 30, 1864, p. 143. *Magnolia Weekly*, March 19, 1864, p. 196. See also *Raleigh* (N. C.) *Semi-Weekly Standard*, Jan. 27, 1863, quoted in Bardolph, "Malice Toward One," 38; J. B. Jones, *Rebel War Clerk's Diary* I, March 29, 1863, p. 281; *Weekly Register*, April 23, 1861, p. 133.

Confederate attention centered on the Northern presidential election in 1864. Southerners were divided on the desirability of Lincoln's reelection. One group, encouraged by the growth of peace societies in the North, hoped that Lincoln would be overthrown and a candidate elected who would make peace on Southern terms. Most men of this persuasion looked to an eventual restoration of the Union, with slavery and the rights of states guaranteed. Alexander Stephens was a proponent of this view. "I know that many of our people think that any allusion to peace on our side is injurious to our cause," the vice president wrote in a published letter to Senator T. J. Semmes. "Some maintain that we cannot entertain any propositions unless they be based upon Independence. I concur in none of this reasoning."[89] Stephens believed that the North teetered on the brink of anarchy and revolution under Lincoln's dictatorship.[90] He was encouraged by the nomination of General George B. McClellan by the Democrats on a peace-and-reunion platform, an event which Stephens hailed as "the first ray of light from the North."[91] When McClellan, in his letter of acceptance, declared that reunion must be a precondition to peace, Stephens feared it would hurt his chances for election and would make an early peace more difficult. "Still," Stephens opined, "I should prefer his election to that of Lincoln."[92]

Senator Benjamin H. Hill of Georgia also desired McClellan's election. In a letter to Stephens, he put their common views succinctly: "Lincoln's defeat in the ensuing election will ensure that crushing [of abolitionism]. Peace will follow. His accession to power was the declaration of war. His continuance in power has been the continuance of war. His ejection from power will be the end of war."[93] Hill knew that Union military victories would quiet Northern criticism and secure Lincoln's reelection. To insure Republican defeat, Hill urged all-out resistance to the invading Union armies and proposed that the South tempt the North with promises of a peace convention should Lincoln be overthrown.[94]

89. Avery, ed., *Recollections of Alexander Stephens*, 77.

90. *Ibid.*, 75.

91. *Ibid.*, 77.

92. Stephens to Richard Malcolm Johnston, Oct. 2, 1864, in Johnston and Browne, *Life of Stephens*, 423.

93. March 14, 1864, in Phillips, ed., *Toombs-Stephens-Cobb Correspondence*, 635.

94. Hill to his wife, Feb. 7, 1864, in Benjamin H. Hill, Jr., *Senator Benjamin H. Hill, of Georgia: His Life, Speeches, and Writings* (Atlanta, 1891), 88–89.

Other Confederates reacted more favorably to the prospects of Lincoln's reelection. John B. Jones, Confederate war clerk, speculated that Lincoln's real motives were to consolidate himself in power in the North. Once safely reelected, Jones pondered, Lincoln might break with the abolitionists and end the war.[95] A large group of Confederates were apprehensive of a McClellan victory. These were men committed to an independent Confederacy. They feared what Stephens hoped for, that a victorious McClellan might seek peace and reunion on terms acceptable to large numbers of Southerners, thus dividing the South and perhaps breaking up the Confederate state. Better Lincoln than McClellan, they reasoned; a Lincoln victory would unite Southerners and strengthen their determination to fight to a triumphant conclusion.[96] President Davis may have shared this view, although he never admitted it publicly. After the election, Stephens accused Davis of preferring Lincoln to McClellan, a charge which Davis denied.[97] These two statesmen never were able to join their considerable talents on behalf of the Confederate cause—a cause on whose nature and ends they were in profound disagreement. For a time, in early 1865, the public was dismayed by the sad spectacle of an open squabble between its two highest elected officials.

Most Confederates probably expected Lincoln to be reelected. They told themselves that Lincoln could hardly lose when he commanded the purse, patronage, and army. "We may rest assured he will shrink from no means, as being too unfair or too low, too illegal or too unconstitutional to retain power," the *Wilmington* (N. C.) *Daily Journal* warned its readers.[98] After Sherman's capture of Atlanta and Republican victories in October state contests signaled the inevitability of Lincoln's reelection, a rebel soldier wrote defiantly in his diary: "From the account I can learn there is very little doubt that Lincoln will be reelected and if he is we may prepare for another four years of it. Well, *let her rip*, I say.

95. J. B. Jones, *Rebel War Clerk's Diary* II, 327. Nov. 8, 1864.

96. For examples of this view, see Spencer G. Welch, *A Confederate Surgeon's Letters to his Wife* (New York, 1911), 114; Kean, *Inside the Confederate Government*, 174; Susan Leigh Blackford, comp., *Letters from Lee's Army, or Memoirs of Life In and Out of the Army in Virginia During the War Between the States* (New York, 1947), 114.

97. Rowland, ed., *Jefferson Davis* VI, 409, 439–45. Kean, *Inside the Confederate Government*, Jan. 13, 1865, pp. 188–89.

98. Sept. 15, 1863, quoted in Bardolph, "Malice Toward One," 39. See also Chesnut, *Diary*, 451; and *DeBow's Review*, OS 34 (July and Aug., 1864), 101.

It is better to fight always than to give up."[99] A less sanguine thought occurred to the New England-born mistress of a Georgia plantation in the path of Sherman's army: "Today will probably decide the fate of the Confederacy," she wrote in her journal on election day. "If Lincoln is reelected I think our fate is a hard one. . . ." With Sherman's avenging hosts descending upon her world, she reflected, "I have never felt that slavery was altogether right. . . ."[100]

Lincoln's victory, then, was not unexpected, but Southerners were dismayed by its magnitude; McClellan carried only Kentucky, New Jersey, and Delaware.[101] All hope of ending the war with the help of a Northern peace movement was dead. No amount of rationalizing propaganda about Lincoln's dictatorship and controlled elections could mask the harsh fact that the North, with its immense populations and resources, was united in its determination to crush the Confederacy. Few Southerners, as they returned wearily to war, would agree with the young New Yorker in Lee's army who said that Lincoln's reelection was "the best thing that could happen for the Confederate States."[102] There seemed no other course save fighting on to the end. Josiah Gorgas, another Northerner in Confederate service, understood: "There is no use in disguising the fact that our subjugation is popular at the North, and the war must go on until this hope is crushed out and replaced by a desire for peace at any cost."[103]

The alternative to fighting on or surrender was a negotiated peace. Peace talks had gone on intermittently throughout the war. Because the "representatives" of one side or the other were not authorized to commit their governments, these unofficial exchanges never amounted to much.[104] High-level negotiations late in the war were frustrated by the basically irreconcilable terms acceptable to the two governments. An understanding of Lincoln's position in these talks is important because

99. Jay Taylor, ed., *Reluctant Rebel. The Secret Diary of Robert Patrick, 1861–1865* (Baton Rouge, La., 1959), 242. Diary entry of Oct. 30, 1864.

100. Dolly S. L. Burge, *A Woman's Wartime Journal* (Macon, Ga., 1927), 25. Nov. 8, 1864.

101. Kean, *Inside the Confederate Government*, 177.

102. Edward Laight Wells to his parents, Nov. 17, 1864, in Smith *et al.*, eds., *Mason Smith Family Letters*, 148.

103. Vandiver, ed., *Gorgas Diary*, Nov. 17, 1864, p. 150. See also *Southern Illustrated News*, Nov. 26, 1864, p. 248; and *Weekly Register*, Dec. 3, 1864, p. 287.

104. Randall, *Lincoln the President* IV, 156–57. Edward Chase Kirkland, *The Peacemakers of 1864* (New York, 1927), 51–206.

Southerners frequently alluded to it in constructing their image of their old enemy. Southerners critical of Lincoln saw in these fruitless negotiations evidence of Lincoln's hostility to the South. Other Southerners, especially after the war, tended to read into Lincoln's terms an excessive generosity and flexibility.

Lincoln made known his peace terms in the summer of 1864:

> Any proposition which embraces the restoration of peace, the integrity of the whole Union, and the abandonment of slavery, and which comes by and with an authority that can control the armies now at war with the United States will be received and considered by the Executive government of the United States, and will be met by liberal terms on other substantial and collateral points. . . .[105]

Lincoln told Congress that he saw little good in negotiations with "the insurgent leader," since Davis would accept nothing less than an independent Confederacy. But there was a growing faction in the South, he said, which desires peace and reunion. He held out his hand to those who would accept emancipation and the restoration of national authority; the door, he said, is "open to all." The President concluded: "In stating a single condition of peace, I mean simply to say that the war will cease on the part of the government, whenever it shall have ceased on the part of those who began it."[106]

Jefferson Davis despaired equally of negotiating with Lincoln. Zebulon Vance, governor of North Carolina, advised Davis that if fair terms were offered Lincoln and rejected, it would strengthen war sentiment in his state. Davis replied that a conference with Lincoln or his representatives was not desirable. After reviewing several abortive offers to negotiate, Davis asked: "Have we not been apprised by that despot that we can only expect his gracious pardon by emancipating all our slaves, swearing allegiance and obedience to him and his proclamations, and becoming in point of fact the slaves of our negroes?" Peace and independence, he concluded, cannot come "until the enemy is beaten out of his vain confidence in our subjugation."[107]

One of the frustrated attempts at negotiations described by Davis in his letter to Vance had been initiated by Alexander Stephens. Stephens

105. "To Whom It May Concern," July 18, 1864, in Lincoln, *Works* VII, 451. See also Lincoln's letter to Horace Greeley, July 9, 1864, *ibid.*, 435.

106. Dec. 6, 1864, *ibid.*, VIII, 151–52.

107. Davis to Vance, Jan. 8, 1864, in Rowland, ed., *Jefferson Davis* VI, 143–46.

thought the military situation in June, 1863—Lee had repulsed Hooker at Chancellorsville, and Vicksburg still held out against Grant—would render the North responsive to overtures for a negotiated peace. He proposed to Davis that he be sent to Washington to confer with federal authorities on the matter of prisoner exchanges. Once there Stephens was confident that he could expand the area of negotiation to a discussion of ways and means to end the war. Stephens did not consider his proposed visit as a peace mission. He wanted to acquaint Lincoln with Confederate war aims and with the dangers to civil liberties should the war continue and to open the way for future negotiations. Privately he hoped that his good relations with Lincoln before the war would give him some leverage with the President. But if Lincoln were unresponsive to his suggestions, Stephens was prepared to appeal to the mass of Northern people by publishing the letters and notes relating to the conference.

Davis summoned Stephens to Richmond, where the vice president was dismayed to learn of Lee's invasion of Pennsylvania. He felt that this turn of military events undermined the success of his proposed mission; Northerners would be less willing to negotiate with a rebel army on their soil. Davis pinned his expectations for peace on Lee's bayonets, not Stephens' diplomatic maneuvers. But he told Stephens to go ahead and authorized him to discuss the treatment and exchange of prisoners "and all kindred subjects" but to take care that the "equal rights of the Confederacy be always preserved." Secretary of War James A. Seddon, realizing the Vicksburg garrison of 30,000 was doomed, hoped that at least a prisoner exchange could be worked out. Stephens, with something less than enthusiasm, set out and got as far as Newport News before being turned back by federal authorities.[108] As Lincoln later explained to Horace Greeley, since Stephens had come on a military mission and was not authorized to treat for peace, Lincoln had no interest in seeing him. Military matters could be handled through established military channels without recognizing Confederate civilian authority.[109] Stephens returned to Georgia. He was to serve his country once more in the cause of peace, as a representative to the Hampton Roads Conference on February 3, 1865.

108. Stephens, *Constitutional View* II, 558–68. John H. Reagan, *Memoirs, with Special Reference to Secession and the Civil War* (New York, 1906), 166. Rowland, ed., *Jefferson Davis* V, 513–19.

109. Lincoln to Greeley, Aug. 9, 1864, in Lincoln, *Works* VII, 490.

As Sherman slashed his way through Georgia and South Carolina and Grant tightened the vise on Richmond, sentiment for peace on terms less than independence was rising throughout the remnants of the Confederacy. Besides Stephens, Secretary of War Seddon and his assistant John A. Campbell, and R. M. T. Hunter and many of his colleagues in Congress hoped for peace and reunion. Campbell had written his former colleague on the Supreme Court bench, Justice Samuel Nelson, asking him to inquire into possible avenues for peace and suggesting a high-level conference. Robert G. H. Kean remembered that Campbell had told him that defeat was inevitable; the only question remaining was whether the South would return to the Union subjugated or with rights and honors. Kean would have none of it. Defeat meant Yankee and Negro rule, and he told Campbell he would emigrate rather than accept it.[110]

A medium through which negotiations might be realized appeared in the unlikely personage of old Francis Preston Blair, who turned up in Richmond in January seeking an interview with President Davis. Blair, who had learned his politics as an intimate of Andrew Jackson, was the patriarch of a powerful political clan; his son Montgomery had been Lincoln's postmaster general, and another son, Frank, Jr., was a congressman and a Union general. Blair was a Southern man, a Marylander, with many connections throughout the Confederacy by blood, marriage, and politics. Jefferson Davis was an old friend and before the war was a frequent guest in Blair's home near Washington. Blair had come to plead for peace. He proposed a course which, he believed, would reconstruct the Union on its old principles, check the rising radical spirit in the Northern Congress, and restore the waning political fortunes of his family.[111]

The Confederacy was doomed, Blair told Davis, and if the war went on much longer, Northern liberties would go too. Slavery was finished whatever happened. Better the war should end now, he asserted, with the nation reunited, its liberties preserved, and slavery abolished. Blair's

110. Kean, *Inside the Confederate Government*, Christmas Day, 1864, p. 182. Several days later, Kean noted, "The number is certainly increasing of those who do not insist on [independence], but would make peace with reconstruction on the old grounds of property and right, and not a few would agree to gradual emancipation." Jan. 13, 1865, *ibid.*, 187–88. See also Coulter, *Confederate States of America*, 533–51.

111. Kirkland, *Peacemakers of 1864*, 196–97.

plan, which he admitted might be the dream of an old man, was that a military convention be concluded between the belligerents, after which Davis, supported by the North, would lead his army to drive Maximilian out of Mexico. A new birth of fraternal nationalism would pour forth out of this common enforcement of the Monroe Doctrine. Jefferson Davis would be a hero to both North and South. And while Blair talked of restoring Mexican liberties, he also evoked the vision of the American eagle spreading over Mexico and Central America.[112]

It *was* an old man's dream, a fantasy which had touched the thoughts of men on both sides whose good sense had been dulled by four terrible years of war.[113] It was impossible that the passions of war could be set aside so easily, that the North should give up its objectives with the victory in sight at last, that hundreds of thousands of men who had been killing each other in unprecedented numbers and who only wanted to see the thing through and go home could be persuaded to march a thousand miles to fight in a politician's foreign adventure.

At any rate, Davis was little moved by Blair's design. He considered the Mexican adventure impractical, and, of course, he disagreed with Blair's premise that slavery and the Confederacy were doomed if the war continued. But Davis was not unwilling to negotiate, with Confederate independence as the *sine qua non* of any settlement reached. He assumed that Blair, armed with a pass from Lincoln, had consulted with the Northern President. Lincoln must be interested in an armistice and talks. An armistice could only benefit the Confederacy. Perhaps, under its aegis, an agreement for peace and independence could be worked out. At the very least, Lee's army would be granted a much-needed rest to gather supplies and recruits. So Davis reasoned, and Stephens agreed. Davis sent Blair back to Washington bearing a letter expressing Davis' willingness "to enter into a conference with a view to securing peace to the two countries."[114]

As a matter of fact, Lincoln had granted Blair a pass without inquiring into that gentleman's purposes. He had not authorized Blair to speak for him and knew nothing of the proposed Mexican venture. When Blair

112. *Ibid.*, 199–203. Davis, *Rise and Fall* II, 614–15.

113. The plan was a pet of James Gordon Bennett's *New York Herald*. See Randall, *Lincoln the President* IV, 282–83, 324.

114. Jan. 12, 1865, in Rowland, ed., *Jefferson Davis* VI, 468. Davis, *Rise and Fall* II, 614–15. Stephens, *Constitutional View* II, 593.

returned Lincoln quickly disabused the old man of any expectations that his government would back a military convention leading to a joint expedition to oust Maximilian. He gave Blair a letter to show Davis, in which he wrote that he would receive informally any Confederate agent "with the view of securing peace to the people of our one common country." The reference to "one common country" was a pointed answer to Davis' "two countries." The substance and tone of the message were consistent with Lincoln's July 18, 1864, statement on negotiations, although he omitted direct reference to emancipation as a prerequisite to peace and reunion.[115]

"Two countries" or "one common country": that was the measure of difference between Jefferson Davis and Abraham Lincoln. The fate of the Hampton Roads Conference was written in those few contrary syllables. But both presidents were willing to talk. After receiving Blair a second time, on January 21, Davis decided to send commissioners to meet with Lincoln or his representatives. The Mexican plan meant nothing to Davis, but Lincoln seemed ready to negotiate. He appointed Stephens, Campbell, and Hunter as commissioners, all of whom personally favored peace and reunion, and instructed them not to compromise on independence. Lincoln sent Seward to meet the Confederates at Fortress Monroe, with instructions to insist on three points as the basis of a settlement: restoration of national authority in the South, emancipation, and no armistice short of an end to the war.[116] After reading a telegram from Grant, who had met Stephens and Hunter as they passed through his lines and who testified to their sincere intentions, Lincoln decided to go himself. Lincoln's sudden decision to participate personally in the conference may have been influenced by an interview he had the day before with General James W. Singleton, Democratic congressman from Illinois and recently returned from a visit to Richmond. Singleton had told the President that the South longed for peace and might accept reunion on the basis of compensated emancipation, guarantees of states' rights, and liberal terms of reconstruction.[117]

Lincoln and Seward met the Confederate commissioners on a steamer

115. Lincoln to Blair, Jan. 18, 1865. Lincoln, *Works* VIII, 220. Stephens, *Constitutional View* II, 600.

116. Lincoln to Seward, Jan. 31, 1861, in Lincoln, *Works* VIII, 279.

117. Randall, *Lincoln the President* IV, 331.

anchored in Hampton Roads off Fortress Monroe.[118] Only the five men were present and no notes were taken. After an exchange of pleasantries and reminiscences of happier times, the five settled down to four uninterrupted hours of debate. Stephens hoped that the question of reunion or independence for the South could be set aside. He pressed for a variation of Blair's proposal: an armistice to be followed by an enforcement of the Monroe Doctrine in Mexico. Stephens considered the Monroe Doctrine an extension of the principle of "the Sovereign right of local Self-government" (which was the point of departure for all of Stephens' thinking about public affairs). He suggested that the enforcement of that principle in Mexico would allow time for blood to cool on both sides in the United States and would bring about a clearer understanding of the principles upon which the Union ought to be restored. Stephens meant that Northern troops should carry out the task of rescuing Mexico. "We had determined not to enter into any agreement that would require the Confederate arms to join in any invasion of Mexico," he wrote years later. The Confederate commissioners understood among themselves that Lee's army ought to be spared to make maximum use of any armistice to strengthen itself.

Seward showed interest in this dubious proposal. Perhaps he recalled his own similar and equally bizarre proposal to Lincoln, nearly four years before, to restore the Union by foreign wars. Lincoln let Stephens go on for awhile, although he tried constantly to nudge the discussions back to the real issue of Confederate refusal or acceptance of reunion. There can be no armistice, Lincoln asserted finally, until the question of reunion is decided. Stephens asked about the status of slaves. Lincoln replied that he believed the Emancipation Proclamation to be a war measure that would cease freeing slaves after peace, but that this was a question for

118. Lincoln's and Seward's accounts of the meeting are in Lincoln, *Works* VIII, 274–85, 286–87. The Confederate Commissioners' report to Davis is in Rowland, ed., *Jefferson Davis* VI, 466–67. R. G. H. Kean describes the conference as he heard it from his friend Campbell, in *Inside the Confederate Government*, 194–98. Campbell's own account is in "Campbell Papers," 45–52. For Stephens' account, see *Constitutional View* II, 599–619. Hunter gives his impressions in a letter to James M. Mason, Sept. 12, 1870, in Fitzhugh Lee, "The Failure of the Hampton Conference," *The Century Magazine*, 52 (July, 1896), 478. For Davis' recollections, see *Rise and Fall* II, 608–25. A good narrative of the conference may be found in Kirkland, *Peacemakers of 1864*, 206–58.

the courts. Seward read a copy of the Thirteenth Amendment, which had passed Congress a few days before, and suggested that the Southern states, once returned to the Union, could defeat the amendment by voting against it as a bloc and denying it the three-fourths necessary for ratification.

According to Stephens, Lincoln added that he did not want to interfere with slavery in the states and would not have proclaimed emancipation except as necessary to save the Union; he favored freeing the slaves but not immediately. He urged the Southern states to recognize the inevitable doom of slavery and to ratify the Thirteenth Amendment "prospectively," to take effect in five years. This meant, without saying it, the abandonment of the Confederacy and return to the Union.[119] As the conference neared its end Lincoln assured the Confederates that the Southern people and states, when restored to the Union, would be under the protection of the Constitution; he, Lincoln, would use the executive power, as regards confiscations, pardons, and restoration of rights of citizens, "with the utmost liberality," and the Congress and courts would act in the same spirit. He added that he believed the North to be as much responsible for slavery as the South, and that he would be willing to be taxed to indemnify slaveholders in states voluntarily giving up slavery. Lincoln emphasized that he could give no assurance on this matter but only was expressing his personal views and those of many Northerners.[120]

"The conference ended without result," Lincoln told Congress.[121] The two sides were committed to irreconcilable positions; there was no room for compromise between disunion and reunion. The three Confederate commissioners, who longed for an agreement which would permit them to reenter the Union with honor—as they defined honor—agreed that Lincoln offered no acceptable terms. To consent to reunion without a treaty or written guarantees of state and individual rights, said

119. Stephens, *Constitutional View* II, 614–15. This incident is not mentioned in Campbell's memorandum, which was written very soon after the conference.

120. On Feb. 5, Lincoln submitted to his cabinet a proposed recommendation for a joint congressional resolution which would empower the President to distribute $400 million to the slave states to compensate slaveholders, once resistance to the federal government had ceased and the Thirteenth Amendment became law. The cabinet unanimously disapproved, and Lincoln withdrew the proposal. Lincoln, *Works* VIII, 260–61.

121. Feb. 10, 1865, *ibid.*, 285.

Hunter, amounted to "unconditional submission."[122] Davis concurred and charged Blair and Lincoln with bad faith. Years later Davis wrote that Lincoln must have changed his mind about negotiations after Blair returned to Washington. As Davis saw it, Lincoln was ready to negotiate a settlement favorable to Southern independence until Blair reported the existence of a large and active peace faction in the Confederate government. Encouraged, Lincoln decided to demand unconditional surrender.[123]

After the collapse of the Hampton Roads Conference, Davis carried to his people the message that Lincoln had refused peace and was determined to conquer and exterminate them. In a series of fiery and uncompromising speeches—one of which occasioned Davis' old enemy, E. A. Pollard, to remark that he had never "been so much moved by the power of words spoken for the same space of time"—Davis and his supporters rallied their people back to war.[124] Although temporarily raising the temperature of Richmond and her citizens, these rhetorical pyrotechnics did nothing to stop Grant or Sherman or to check the deterioration of the Confederacy's capacity to wage war.

After the war some Southerners misread Lincoln's position at the Hampton Roads Conference. Frequently, these men were critics of Jefferson Davis, and they contrasted what they believed to be the narrow and conventional statesmanship of Davis with Lincoln's magnanimity and wisdom. Gifted with hindsight, these critics, of whom the editor Henry Watterson was prominent, charged that Davis ought to have realized that the game was pretty much up by February, 1865, that slavery and independence were doomed, and that he should have sought the best and most honorable terms for the defeated South. Such a course probably would have prevented a punitive reconstruction period. According to these critics Lincoln offered honorable terms. His position at the conference was magnified to include a concrete offer of $400 million to compensate Southern slaveholders if they but would return to the

122. Stephens, *Constitutional View* II, 616. *Southern Historical Society Papers,* 4 (July to Dec., 1877), 306.

123. Davis, *Rise and Fall* II, 618–19. Alexander Stephens later wrote that Davis had attributed Lincoln's supposed change of policy to the fall of Fort Fisher and the closing of Wilmington, N. C., the Confederacy's last port. *Constitutional View* II, 619–21.

124. Pollard, *Life of Jefferson Davis,* 471.

Union and a willingness to let the South write the terms once reunion was agreed upon.[125] Whether Davis deserves censure or praise for clinging to the reed of independence until his capital had fallen, his armies scattered, and he himself was a prisoner, depends upon the perspective of the reader surveying these events. Nevertheless, it was a curious spectacle when Southerners exaggerated the virtues of their late enemy to discredit the reputation of their old chief.

John Wilkes Booth, an actor and Confederate sympathizer, shot and mortally wounded Abraham Lincoln in a Washington theater on the night of Good Friday, April 14, 1865. The President's death, coming only a few days after his armies entered Richmond and forced Lee's surrender, permitted the defeated and demoralized Southerners once again to focus their thoughts and passions upon the man who had been the architect of their ruin.

Although no American President had been assassinated before 1865, it should not have surprised Southerners to hear of Lincoln's murder. No President had engendered so much hate. For years Confederates had been told that countless Northern assassins lay in wait for Lincoln, so deep was the loathing for him among his own people. Rebel newspapers from time to time carried private advertisements placing a price on Lincoln's head.[126] Yet many Southerners refused to believe the news as it filtered south. The collapse of the Confederacy, like all apocalyptic events, was attended by a thousand rumors. "If we are poor in every thing else we are least rich in rumors," a Georgia girl remarked to her diary.[127] In their eleventh hour as an independent people, Confederates heard not only of Lincoln's death, but also that an armistice had been agreed upon, that the European powers had recognized the Confederacy, and that a French fleet stood off New Orleans (in other versions Napoleon III had landed troops in Texas or bombarded occupied Charleston). "None of our people believe any of the rumors," observed army nurse Kate Cum-

125. Reagan, *Memoirs*, 166–79. Julian Shakespeare Carr, *The Hampton Roads Conference. A Refutation of the Statement that Mr. Lincoln Said if Union was Written at the Top the Southern Commissioners Might Fill in the Balance* [Durham, N.C.? 1917].

126. *Berryville* (Va.) *Cultivator*, March 12, 1862, reprinted in *Magazine of History with Notes and Queries*. Extra Number—No. 157. Rare Lincolniana No. 38 (Tarrytown, N.Y., 1930), 21. *Charlotte* (N.C.) *Bulletin*, May 28, 1861, quoted in Bardolph, "Malice Toward One," 36.

127. April 27, 1865, in Hardin, *Private War of Lizzie Hardin*, 235.

ming, "thinking them as mythical as the surrender of General Lee's army. They look upon it as a plot to deceive the people."[128]

For many Southerners the hatred born of four years of terrible war spilled forth as undisguised joy at the news of Lincoln's death. In Fort Delaware rebel prisoners greeted the event with cheers and threw their hats in the air; one hospitalized prisoner said he would gladly share his last crust of bread with Booth.[129] The demonstration so alarmed the federal commandant that he leveled his guns on the prisoners and threatened to fire on any rebel expressing delight at the news. For a refugee soldier from Lee's army, sunk in despair and grieving over the recent death of a brother in battle, "Lincoln's death seemed . . . like a gleam of sunshine on a winter's day."[130] Lizzie Hardin realized assassination was wrong, but after all the killing and suffering, "it seems a wrong for which there are many excuses." She found the day bright with hope for her country.[131] Another Southern girl regretted only that Booth had waited so long, and a rebel private wished Old Abe had been killed four years before.[132] Booth's act, with its theatrical flourishes—the handsome young actor brandished a dagger and shouted "Sic semper tyrannis," escaping across a stage in full view of hundreds—appealed to the morbid romanticism that lay coiled in the breasts of many fair Southern ladies. Kate Stone, driven from her plantation home and exiled in Texas, thought Booth had earned the applause of generations and hoped he would find refuge in the South.[133] Emma LeConte, whose home city of Columbia, South Carolina, had been reduced to ashes by Sherman's men, confessed that she trembled with joy at the news and feared only that the story was

128. April 22, 1865, Cumming, *Kate*, 275. William W. Heartsill, *Fourteen Hundred and 91 Days in the Confederate Army. . . .*, ed. Bell I. Wiley (Jackson, Tenn., 1954), May 7, 1865, p. 241. Taylor, ed., *Reluctant Rebel*, 27.

129. "Diary of Captain Robert E. Park," in *Southern Historical Society Papers*, 3 (May and June, 1877), 245–46. Opinion in the camp was divided on the desirability of Lincoln's assassination. Many of the officers felt it would do great harm to the South. Ben Crampton Papers, Maryland Historical Society (taken from the E. B. Long–Bruce Catton Notes for *Centennial History of the Civil War*, 1865/249/51, Manuscripts Division, Library of Congress, Washington, D. C.).

130. W. O. Harris, in *Lincoln Centenary Services, 1909, Temple Adeth Israel* (Louisville, Ky., 1909), 15–17.

131. April 23, April 26, 1865, in Hardin, *Private War of Lizzie Hardin*, 233–35.

132. April 23, 1865, in Edmonston, *Journal*, 104–105. Diary entry of Pvt. R. W. Waldrop, April 19, 1865, in Wiley, *Common Soldier of the Civil War* II, 312.

133. Anderson, ed., *Brokenburn*, April 28, 1865, p. 333.

a Yankee lie. "Sic semper tyrannis," she scribbled rapturously in her diary, "Could there have been a fitter death for such a man?"[134] Opinion in Texas, of all Confederate states the one touched least by the war, may have been the most uncompromising in its approval of the murder. Booth, said Texas newspapers, surely was a Divine instrument sent to remove the bloody-handed despot who "had not only gloated over our suffering, but was preparing new measures of vengeance to mete out to us."[135] Said the Marshall *Texas Republican*: "It is certainly a matter of congratulation that Lincoln is dead, because the world is happily rid of a monster that disgraced the form of humanity."[136]

In contrast to these widespread endorsements of Booth's act, mass meetings were held in New Orleans, Nashville, Savannah, Natchez, Charleston, and other Southern cities in which speakers deplored Lincoln's assassination and resolutions of disapprobation of the deed were passed.[137] One must not make too much of these meetings as expressions of sincere Southern sentiment toward Lincoln. By mid-April, 1865, most Southern cities were under Union occupation, and thousands of troops, freedmen, and Union sympathizers could be marshalled to fill public squares and churches. Ex-rebels no doubt found it politic under the circumstances to attend these meetings, thereby disassociating themselves from Booth's deed. For example, Dr. Richard D. Arnold, the secessionist mayor of Savannah who had seen his city delivered as a "Christmas present" to Lincoln from Sherman, helped organize a mass meeting of citizens to express sorrow at the assassination.[138] Prudence suggested

134. Earl Schenck Miers, ed., *When the World Ended: The Diary of Emma LeConte* (New York, 1957), April 21, 1865, pp. 91–93.

135. *Dallas Herald*, May 4, 1865, and *Galveston News*, April 28, 1865, quoted by Steen, "Texas Newspapers and Lincoln," pp. 202, 203.

136. April 28, 1865, quoted in *ibid*., 201.

137. J. S. Whitaker, *Louisiana's Tribute to the Memory of Abraham Lincoln. . . . Public Demonstrations in the City of New Orleans* (New Orleans, La., 1881). [J. W. Davidson], *Resolutions Adopted at a Meeting of the Officers of the Army and Navy and Citizens of Natchez on the Death of the President of the United States* (Natchez, Miss., 1865). *Tribute to the Late President Lincoln. Report of the Great Mass Meeting in Savannah, the Largest Ever Held in the City. . . . On Saturday, April 23, 1865* (Savannah, Ga., 1865). See also Martin Abbott, "Southern Reaction to Lincoln's Assassination," *Abraham Lincoln Quarterly*, 7 (Sept., 1952), 119–23.

138. Richard D. Shryock, ed., *Letters of Richard D. Arnold, M. D., 1808–1876. Papers of the Trinity College Historical Society, Double Series XVIII–XIX* (Durham, N. C., 1929), 119n.

that public lamentations would spare life and property from avenging Yankee soldiery. Sarah Dawson observed sardonically that New Orleans was draped with the black crepe of mourning: "the more violently 'secesh' the inmates, the more thankful they are for Lincoln's death, the more profusely the houses are decked with emblems of woe.... Men who have hated Lincoln with all their souls, under terror of confiscation and imprisonment which they *understand* is the alternative, tie black crape from every practicable knob and point to save their homes."[139] When these meetings shouted hosannas to the Union army and called down God's wrath upon traitors and rebels, one begins to doubt that they reflected faithfully the sentiments of the majority of the citizenry.

Yet, there is ample record that many Southerners truly were appalled by Lincoln's murder. Sergeant W. W. Heartsill, a Texas cavalryman who wanted to continue the fight, deemed it unfortunate that Old Abe had "Gone up the spout."[140] Some were not displeased that the tyrant had met his end but deplored the manner of it; assassination, they declared loftily, was not the way of Southern gentlemen.[141] The bishop of Natchez feared the assassination would bring down the wrath of God upon the South, and he called upon his parishioners to atone for the crime with prayers and the taking of sacraments.[142] More mundane Southerners feared the immediate wrath of the Yankees. The ascension to power of Andrew Johnson—"that vulgar renegade"—filled Southern hearts with fear and disgust. Mrs. Chesnut learned of the assassination on the day before her silver anniversary—"the unhappiest day of my life"—and believed it would bring down even worse miseries upon the South.[143] A Baptist minister in Richmond told his congregation that Lincoln's murder "was a stupendous crime against the South. . . . Its tendencies are to inflict a deeper injury upon us. . . ."[144]

139. Sarah Morgan Dawson, *A Confederate Girl's Diary* (Bloomington, Ind., 1960), April 22, 1865, pp. 437–38.

140. Heartsill, *Fourteen Hundred and 91 Days*, May 7, 1865, p. 241.

141. T. C. DeLeon, *Four Years in Rebel Capitals; An Inside View of Life in the Southern Confederacy from Birth to Death* (Mobile, Ala., 1890), 367. *John Dooley, Confederate Soldier; His War Journal*, ed. Joseph T. Durkin, S. J. (Notre Dame, Ind., 1963), 195–97.

142. Pastoral message of Bishop William Henry Elder, Bishop of Natchez, in Willard E. Wright, ed., "The Bishop of Natchez on the Death of Lincoln," *Lincoln Herald*, 58 (Fall, 1956), 13–14.

143. Chesnut, *Diary*, April 22, 1865, p. 380.

144. "Extract from a Sermon Preached at the First Baptist Church, Sunday,

For Alexander Stephens, Lincoln's death caused deep, personal sorrow. Stephens thought the South would have been safe remaining in the Union with Lincoln as President and would have been safer returning to it had Lincoln lived. They had been something other than enemies, and Stephens had a special reason for cherishing the memory of the late President. As the Hampton Roads Conference broke up, Lincoln had asked Stephens if he could do anything for him. Stephens requested the release of his nephew, Lieutenant John A. Stephens, a prisoner of war since the fall of Port Hudson a year and a half before. Lincoln immediately had the young man released and sent South, an act of generosity for which the elder Stephens was deeply grateful. Soon after the collapse of the Confederacy, Stephens was imprisoned in Boston's Fort Warren. On a day officially set aside for fasting and mourning, the ailing Stephens joined in abstention in tender tribute to his late friend.[145]

Many ranking Confederate officers were dismayed on hearing of Lincoln's death. They believed that they had lost a generous foe and that Northern opinion would be inflamed against the Southern people. General Joseph E. Johnston received the news as he was negotiating the surrender of his army to Sherman; he told Sherman he believed Lincoln's death to be "the greatest possible calamity to the South." Like sentiments were expressed by Admiral Raphael Semmes, Generals Lee, George Pickett, and Richard S. Ewell, and by other officers in flight or prison.[146]

Reports of the assassination overtook Jefferson Davis at Charlotte,

---

April 23, 1865, Upon the Assassination of Abraham Lincoln, President of the United States," in J. Lansing Burrows, D. D., *Palliative and Prejudiced Judgments Condemned. . . .* (Richmond, Va., 1865). For similar sentiments see J. B. Jones, *Rebel War Clerk's Diary* II, 479; and Eliza Frances Andrews, *The War-Time Journal of a Georgia Girl, 1864–1865*, ed. Spencer Bidwell King (Macon, Ga., 1960), 172–73.

145. Avery, ed., *Recollections of Alexander Stephens*, 141. Lincoln, *Works* VIII, 259, 287. Marta Lockett Avery, "A Lincoln Souvenir in the South. A Letter from Abraham Lincoln to Alexander Stephens, Which Hangs on the Walls of a Southern Home," *Century Magazine*, 73 (Feb., 1907), 506–508. *Lincoln Herald*, 45 (June, 1943), 18–21.

146. Joseph E. Johnston, *Narrative of Military Operations* (Bloomington, Ind., 1959), 402. Eva and Mary Parrish, "What the South Thinks of Lincoln," *The Epworth Herald*, Feb., 6, 1909, p. 941. Mrs. General Pickett, "President Lincoln: Intimate Personal Recollections," *Lippincott's Magazine*, May, 1906, p. 560. Beverley Tucker, *Address of Beverley Tucker, Esq., to the People of the United States, 1865*, ed. James Harvey Young (Atlanta, 1948), 17. Letter of Richard S. Ewell to U. S. Grant, April 16, 1865 (Long-Catton-Centennial History notes: 1865/249/49).

North Carolina, where he had paused in flight with the remnants of his government. Davis later would be accused of masterminding the assassination; a price was put on his head, and a dungeon and felon's chains awaited him.[147] No one will know what thoughts surged through his mind as he read the telegram announcing the death of his great adversary. Four long years before, the man and his hour had met in Montgomery and launched a great nation. Now all was reduced to this fugitive and his pitiable corporal's guard in a Carolina piney wood. But there seems to have been no malice in Jefferson Davis' heart. According to various accounts he received the news calmly, remarked briefly that it brooked ill for the South, quieted the few, scattered cheers with a short speech. The slight details of the scene vary with the witness.[148] Davis himself wrote years later that he considered Lincoln a kind-hearted man who was preferable to Andrew Johnson. "For an enemy so relentless in the war for our subjugation, we could not be expected to mourn; yet, in view of its political consequences, it could not be regarded otherwise than as a great misfortune to the South." Had Lincoln lived, Davis concluded, perhaps reconstruction would have been less destructive to Southern liberties.[149]

On June 1, 1865, the day set aside by President Andrew Johnson for public fasting and mourning in the memory of his late predecessor, the Reverend J. Lansing Burrows mounted the pulpit of his First Baptist Church of Richmond, opened his text, and began to speak to his fellow Southerners about Abraham Lincoln. As "Christians and honest men," Burrows said, it is right and proper for Southerners to join the nation in mourning and to express horror and grief for the assassination. There

147. Seymour J. Frank, "The Conspiracy to Implicate the Confederate Leaders in Lincoln's Assassination," *Mississippi Valley Historical Review*, 40 (March, 1954), 629–56.

148. *New York Times*, Feb. 10, 1909. *Richmond Dispatch*, Feb. 21, 25, 1900. Basil W. Duke, "Last Days of the Confederacy," in Robert Edward Johnson and Clarence Clough Buel, eds., *Battles and Leaders of the Civil War* (New York, 1956), IV, 762–67. Reagan, *Memoirs*, 208. Burton N. Harrison, "Extracts from a Narrative, Written Not for Publication but for the Entertainment of My Children Only," in Rowland, ed., *Jefferson Davis* VII, 1–3. William Johnston to Davis, March 29, 1882, in *ibid.* IX, 158. Stephen R. Mallory, Diary, Southern Historical Collection, University of North Carolina (Long-Catton-Centennial History notes: 1865/253/54–55).

149. Davis, *Rise and Fall* II, 683–84, 685–86. Jefferson Davis to Crafts J. Wright, May 11, 1876, in Rowland, ed., *Jefferson Davis* VII, 514.

is no hypocrisy in this, even though Lincoln represented principles against which the South fought and bled. "We accept the settlement of these principles by the arbitration of war and by the providence of God," declared Burrows. "We mean to be what we have sworn to be, faithful and loyal subjects of that government, to maintain and uphold its authority and influence." As for Abraham Lincoln, the South's late foeman:

> We believe he was disposed to be generous and liberal in his measures for the reconstruction of the government. No harsh or vengeful or malignant thoughts toward our people seemed to find place in his heart, in arranging for the settlement of the great controversy. He would, I doubt not, as leniently and benevolently as possible, have exerted his great influence and authority. His death is, therefore, a calamity to us for which we mourn.[150]

It is impossible to say how many Southerners at the end of the war shared Reverend Burrows' spirit. With the ruins of their cause and country fresh about them, with so many graves newly closed, it perhaps would have been asking too much of Southerners to think dispassionately of their fallen foe. But the shock of the Confederacy's collapse and the President's assassination forced many Southerners to see Lincoln in a new light. The thoughts of Burrows and other of his fellow ex-rebels—acceptance of the decisions of war, belief in Lincoln's personal magnanimity and in his plans for a gentle reconstruction—were to take hold in millions of Southern minds in the years after the war. The conjecture that had Lincoln lived he would not have permitted Radical Reconstruction grew into an article of Southern faith. Many ex-rebels, and their children, never would forgive nor forget. But a new image of Lincoln was taking shape in the South, one which was to become an instrument for eroding old sectional hatreds and for rebuilding a new American national consciousness.

150. J. Lansing Burrows, "A Discourse Delivered in the First Baptist Church, Richmond, Va., June 1, 1865, the Day Appointed by the President of the United States for Humiliation and Mourning on Account of the Assassination of President Lincoln," in *Palliative and Prejudiced Judgments Condemned*, 3–8.

4.

Lincoln and the Lost Cause

On November 6, 1865, nearly seven months after the surrender of Robert E. Lee, the Confederate cruiser *Shenandoah* sailed into the River Mersey at Liverpool and permitted herself to be interned by British authorities. The last Confederate battle flag had been struck, the last island of Confederate sovereignty had surrendered. The Confederate States of America disappeared forever as a sovereign republic.

Few nations seemed so utterly defeated as the South in 1865. The foundation of the Southern world had been turned upside down. Her dreams of independence were crushed. A quarter million of her sons were dead. Two billion dollars in slave properties were wiped out, and three and one-half million former slaves were loosed upon the land. The countryside had been ravished by invading armies, and the soil lay fallow for want of labor. Many of the South's cities were in ashes and her infant industries in ruins. Her leaders were proscribed, imprisoned, or in exile. The spirit of defeat and despair hung heavily upon her people. The states of the late Confederacy were wretched, impoverished, and demoralized. It was all too much for venerable Edmund Ruffin, the fire-eating Virginian who had long agitated for an independent Southern republic.

Swearing undying hatred for all things Yankee, he put a bullet into his brain.[1]

The spirit which moved old Ruffin to the ultimate act of defiance could have poisoned sectional relations for generations. But that spirit did not abide. Although Southerners drank deeply at the well of bitterness and humiliation, they generally followed the example of Robert E. Lee in accepting the result of the war and in working to rebuild the South within the Union. After this long and cruel brothers' war there were those, to be sure, who would make political capital out of these honest sentiments. But the most remarkable achievement in the generation after the close of the war was the quiet rebuilding of American nationalism to replace the bitter sectional animosities of the 1860's. By the turn of the century a spiritual reunion had been consummated to complement the political reunion sealed at Appomattox.[2]

Among the many factors contributing to this growing spirit of reconciliation, perhaps the most important was the relative gentleness of the reconstruction process. Republican radicals, motivated by political opportunism and by a genuine concern to preserve their war aims of reunion and emancipation, sought to impose their will upon the defeated South through Negro and carpetbag governments backed by federal bayonets. But these alien regimes survived no more than a decade. After 1877, with Northern consent, Southern Democrats were in control of every statehouse in the late Confederacy. When one considers the usual fate of rebels, the South's reconstruction experience was benign indeed. No Confederate was convicted of treason and, with the exception of the unfortunate Major Wirz, none was executed for alleged war crimes. Jefferson Davis was released and pardoned to return to Mississippi and quietly live out his days. Amnesties and pardons were generous, and Confederate leaders soon returned to political life. Although "bloody shirt" politics in the North and the equating of Republicanism with "nigger rule" in the South periodically soured sectional relations at election time, in the long run the return of the South to national politics proved a force for peace and reconciliation. The Democratic party pro-

1. Avery O. Craven, *Edmund Ruffin, Southerner: A Study in Secession* (New York, 1932), 259.

2. For ideas about sectional reconciliation expressed in this and following paragraphs, I am heavily indebted to Paul H. Buck's excellent study, *The Road to Reunion, 1865–1890* (New York, 1937).

vided Southerners with a vehicle to return to political respectability and, in a limited measure, power. The administrations of Grover Cleveland (who appointed two ex-rebels to his first cabinet) demonstrated to the North that the nation was safe in the hands of the party so recently associated with treason. To Southerners Democratic victory meant that they were no longer political pariahs.

Other influences worked to heal the wounds of war. A common language and a common history before separation made reunion less painful. The great economic issues of the last quarter of the nineteenth century showed little respect for sectional lines. Men of the New South sought Northern capital in their campaign to industrialize their states, and Southern farmers joined their Western brethren against the interests which they believed denied them a fair share of American prosperity. The passing of time also softened the rancor of those most immediately involved in the war—the veterans of the Union and Confederate armies. The formal veterans' organizations—the Grand Army of the Republic and the United Confederate Veterans, and their auxiliaries—remained citadels of partisanship in defending their respective interpretations of the cause and conduct of the war. Nevertheless, there were growing bonds of esteem and even affection between these old soldiers: the common mourning of the dead, mutual respect for brave and honorable foemen, and appreciation of the sincerity which lay behind the sacrifices of both sides. One of the most poignant symbols of the new spirit of reconciliation was seen in aging veterans marching together in parades and meeting together in occasional joint reunions.

What finally sealed the reconciliation of the sections was the South's discovery that its defeat had not been so total after all, that a measure of victory could be salvaged from the wreckage of the Confederacy. There was a remarkable continuity of interests in the South throughout much of the nineteenth and twentieth centuries. Those interests largely were defined by the presence in the South of great numbers of Negroes believed to be inferior and unassimilable in the white culture. The Southern states endeavored constantly to administer their own affairs without compulsory federal interference. Particularly, they desired to control their Negroes to guarantee white supremacy.[3]

3. Ulrich B. Phillips, "The Central Theme of Southern History," *American Historical Review*, 34 (Oct., 1928), 30–43.

In ante bellum days the institution of slavery regulated the Negro population, and local self-government was protected by a *cheval-de-frise* of constitutional guarantees, states' rights theories, and the proscription of liberal ideas. When these defenses proved inadequate the South sought safety in secession and an independent Confederacy. When the contest of arms destroyed slavery and independence, only the South's methods changed, not her fundamental interests as she saw them. Within the broad limits set by the Lincoln and Johnson plans of reconstruction, the Southern states sought to impose restraints upon the freedmen through the Black Codes.[4] The decade of military-carpetbag regimes which followed only strengthened Southern desire for home rule and local control of the Negro population.

Radical Reconstruction climaxed in 1868 with the impeachment of President Johnson and the death of Thaddeus Stevens, the vindictive Pennsylvania congressman who was the driving spirit of radicalism in Congress. Although more reconstruction acts followed, there soon began a steady erosion of public support for the congressional radicals. The majority of Northerners wearied of Southern problems and echoed General Grant's wish, "let us have peace." Northern attention increasingly was absorbed by the problem of political corruption and by the social and economic difficulties wrought by industrialism. Northern businessmen desired a return to home rule and stability in the South to create a favorable climate for their enterprise.[5] Moreover, the North abandoned its commitment to the freedman. Republicans gave up ambitions to build a Southern Republican party based on black votes and looked instead to an alliance with the reemerging Whiggish leadership in the South.[6] The vast majority of Northern people was not willing to sustain the radicals' efforts to protect the political and civil rights of Negroes. However much they deplored slavery and rejoiced in its destruction, most Northerners did not believe in the equality of races and had no desire to see Negroes elevated legally to the status of white Americans. After the excitement of the immediate postwar years died down, the North stood by while the Supreme Court systematically dismantled the framework of

4. Randall and Donald, *The Civil War and Reconstruction*, 571–74.

5. William B. Hesseltine, "Economic Factors in the Abandonment of Reconstruction," *Mississippi Valley Historical Review*, 22 (Sept., 1935), 191–210.

6. C. Vann Woodward, *Origins of the New South, 1877–1913* (Baton Rouge, La., 1951), 28–29.

radical legislation constructed to protect Negro rights.[7] With slavery gone forever, most Northerners and Southerners could agree that the Negro was an inherently inferior and potentially dangerous creature who ought to be placed in a social position somewhere between absolute equality and absolute servility.

Sectional recognition, then, was realized at the expense of the Negro. In effect, a compromise was reached between the late belligerents. The South surrendered forever her rights to slavery and secession; in return, she was granted a broad measure of freedom in controlling her Negro population. The South took advantage of this freedom to fix the Negro in a rigid economic and social caste structure. Southern leaders first sought to control the Negro vote; then, as redneck politicians overturned the Redeemer governments, the black man was disfranchised and subjugated by Jim Crow laws.[8]

For many Southerners these developments justified in part the great sacrifices made in the 1860's. Three years after Appomattox, Edward A. Pollard wrote that the cause for which Southerners fought and died was much misunderstood even in Dixie. The South, he argued, fought not primarily for slavery and independence, but to guarantee white supremacy and "the preservation of the political traditions of the country."[9] Southerners who witnessed the redemption of their state governments to home rule and the imposition of segregation upon the freedman well could believe that, to a significant extent, the Lost Cause had been regained.

What the South gained in the long run, of course, was not victory nor even a lasting compromise, but only a reprieve. The South could not aspire to merge itself within the new American nationalism nor could it covet the loaves and fishes of the new industrial order without being affected by the social dynamics which accompanied these phenomena. The acids of modernity continued to dissolve the traditional Southern order of things. The specter of Negro rights, backed by the

7. *Slaughterhouse Cases*, 16 Wall. 36 (1873), placed most individual civil rights under state, not federal, protection. *Civil Rights Cases*, 109 U. S. 3 (1883), said that the Fourteenth Amendment did not protect civil rights invaded by individuals unaided by state authority. *Plessy* v. *Ferguson*, 163 U. S. 537 (1896), upheld "separate but equal" accommodations for Negroes.

8. C. Vann Woodward, *The Strange Career of Jim Crow*, 2nd rev. ed. (New York, 1966), 31–109.

9. Edward A. Pollard, *The Lost Cause Regained* (New York, 1868), 13–14.

national government, would return nearly a century later to shake the South more profoundly than before.

The image of Lincoln in Southern minds in the postwar years depended to a large degree upon the way individual Southerners surveyed the events which they and their section experienced. If one viewed the Old South as the most brilliant of all possible cultures, if one lamented the unrealized promise of the late Confederacy, then one's estimate of Lincoln was apt to be harsh and uncompromising. Such an unreconstructed rebel might acknowledge Lincoln's individual acts of humanitarianism and concede that reconstruction might have been different had Lincoln lived. But generally his impressions of Lincoln differed little from those of Confederates at war. On the other hand, the Southerner who believed that the South was liberated by the end of slavery and fanatical sectionalism and who looked to the building of a new and prosperous South within the Union was likely to entertain a more liberal image of Lincoln. With a few exceptions, Southerners remained immune from the apotheosis of Lincoln which swept the North immediately after his assassination. But for the Southerners of sanguine temper, the way was open to a more generous appreciation of Lincoln's character and place in history.

Southerners frequently expressed their feelings about Abraham Lincoln in the years after Appomattox because they were thinking and writing about their history as they had at no other time. Southerners had not been a historically conscious people. Circumstances of Southern life—persistent frontier conditions, careless preservation of records, a stout individualism which did not lend itself to introspection—had conspired to turn the thoughts of Southerners from their past. Intellectual energies were absorbed by politics, religion, and the defense of slavery.[10]

The Civil War was the South's most traumatic historical experience. The drawing together of the Southern states in defense of slavery and states' rights forced Southerners to raise their mental horizons beyond state lines and to think regionally. The war itself united the South as had no other event; it seemed to Southerners that a great confluence of human and divine purposes had met at Appomattox.[11] It was natural

10. E. Merton Coulter, "What the South Has Done About Her History," *Journal of Southern History*, 2 (Feb., 1936), 3–28.

11. *Ibid.*, 16–17. Thomas J. Pressly, *Americans Interpret Their Civil War* (Princeton, N. J., 1954), 73–95.

and proper for men to write about the causes and results of this great war and to describe their part in the events which so profoundly turned their lives.

Southerners were moved to take up their pens in self-defense against a rising flood of Northern books on the war. The North seemed determined to nail down its military victory by fixing all responsibility for the war upon the South. Histories by John W. Draper (1867–1870) and the radical Henry Wilson (1877) and the memoirs of William T. Sherman (1877) and other Northern military men put the burden of blame for the war upon Southern slaveholders. In the face of these hostile interpretations Southern writers closed ranks to defend the legality of states' rights and secession and to charge Yankee abolitionists with culpability in destroying the Union.[12]

Most of these Southern histories and memoirs were of the nature of *apologiae*. Southerners, having lost the decision on the battlefield, sought to justify their deeds while accepting the results of the trial by combat. Although frequently prefaced by appeals to the truth, these works little disguised their partisanship. In an oft-repeated phrase, Southerners were appealing to "the bar of history"; the expression suggests that there was more interest in preparing a lawyer's brief for the defense than in attempting an objective analysis of events. General John Brown Gordon, writing as late as 1903, thought that the man probably was unborn who could write a history of the war with full justice to both sides.[13] The president of the late Confederacy scorned so-called objective history. "I would distrust the man who served the Confederate cause and was capable of giving a disinterested account of it," said Jefferson Davis. "I would not give a twopence for a man whose heart was so cold that he could be quite impartial."[14]

Edward A Pollard, the Richmond editor, was the first Southern historian of the war, and neither was his heart cold nor his account impartial. His war chronicles, three volumes of which appeared while the fighting was in progress, commanded wide attention. After Appomattox,

12. Pressly, *Americans Interpret*, 85. Howard K. Beale, "What Historians Have Said About the Causes of the Civil War," *Theory and Practice in Historical Study: A Report of the Committee of Historiography* [of the Social Science Research Council] (New York, 1946), 58–61.

13. John B. Gordon, *Reminiscences of the Civil War* (New York, 1903), xi.

14. *Southern Historical Society Papers*, 10 (May, 1882), 228.

Pollard published several more volumes of history and comment on the war, much of them being hashed-over versions of his earlier work. Alexander H. Stephens followed with his massive treatise, *A Constitutional View of the Late War Between the States* (1868, 1870), and Jefferson Davis' account of his services, *The Rise and Fall of the Confederate Government*, appeared in 1881. These three authors differed widely on many points of interpretation: Pollard had been a zealous defender of Southern independence and a caustic critic of Davis' handling of the war; Stephens did not believe Lincoln's election to be sufficient cause of secession and was never enthusiastic about a Southern republic; Davis, of course, defended his administration. But all agreed in retrospect that the South had championed the loftiest constitutional principles and that Northern aggression upon those principles forced her to war. They concurred that slavery was not the cause of the war but—in a phrase frequently used by Southern apologists—was merely the immediate "occasion" of war; the true causes arose from deeper and more honorable differences between the sections.

Pollard, Davis, and Stephens also reached a consensus of sorts on the character of their late enemy, Abraham Lincoln. They put the ultimate responsibility for war itself upon Lincoln because he had the power to let the seceded states go in peace. They deplored many of Lincoln's wartime acts as unconstitutional, despotic, or cruel; the Emancipation Proclamation especially was singled out for condemnation. On the other hand, the three writers believed that Lincoln's assassination was a misfortune to the South. Lincoln, they were convinced, had no personal ill-will toward the South, wished a speedy and peaceful reconciliation, and would have frustrated the vengeful Republican radicals.[15] Stephens went furthest in distinguishing between what he deemed Lincoln's excellent personal character and the official sins he committed as President:

> His many private virtues and excellencies of head and heart, I did esteem. Many of them had my admiration. In nothing I have said, or may say, was it or will it be my intention to detract from these. In all such cases in estimating character, we must discriminate between the man in private life,

15. Edward A. Pollard, *The Lost Cause: A New Southern History of the War of the Confederates. . . .* (New York, 1867), 743–44. Pollard, *Lost Cause Regained*, 65. Davis, *Rise and Fall* II, 683–84. For Davis' postwar views on Lincoln, see Rowland, ed., *Jefferson Davis* VIII, 197–98, and *Confederate Veteran*, 16 (June, 1908), 245–47.

> and the man in public office. . . . Power generally seems to change and transform the character of those invested with it.[16]

Not all ex-Confederates wrote to defend the Lost Cause. Foote's *War of the Rebellion, or Scylla and Charybdis* (1866) blamed the war on fanatics of both sections, but especially on a conspiracy of slaveholders in the South. Foote had been a strong unionist and a supporter of the Compromise of 1850. A former United States senator and governor from Mississippi, he was a bitter political and personal enemy of Jefferson Davis; Foote had defeated Davis for governor in 1851, and at one time the two men actually had come to blows. His growing unpopularity caused Foote to move to California and then to Tennessee. When secession came he reluctantly went with his new state. Tennessee sent Foote to the Confederate Congress, where he continued to make life difficult for his old enemy, agitating for peace and charging Davis with despotism. His peace designs frustrated, he abandoned the Confederacy for the North, where he was received coolly, and thence for Europe. Foote's book is a condemnation of Davis and the war, interspersed with praises of Lincoln. He charged Davis with conspiring to bring on the war, incompetency and tyranny in administration, and refusing generous peace terms. Lincoln's conduct, on the other hand, was "marked with moderation, elevated patriotism, and true practical wisdom."[17] Foote returned to the South after the war and managed to live more or less peacefully, but his singular views were shared by few of his contemporaries.[18]

One of the ablest defenders of the Lost Cause, and a powerful critic of Lincoln, was Albert Taylor Bledsoe. A man of vigorous intellect and diverse interests, his multifarious career included tenures as a soldier, lawyer, theologian and minister, mathematician, professor, Confederate bureaucrat, author, and editor.[19] Born in Kentucky the same year as

16. Stephens, *Constitutional View* II, 448.

17. Henry S. Foote, *War of the Rebellion, or, Scylla and Charybdis. . . .* (New York, 1866), 323–24.

18. Charles S. Sydnor, "Henry Stuart Foote," *Dictionary of American Biography* VI, 500–501.

19. Biographical details on Bledsoe have been drawn from Harry E. Pratt, "Albert Taylor Bledsoe: Critic of Lincoln," *Illinois State Historical Society, Transactions for the Year 1934,* Illinois State Historical Library Publication No. 41 (Springfield, Ill., n.d.), 153–83; Edwin Mims, "Albert Taylor Bledsoe," *Dictionary of American Biography* II, 364–65; and two articles by Bledsoe's daughter, Sophia Bledsoe Herrick, "Personal Recollections of My Father and Mr. Lincoln and Mr.

Lincoln, Bledsoe entered West Point at fifteen; Jefferson Davis and Robert E. Lee were among his fellow cadets. After graduation, he served on the Indian frontier for the required two years of duty and in 1832 resigned to study law and theology. Ordained into the Episcopal ministry in 1835, he served two Ohio congregations and taught mathematics at Miami University. Unwillingness to accept certain points of doctrine regarding baptism and regeneration led Bledsoe to resign his ministry in 1839, although he remained an Episcopal communicant most of his life. For the next eight years he practiced law in Springfield, Illinois, Cincinnati, Ohio, and Washington, D. C. In 1848, Bledsoe was called to the chair of mathematics at the new University of Mississippi, where, according to a biographer, he found the students "to be idle, uncultivated, and ungovernable, and given much to rowdiness and drunkenness." Four years later he removed to the more genteel environment of the University of Virginia, where his election as professor of mathematics had been secured by his friends Davis and Lee. One of the candidates passed over for the vacant chair was an unknown young instructor from the Virginia Military Institute, Thomas J. Jackson.[20]

Although Bledsoe had left the ministry for the courtroom and campus, his consuming interest continued to be theology. He abhorred the doctrine of predestination and spent much of his time and intellectual energy constructing arguments against Calvin and Jonathan Edwards. Bledsoe's most forceful theological treatise, *A Theodicy: or Vindication of the Divine Glory, as Manifested in the Constitution and Government of the World* (1854), was an attempt to reconcile the perfect nature of God with the existence of evil in the world. Although he had some difficulty in finding a publisher, Bledsoe had some impact on theological circles through his book. One minister pronounced *The Theodicy* "one of the greatest works the human mind has ever produced";[21] another testified that a chance reading of Bledsoe's work saved him at the last moment from the clutches of Presbyterianism.[22]

Davis," *Methodist Review*, 64 (1915), 665–79, and "Albert Taylor Bledsoe," *Virginia University Alumni Bulletin*, 6 (May, 1899), 1–6.

20. Pratt, "Albert Taylor Bledsoe," 163.

21. J. M. Hawley, "An Intellectual Giant," *Christian Advocate*, May 7, 1915, 9 (585).

22. S. A. Steel, "Albert Taylor Bledsoe," *Methodist Review*, 64 (April, 1915), 211–28.

Bledsoe's study of the Bible convinced him that a paternal system of slavery was sanctioned by holy writ; yet he was never an enthusiastic slaveholder, and he deplored the commercial side of the peculiar institution. His wife, a New Jersey woman, permitted the family servants to work for pay and buy their freedom.[23] While at the University of Virginia, Bledsoe wrote a Biblical and constitutional defense of slavery (1856), which was incorporated later into the massive Southern apology, *Cotton is King, and Pro-Slavery Argument* (1860).

The coming of war found Bledsoe quietly teaching in Charlottesville. The decision to go with Virginia was a bitter one, but he remained loyal to the South and accepted a commission in the Confederate army.[24] Soon he moved to the civil government as chief of the Bureau of War and then assistant secretary of war. John B. Jones, the rebel war clerk, described Bledsoe as a man of mercurial moods, a fat, grumbling paper-shuffler, and a carping subordinate to the two secretaries he served.[25] Bledsoe was not happy in the War Department; he later called it a "purgatory."[26] An elevated clerkship was not a post suited to his particular talents. Still, Jones' description was too severe; he never liked his chief and always permitted his prejudices free rein in his diary.

President Davis soon found an ideal job for his friend. He commissioned Bledsoe to prepare a massive constitutional defense of the right of secession. Bledsoe embraced the project with enthusiam, and, finding that the necessary documents were not available in the embattled South, he ran the blockade to Great Britain. He spent the better part of two years in the British Museum accumulating evidence to buttress his arguments. Returning in January, 1866, Bledsoe found Jefferson Davis in prison and facing a trial for treason. He hurried the result of his labors into print. *Is Davis a Traitor; or, Was Secession a Constitutional Right Previous to the War of 1861?* proved a powerful argument for the compact theory of government and a vindication for the actions of the secessionists. Davis' attorney later told Bledsoe that the book's argument would have been the cornerstone of the defense's brief had Davis been brought to trial.[27]

A year after his return to the United States, Bledsoe founded the

23. Herrick, "Personal Recollections of My Father," 670–71.

24. *Ibid.*, 673.

25. J. B. Jones, *Rebel War Clerk's Diary* I, 40–116 (numerous scattered references).

26. *The Southern Review*, 11 (July, 1872), 148.

27. Herrick, "Personal Recollections of My Father," 673.

Southern Review in Baltimore. Into this remarkable journal he poured all his energies and the full resources of his fertile mind during the twelve years of life remaining to him. Dedicated "to the despised, the disfranchised and downtrodden people of the South," the *Southern Review* was almost wholly an extension of its editor's ideas in theology, science, literature, and politics. Bledsoe wrote much of the copy himself; to one number he contributed every article but one—a total of 250 pages.[28] He liked to quote what General Lee said to him: "You have a great work to do; we all look to you for our vindication."[29] He committed his *Southern Review* to that end and never surrendered his ante bellum principles; in the words of Douglas Southall Freeman, Bledsoe was always "counsel for the defense."[30] In the columns of his journal, Bledsoe justified secession as a legal right and slavery as a moral one, likened democracy to mob rule, opposed industrialism as a destroyer of chivalry and beauty, and damned modern science as an enemy of faith. Women's suffrage, heterodoxy in religion, and public schools were among his favorite targets. Bledsoe also could be a devastating personal critic. A book sent to him for comment occasioned his displeasure, and he wrote the author: "Your book has in it many new things and many true things; but, unfortunately, none of the true things are new, and none of the new things are true."[31] Bledsoe's uncompromising principles and want of tact earned him a legion of enemies as well as admirers.

Widely praised in the South but little read, the *Southern Review* always stood at the door of bankruptcy. Bledsoe was no businessman, and more copies were given away than sold.[32] Kept alive by the energy of its editor and the earnings of his school-teacher daughters, the *Southern Review* survived Bledsoe's death only about a year.

Religious conservative, unreconstructed Confederate, and defender of slavery, Bledsoe only could be unfriendly to the memory of the man whose coming to power occasioned secession, war, and the destruction of Bledsoe's world. He published his most detailed estimate of Abraham Lincoln in the columns of the *Southern Review* seven years after the

28. *The South in the Building of the Nation* (Richmond, Va., 1909–1913) VII, 463–65.

29. Mims, "Albert Taylor Bledsoe," *DAB* II, 364–65.

30. Douglas Southall Freeman, *The South to Posterity* (New York, 1939), 34.

31. Herrick, "Albert Taylor Bledsoe," 6.

32. Herrick, "Recollections of My Father," 674. Pratt, "Albert Taylor Bledsoe," 168.

President's death. In *Is Davis a Traitor?* Bledsoe had made the old charges that Lincoln decided on war to save his tariff revenue and that abolitionists controlled the Washington government.[33] In 1872, the publication of Ward Hill Lamon's *The Life of Abraham Lincoln* provided Bledsoe with the biographical details for a full-scale assault upon the character and conduct of the late President.

Lamon was a burly Illinois lawyer who had been Lincoln's friend and bodyguard and marshall of the District of Columbia. His biography of Lincoln, actually ghostwritten by Chauncey F. Black, son of President Buchanan's attorney general, was written from materials collected by William H. Herndon, Lincoln's law partner in Springfield. The three men were disgusted by the many eulogistic biographies of Lincoln which had appeared since the assassination. In their procrustean efforts to make Lincoln into a model Christian hero and fit moral example for American youth, these admiring biographers twisted Lincoln's life into a shape which the late President's friends hardly recognized. Lamon, Black, and Herndon thought that Lincoln's true greatness best could be illustrated by contrasting the wisdom and great deeds of his presidency with the meanness of the environment into which he was born. "We must point mankind to the diamond glowing on the dunghill," wrote Black to Lamon, "and then to the same resplendent jewel in the future setting of great success and brilliant achievements."[34] The amazing growth of Lincoln's character and abilities was to be the main theme of the projected biography.

To describe Lincoln's boyhood, the authors drew upon testimonies of Lincoln's neighbors and of the old-timers in New Salem and Springfield. Many of these rumors and stories had been circulating for years, but Lamon's book collected and presented them in a systematic way to an incredulous public accustomed to worshiping Lincoln's memory. The probable illegitimacy of Lincoln's mother, Nancy Hanks, was described, and it was alluded that Old Abe himself might have been a bastard. The brutality and coarseness of frontier life were portrayed vividly. Rather than a model boy, Lincoln was represented as one of a gang of frontier rowdies, skilled at fighting, drinking, and cruel practical jokes, and dis-

33. Albert T. Bledsoe, *Is Davis a Traitor; or, Was Secession a Constitutional Right Previous to the War of 1861?* (Richmond, Va., 1907), 143–44, 150–52.

34. Quoted in Benjamin Thomas, *Portrait for Posterity; Lincoln and His Biographers* (New Brunswick, N. J., 1947), 36–37.

tinguished from his fellows only by a superior native intelligence. Lincoln showed a streak of lascivious humor and delighted in telling smutty jokes. Worse, Lincoln was said to have been a confessed "infidel," an open scoffer at Christianity, whose blasphemous conduct was so outrageous that most Springfield ministers denied him political support. Lincoln's unchivalrous conduct toward Mary Owens, the woman who rejected his suit and whom he lampooned in an unkind letter, was described and documented. Lamon and Black told Herndon's story that Ann Rutledge was Lincoln's only real love and that life with Mary Todd had been a succession of woes.[35]

Unfortunately, neither Lamon nor Black brought out the planned second volume. Without the complementary work, the purpose of the authors was frustrated and their achievement distorted. The record of the brilliant presidency was obscured; the dunghill remained. Northern reaction was mixed but generally unfriendly. Southern critics of Lincoln seized upon the book as a mine of evidence revealing the shabbiness of Lincoln's life and meanness of his character. Since Lamon had been Lincoln's friend, the incidents he described were assumed to be of unimpeachable authenticity. Praising Lamon's just and conscientious use of evidence, William Hand Browne wrote in the *Southern Magazine*:

> The whole story of his [Lincoln's] career from beginning to end is so dreary, so wretched, so shabby, such a tissue of pitiful dodging and chicanery, so unrelieved by anything pure, noble, or dignified, that even to follow it as far as we have done, has well-nigh surpassed our limits of endurance; and when, putting all partisan feeling aside, we look back at the men who once were chosen by their countrymen to fill the places that this man has occupied—a Washington, a Jefferson, a Madison, an Adams, or later, a Webster, a Clay, or a Calhoun— men of culture and refinement, of honor, of exalted patriotism, of broad views and wise statesmanship—and measure the distance from them to Abraham Lincoln, we sicken with shame and disgust.[36]

Unlike Browne and the great majority of Southerners, Bledsoe had known Lincoln and once had called him friend. The two had practiced law in the same Illinois courts and occasionally had opposed each other on a case. Both were active Whigs and in 1843 had worked together to

35. For background to Lamon's book, see *ibid.*, 3–90, and Roy P. Basler, *The Lincoln Legend: A Study in Changing Conceptions* (Boston, 1935), 9–11, 166–67.

36. *Southern Magazine* (Baltimore, Md.), II (Sept., 1872), 374.

draft their party's "Address to the People of Illinois."[37] The Bledsoes and the Lincolns lived for a time in the same Springfield boardinghouse. Bledsoe's wife helped care for Mary Todd Lincoln after the birth of her first son, Robert, and six-year-old Sophia Bledsoe romped with the Lincoln baby.[38] When Bledsoe was serving the Confederacy in the British Museum, Lincoln granted Mrs. Bledsoe a pass through Union lines so she could return South after a visit with her family.[39]

Despite these intimacies, the war purged Bledsoe's heart of any affection for Lincoln. Compassion did not replace bitterness after Lincoln's assassination. In a lengthy review of Lamon's book, Bledsoe said of his sometime friendship with Lincoln:

> Some persons will think it a great honor, and some a great disgrace, that we have lived eight long years in the same region with Abraham Lincoln, and held almost daily intercourse with him at the Bar. We think it neither an honor nor a disgrace. We regard it, on the contrary, merely a piece of good fortune, that we have had the opportunity of seeing, scrutinizing, and forming an opinion of one of the most extraordinary human beings that has figured in history. The world will, perhaps, know him a little better because we have known him.

Lincoln, Bledsoe admitted, had a "powerful intellect" and enjoyed great success at the bar. His great natural abilities overcame his lack of formal education. By hard work and self-discipline he mastered a simple, direct style of address that all preachers of the gospel ought to imitate. Bledsoe believed Lincoln was a great man. "His success, in this world at least, has been the wonder of all nations, and will, perhaps, be the wonder of all ages."

Bledsoe confessed that he never had understood Lincoln's "ruling passion" until he read Lamon's book. That passion, he concluded, was not a love of freedom or hatred of oppression, but rather was a thirst for popularity and distinction. Having no faith in God and the hereafter, "the one thought . . . which haunted and tormented his soul, was the reflection that he had done nothing, and might die without doing anything, to link his name and memory forever with the events of his time." It was this vain passion which led Lincoln to overcome his unfortunate

37. Lincoln, *Works* I, 297, 308, 309–18.
38. Herrick, "Recollections of My Father," 667–68.
39. Lincoln, *Works* VIII, 218.

birth and the squalid circumstances of his youth. It was this mundane political ambition which caused him to deceive the public—for in private affairs he was an honest, candid man—and to disguise his love for the obscene and his terrible heathenness. "This reticent, secretive, scheming art of deception," Bledsoe wrote, "was the most conducive to the successful prosecution of his ambitious designs."

Evaluating Lincoln's place in history, Bledsoe, Southerner and theologian, concluded that if the North

> was the cause of brute force, blind passion, fanatical hate, lust of power, and the greed of gain, against the cause of constitutional law and human rights, then who was better fitted to represent it than the talented, but the low, ignorant and vulgar, rail-splitter of Illinois? Or if, as we also believe, it was the cause of infidelity and atheism, and against the principles and the spirit of the Christian religion, then who more worthy to muster its motley hosts, and let them slip with the fury of the pit than the lowbred infidel of Pigeon Creek, in whose eyes the Saviour of the world was "an illegitimate child," and the Holy Mother as base as his own?[40]

Bledsoe sought to condemn Lincoln by the testimony of his friends, a device which would become familiar in the anti-Lincoln literature. Confederates had vilified Lincoln by quoting the President's many Northern critics. After the war, many Lincoln biographies, especially those by Lamon and Herndon, offered a mine of materials from which anti-Lincolnians could extract anecdotes to diminish Lincoln's reputation. Little attempt was made to verify these anecdotes. Southern critics like Bledsoe reasoned that if a Yankee related a story that would tarnish Lincoln's halo it must be true.

Bledsoe was among many criticizing the use of Northern textbooks in Southern schools. On few points were Southerners more sensitive than on the teaching of history to their children. Ex-Confederates feared Southern youth were being taught that their fathers were rebels and traitors. Veterans' groups and self-appointed patriots periodically reviewed classroom texts and the conduct of teachers to detect any deviations from the orthodox Southern interpretation of things. Less than three years after the close of the war the *Southern Review* examined eleven history texts proposed for use in schools and found that "the one

40. *Southern Review*, 26 (April 1873), 328–64.

grand moral of these books is, that the people of the North alone are fit to rule, while the people of the South deserve only to be ruled by them. They continually feed the mean pride of the North, and inspire its people with an abhorrence and contempt of the South." Critics demanded that offensive books be replaced by texts which emphasized the South's contributions to the Union, defended the constitutional right of secession, and gave due recognition to the valor of Southern men-at-arms. Among Southern books recommended were school histories by Susan Pendleton Lee, Alexander H. Stephens, John William Jones, George F. Holmes, Joseph Tyrone Derry, and John S. Blackburn and W. N. McDonald. Jabez L. M. Curry's powerful defense of states' rights and Robert Dabney's apology for slavery were highly regarded. George Lunt's *Origin of the Late War* (1866) received special attention because it was written by a Northern man from a Southern point of view.[41]

Instructors were persuaded, if they were not already so inclined, to teach the approved Southern interpretation of the war. William E. Dodd recalled teaching as a young man in rural North Carolina schools in the early 1890's:

> In the South, and particularly in the older sections of it, public opinion is so thoroughly fixed that many subjects which come every day into the mind of the historian may not with safety even so much as be discussed. . . . To suggest that the revolt from the union in 1860 was not justified, was not led by the most lofty minded of statesmen, is to invite not only criticism but an enforced resignation.[42]

These were not idle threats. As late as 1911, a Georgia-born professor at the University of Florida was fired for publishing an article in a national magazine in which he expressed this belief that the North was right in opposing secession and that Lincoln was a greater statesman than Jefferson Davis. Ironically, the professor, Enoch Banks, had expressed hope

41. *Ibid.*, 3 (Jan., 1868), 155. *Southern Magazine*, 10 (April, 1872), 503; 12 (May, 1873), 609; 16 (May, 1875), 530. *Confederate Veteran*, 33 (June, 1895), 170; 7 (Nov., 1899), 500–509. *Southern Historical Society Papers*, 14 (1886), 576. *Richmond Dispatch*, May 12, 1900. Buck, *Road to Reunion*, 58–61. Hunter McGuire and George L. Christian, *The Confederate Cause and Conduct in the War Between the States, as Set Forth in the Reports of the History Committee of the Grand Camp, Confederate Veterans, of Virginia* (Richmond, Va., 1907).

42. William E. Dodd, "Some Difficulties of the History Teacher in the South," *South Atlantic Quarterly*, 3 (April, 1904), 119.

that the appearance of his article would testify to the increasing tolerance of dissent in the South.[43]

Northern history texts had high praise for Abraham Lincoln. The apotheosizing of Lincoln was at full tide in the North in the generation following the war. Lincoln was not only characterized as the greatest American but sometimes deemed the greatest man since Christ. The excessive laudations disgusted true-believing Southerners. A Texas outfit of Confederates condemned *Montgomery's History for Beginners* because it was partisan to Lincoln. They demanded that it be replaced or that a like number of pages praising Jefferson Davis be added to the text. At the very least, resolved the veterans, the students should be told that Lincoln and his party "were in fact the revolutionaries and are morally responsible for all the loss of life and destruction of Southern homes and property that ensued."[44] Many Southerners resented Lincoln's being presented to students as a moral example worthy of emulation. Southern youths were urged to look to Davis, Lee, and Jackson as heroes. By deliberate censorship or by disposition of the instructor, Lincoln frequently was abused or ignored in Southern classrooms. "I went through school without ever having heard of the Gettysburg Address or First Inaugural," recalled author and poet Archibald Rutledge of South Carolina. "Hayne and Calhoun were my Webster and Lincoln."[45]

The glorification of Lincoln in the North seemed to many Southerners as direct threat to the reputation and self-respect of the South. As Lincoln and the cause he represented were elevated in the public fancy, reasoned these unreconstructed rebels, the South and her heroes were that much diminished. One could not love both Lincoln and the South. "One of two things is true; there is no middle ground," wrote a Virginian. "If Davis was a patriot, Lincoln was a tyrant. . . . Lincoln conquered the South and built up a powerful nation, in which true lovers

43. Enoch M. Banks, "A Semi-Centennial View of Secession," *Independent*, 70 (Feb. 9, 1911), 299–303. For commentary on the Banks affair, see *ibid.* (April 13, 1911), 806–807, and (April 27, 1911), 900; and Virginius Dabney, *Liberalism in the South* (Chapel Hill, N. C., 1932), 341–42.

44. "From Minutes of Confederate Reunion, Belton, Texas, July 2–3–4, 1901. Report of Committee of School Histories, Camp 122, Bell Co. Confederate Association," *Confederate Veteran*, 9 (July, 1901), 331.

45. Archibald Rutledge, "Lincoln: A Southern View," *The Reviewer*, Jan. 1925, pp. 4–5. *Richmond Dispatch*, Jan. 7, 1900. *Southern Historical Society Papers*, 14 (1886), 576.

of liberty cannot rejoice, for it cost the lives of two noble republics, the old United States of America and the Confederate States of America."[46] Many whose hearts dwelt in the Old South deplored what they believed to be the handmaidens of modernity—impiety, centralism, trusts, corruption, and miscegenation. These heresies were Lincoln's avowed purposes, they charged, and Lincoln's war brought them upon the country.[47]

Some of the attempts to discredit Lincoln were contrived and bizarre, such as "A Plain Farmer's" attempt to show that the life, death, and crimes of Lincoln were foretold in the Book of Ezekiel.[48] Other disclaimers were the spontaneous outpourings of impassioned hearts. Paul Hamilton Hayne, the well-born Charleston poet, had been broken in health and fortune by the war and was living out his days in a back-country Georgia shack. On reading some praiseful poetry on Lincoln by his Northern friend Richard Henry Stoddard, Hayne wrote bitterly to Margaret Preston:

> These "Homeric lines" on *Lincoln* may be good, but I see continually between each stanza, the gawky, coarse, not-over cleanly, whisky drinking, and whisky smelling Blackguard, elevated by a grotesque *Chance* (nearly allied to *Satan*) to the position for which of all others, he was most unfit:—and whose memory has been *idealized* by the Yankee fancy, & Yankee arrogance, in a way that *would* be ludicrous, were it not *disgusting*, and calculated, finally, to belie the facts of History, and hand down to future times as Hero and Martyr, as commonplace a *Vulgarian* as ever patronized bad Tobacco and mistook *blasphemy* for *wit*.[49]

The most systematic attack upon Lincoln by a Southerner came from the pen of Charles Landon Carter Minor. Minor was a Virginia aristocrat, Confederate veteran, and, after the war, president of Virginia A&M College (later Virginia Polytechnic Institute). After retirement, he devoted himself to his church and to writing on history and politics.

46. Berkeley Minor, in *Baltimore Sun*, Feb. 4, 1903, and reprinted in *Southern Historical Society Papers*, 30 (1902), 338.

47. J. Clarence Stonebreaker, *The Unwritten South; Cause, Progress and Result of the Civil War. . . .* 5th ed. (n.p., 1908), 185. *Southern Historical Society Papers*, 30 (1902), 332–38.

48. A Plain Farmer, *Abraham Lincoln, Late President of the United States, Demonstrated to be the Gog of the Bible, as Foretold by the Prophet Ezekiel. . . .* (Memphis, Tenn., 1868). For a favorable comment on the Plain Farmer's effort, see *Land We Love*, 6 (Jan., 1869), 259.

49. Dec. 15, 1871, quoted in Basler, *The Lincoln Legend*, 57.

Angry at the canonization of Lincoln in the North, Minor compiled an anti-Lincoln brief based exclusively upon Northern sources. Publication of Lincoln's letters, official records, and the memoirs of Lincoln's contemporaries made available an enormous amount of material from which testimony could be abstracted that might compromise Lincoln's claim to greatness. Minor assembled a pamphlet, *The Real Lincoln* (1901), later expanded into a book, in which he attempted to dismantle the legend which had grown up around the late President.[50]

"To try to reawaken or to foster ill will between the North and the South would be a useless, mischievous and most censurable task," Minor explained, "and it will be seen that this sketch has exactly an opposite purpose."[51] Minor declared that his real object was to allay sectional bitterness by showing just what kind of man Lincoln really was, for it was the undeserved apotheosis of Lincoln which angered the South and helped to keep sectional animosities alive. Minor chose Northern witnesses exclusively because his book was aimed at Northern readers who would tend to dismiss Southern testimony against their hero. The book was frankly one-sided, for Lincoln's alleged virtues "are familiar to all who have given the least attention to Lincoln's place in world esteem."[52] Minor's book, little more than hundreds of quotations (not all of them accurate) strung together, showed Lincoln to be a coward, an infidel, unkind to his mother, fond of indecent jokes, unchivalrous in his relations with women, and lacking the support of the leading men of his party. Lincoln's speech in the House of Representatives in 1848, in which he endorses the right of revolution, was introduced as evidence that most Americans, including Lincoln, accepted the legality of secession before 1860, and that Lincoln betrayed his own principles in denying that right once he was President. The North and West did not want to fight, according to Minor's collage of "evidence," but were maneuvered into war with the South by the Republicans. Lincoln's emancipation policy was unpopular, and his army was at the point of mutiny. Civil liberties were

50. Charles L. C. Minor, *The Real Lincoln; With Article by Lyon G. Tyler*, ed. Kate Mason Rowland (Richmond, Va., 1901). Minor, *The Real Lincoln, From the Testimony of His Contemporaries*, 2nd. ed., revised and enlarged (Richmond, Va., 1904). There is a brief sketch of Minor in these volumes and also in L. G. Tyler, ed., *Encyclopedia of Virginia Biography* (New York, 1915), III, 188–89.

51. Minor, *The Real Lincoln* (1901), 7–8.

52. Minor, *The Real Lincoln* (1904), 12.

suppressed, and the Yankees fought with bayonets in their backs as well as at their fronts.

Minor, of course, made no attempt at an honest assessment of Lincoln. In order to show a Lincoln portrait with warts, he painted a toad. One wonders how such a miserable specimen of humanity as Minor's Lincoln came to be respected, much less canonized, by the North. Minor asks the question, but he cannot answer it. His query "in the interest of truth" was another partisan attempt, somewhat after the manner of Bledsoe, to uphold the righteousness of the Lost Cause by discrediting the man who defeated it.

Minor's book was popular in the South and ran through several editions after his death in 1903. The United Confederate Veterans and the United Daughters of the Confederacy endorsed it. A Southern reviewer noted gleefully that Union veterans in Massachusetts had forced the book off the shelves of local libraries and had actually destroyed many copies, proof that the North would go to any lengths to suppress the truth about its hero.[53] *The Real Lincoln* served as a source book for later Lincoln critics such as Lyon Gardiner Tyler, Mildred Lewis Rutherford, and Edgar Lee Masters.

Elizabeth Avery Meriwether was a Mississippi lady who had read Minor's book and imbibed its message. She hated Lincoln for what she believed he did to the South, and she was convinced that his deification was a deliberate Republican conspiracy to perpetuate the party in power. In *Facts and Falsehoods* (1904), her defense of the South, she described the many acts of cruelty attributed to Lincoln, the frontier bully—sewing up the eyes of hogs, beating an old mare, and passing counterfeit money onto unsuspecting citizens. "Is it insanity or pure mendacity," she asked,

> to liken a man of this nature to the gentle and loving Nazarene? Who for an instant can imagine Jesus swinging a bottle of whisky around his head, swearing to the rowdy crowd that he was the "big buck of the lick"? Or with a whip in his hand, lashing a faithful old slave at every round of her labor? Who can imagine Jesus sewing up hogs' eyes? What act of Lincoln's life betrays tender-heartedness? Was he tender-hearted when he made medicine contraband of war? When he punished women caught with a bottle of quinine going South? . . . Was it tender-hearted to despise Greeley's prayer [for peace], rush on carnage, and for four years

53. *Confederate Veteran*, 14 (April, 1906), 166.

> drench the whole Southland with human blood? And when Lincoln's legions were devastating the South, when with wanton cruelty, at the point of the bayonet, Sherman drove 15,000 women and children of Atlanta, Georgia, out of their homes, out of their city, to wander in the woods, shelterless, foodless, and then laid the whole city in ashes, did Lincoln give one thought to the suffering of those innocent women and children? Did he once, during the four years of the cruel war, utter or write one kind word of the people on whom *he* had brought such unspeakable misery?[54]

In her animus for Lincoln, Elizabeth Meriwether was a spiritual descendant of Confederates Kate Cumming and Catherine Edmondston. A generation and more after the guns fell silent at Appomattox, hatred for the memory of Abraham Lincoln—the killer of the dream—burned deep in many a Southern woman's heart.

Strong anti-Lincoln sentiment has persisted in the South into the twentieth century, even unto the present day. Frequently, the critics have been Confederate veterans and their children, writing in honest, if excessive, reaction to the adulation of Lincoln which had swept the country and to which the South itself was not completely immune. Among the most vigorous of the later Lincoln critics were Samuel A'Court Ashe, the North Carolina historian who charged Lincoln with starting the war and thus doing "more evil than any man known to the world"; O. W. Blacknall, for whom Lincoln was a worse tyrant than the kaiser; R. W. Barnwell of South Carolina, who believed Lincoln was insane; Mary Scrugham, a Columbia-trained historian, who wrote that Lincoln never failed to put his party ahead of the country; David Rankin Barbee, North Carolina editor, who encouraged biographer Albert Beveridge to write fairly about Lincoln and the South; and Mildred Lewis Rutherford, the indefatigable and unreconstructed historian general of the United Daughters of the Confederacy, whose career was dedicated to vindicating Jefferson Davis and vilifying Abraham Lincoln.[55]

54. [Mrs. Elizabeth Avery Meriwether] George Edmonds, *Facts and Falsehoods Concerning the War on the South* (Memphis, Tenn., 1904), 49–50.

55. Samuel A'Court Ashe, "Abraham Lincoln, the Citizen," *Tyler's Quarterly Historical and Genealogical Magazine*, 16 (Jan., 1935), 150–56. O. W. Blacknall *Lincoln as the South Should Know Him*, 2nd ed. (Raleigh, N.C., 1915). R. W. Barnwell, *The Lines and Nature of Lincoln's Greatness* (Columbia, S.C., 1931). Mary Scrugham, *The Peaceable Americans of 1860–1861*, Columbia University Studies in History, Economics, and Public Law, XCVI, No. 219 (New York, 1921);

Compiling a check-list of Lincoln critics in the South would be an endless task and is not the purpose of this narrative, which is concerned with Southern attitudes toward Lincoln as they reflect upon civil war and reunion. Besides, most of these cavilers employed familiar arguments already explored. But there was one vociferous Lincoln critic who, because of his career as a historian and educator and because he was the scion of an old and honored Southern family, deserves closer attention.

Lyon Gardiner Tyler was the distinguished son of two distinguished families. Through his mother he was descended from the rich and aristocratic Gardiners of New York, whose founding father, Lion Gardiner, had landed in America in 1635 and five years later planted the first English settlement on Long Island.[56] But it was from his father's family that Lyon Tyler imbibed his legal and moral principles and his love of Virginia which would shape his response to the memory of Lincoln. He was the fourteenth of sixteen children of John Tyler and the fifth of seven by Tyler's second wife, Julia Gardiner. Family tradition claimed descent from Wat Tyler, who led a revolt against Richard II; rebellion thus was rooted deep in the family tree. The Tylers came to the New World about eighteen years after Lion Gardiner and within two generations had established themselves as prominent Virginia landowners, slaveholders, and public men. Lyon Gardiner Tyler's grandfather, John Tyler, Sr., was a revolutionary war patriot, opponent of the Constitution, and governor of Virginia. His father was tenth President of the United States.[57]

President Tyler's son was not without advantages in Virginia, and Lyon Tyler enjoyed a long and useful career. He entered the University of Virginia in 1870, took two degrees, and studied law under John B. Minor. After teaching briefly at College of William and Mary, he settled in Memphis, Tennessee, as principal of a school. In 1882 he returned to Richmond to practice law, became active in public affairs, and was

---

and the same author's *Force or Consent as the Basis of the American Government* (Lexington, Ky., 1920). David Rankin Barbee, *An Excursion into Southern History....* (Asheville, N. C., 1928). Of the many writings of "Miss Milly" Rutherford, see especially *Jefferson Davis, the President of the Confederate States, and Abraham Lincoln, the President of the United States, 1861–1865* (Richmond, Va., 1916); and *The South Must Have Her Rightful Place in History* (Athens, Ga., 1923).

56. Robert Seager II, *And Tyler Too: A Biography of John and Julia Gardiner Tyler* (New York, 1963), 17–19.

57. *Ibid.*, 50–51. Lyon Gardiner Tyler, *The Letters and Times of the Tylers* (Richmond, Va., 1884–1885) I, 38, 41–48.

elected to the House of Delegates. As a legislator in 1888, Tyler sponsored a bill appropriating state money to help revive William and Mary, which was nearly bankrupt. The grateful college, which had educated his father and grandfather, chose Tyler as its seventeenth president.

Under the Tyler presidency, the college prospered modestly and evolved from a private to a public institution. In addition to administrative duties, Tyler taught courses in political economy and history and maintained a lively interest in politics as an advocate of prohibition and women's suffrage. Throughout his presidency and in retirement after 1919, he contributed numerous articles and books to the historiography of his family, college, and state. Nor was his fecundity restricted to literature. In the Tyler tradition of big families, he fathered seven children, three of them by his second wife whom he married when he was seventy. A biographer fairly sums up Tyler and his career: "He was a gentleman of great charm, tall, vigorous, and commanding, whose personality impressed itself on the whole political and educational life of Virginia."[58]

"Study hard and be a great man like Papa was and you will astonish the world," wrote Julia Tyler to sixteen-year-old Lonie as he entered the University of Virginia in 1870.[59] Sound enough advice from a President's widow to her son. But Lonie Tyler soon became aware that America in the Gilded Age was not a very hospitable place to a young Virginia gentleman seeking greatness. The war had turned Tyler's world upside down. He had not seen much of the war himself; when McClellan's army pressed close to the family plantation, "Sherwood Forest," Julia Tyler took nine-year-old Lonie and five of her other children to the Gardiner home on Staten Island, New York, to escape the fighting. But the effects of war weighed heavily upon him. His beloved father, who had died in 1862 just after his election to the Confederate Congress, had been condemned by many Americans as a traitor. The family home had been ravaged by war and defiled by the occupation of Negro troops. The Tylers and Gardiners divided their allegiances during the conflict, and some members were permanently estranged from others in the family. Tyler's mother, Julia, while not exactly impoverished, had to struggle

58. Robert Hunt Land, "Lyon Gardiner Tyler," *Dictionary of American Biography*, 21 (Supplement I), 691. *William and Mary College Quarterly Historical Magazine*, 2nd Ser. 15 (Oct., 1935), 319–23, 334–43.

59. Seager, *And Tyler Too*, 641n.

to support her children. As the widow of a President, she was not unwilling to receive the flattery and favors of Republican administrations. But many of John Tyler's sons remained unreconstructed and embittered.[60]

Among those least reconciled to Southern defeat was Lyon Gardiner Tyler. Too young to wear the gray, he enlisted in the ranks of the Lost Cause. In defense of the South, his weapon was the pen and his battlefields were the teacher's lectern and the history book. For Tyler, the battle was over only at his last breath.

Tyler fancied himself an objective historian exposing Northern lies which had infiltrated into the history books and into American minds—lies about the South, the nature of the Union, slavery, civil war, and national heroes. "Real history," he once wrote, "cares nothing for the blare of trumpets and the shouts of the propagandists—it cares only for facts!"[61] But Tyler himself was all trumpets and propaganda, a historian who carefully selected his "facts" to support his fierce prejudices. For Tyler, "objective" history was a broadsword used to defend the Old South and the reputation of one of its first families, the Tylers.

The romance of Old South civilization appealed powerfully to this born aristocrat who had matured in the shabby reality of Reconstruction Virginia and Gilded Age America. Like many other apologists of the Confederacy, Tyler developed a "two nations" theory of American history. During the colonial period, British North America developed two distinct sectional cultures, the one mean, grasping, and commercial, the other democratic, refined, and agricultural. Slavery did not influence the growth of sectional differences, Tyler asserted; rather, "geography had marked out the character of the two sections of the United States before any white man came along."[62]

Tyler had no doubt that the Southern culture produced a superior people: "No people were more energetic, or more capable of bearing hardships and fatigues, and while the energy of the North was, in a measure, one of speculation, or of adding figures in the easy retreat of the counting-room, that of the South was mainly the energy that wrestles with nature in its strength—superintending the farm or holding the

60. *Ibid.*, 537–38.

61. L. G. Tyler, *General Lee's Birthday* (n.p., n.d.), 5. L. G. Tyler, *John Tyler and Abraham Lincoln. Who Was the Dwarf? A Reply to a Challenge* (Richmond, Va., 1929), 4–5.

62. Tyler, *General Lee's Birthday*, 15.

plow."[63] These two peoples, according to Tyler, allied to throw off British tyranny. After the revolution, to which the South contributed the bulk of leadership, men, money, and virtue, the two sections confederated into a new nation for their mutual benefit. But the North reaped most of the benefits of union at the expense of the South. "The South made a fatal mistake," wrote Tyler, ". . . in uniting with a people so differently constituted as the people of the North." After suffering years of abuse, climaxed by the electoral triumph of a sectional party led by ignorant, "self-made" men who hated the South, the South seceded from the Union, just as the American colonies earlier had seceded from the British Empire. Again, slavery was of little historical importance in bringing about disunion; "the war was nothing more than the outcome of a tyranny exerted for seventy two years by the North over the vital interests of the South."[64]

Tyler believed that Confederate defeat was one of the great tragedies of all time. Had the South won, he maintained, she would have been a great nation, secure in her institutions (but without slavery, which would have been ended as unprofitable), peacefully trading with all mankind, and "a great outstanding figure in the affairs of the World."[65]

For a Southern gentleman, a Virginian, and a Tyler, the modern Union was an intolerable place. "What we have is a great Northern Nation," he wrote bitterly in 1929,

> controlled by Northern majorities to which the South has had to conform all its policy and sacrifice all its ideals for sixty years. The national authority is only Northern authority. The South, growing every day more commercialized, is little more than a neglected part of the Great North. The old Union was one of consent, the present Nation is one of force, imperialistic in every sense and masquerading under the name of Union.[66]

For Tyler, the great villain in this historical drama was Abraham Lincoln. Not only was Lincoln the very incarnation of the rude, self-made men whose rise destroyed the Old Union, but it was Lincoln who refused to let the South go in peace as was her constitutional and moral right, and it was Lincoln who chose to wage war upon the South and

63. Tyler, *Letters and Times of the Tylers* II, 572.

64. *Ibid.*, 567, 573. Tyler, *General Lee's Birthday*, 12–17, 21. L. G. Tyler, *A Confederate Catechism. The War of 1861–1865.* 5th ed. (Holdcroft, Va., 1930), 3–4.

65. Tyler, *General Lee's Birthday*, 21.

66. *Ibid.*, 17.

deny her her rightful place among the nations. For over fifty years, with increasing bitterness, Tyler attacked the martyr-heroic image of Lincoln as a false image foisted upon the nation by lying Yankee propagandists for nefarious purposes.

Tyler rarely resisted a chance to strike a blow against the memory of his nemesis; every anti-Lincolnian in America could look to "Dr. Tyler" for a multitude of helpful citations or quotations. From "Lion's Den," Tyler's country seat, poured scores of critical articles, reviews, and pamphlets. *Tyler's Quarterly Historical and Genealogical Magazine*, edited by the bearded lion himself until his death, was an encyclopedia of anti-Lincoln literature. When William Barton suggested that Lincoln might be descended through Nancy Hanks from the Virginia Lees, Tyler was quick to the defense; any Lee blood in Lincoln, he replied, was not from the distinguished family of Robert and Light Horse Harry, but from an obscure family of servants. When Virginia considered adopting for public schools a history textbook not unfriendly to Lincoln, Tyler led the fight against it. When the Virginia legislature in 1928 passed a resolution honoring Lincoln's birthday, Tyler informed the lawmakers that Lincoln hardly deserved the respect of the commonwealth upon which he waged "inhuman" war.[67]

Tyler's bill of indictment against Lincoln is familiar. Lincoln, he admitted, possessed some rough talents but was an odious man. Lincoln caused the war by denying the South's right to peacefully secede. He established a despotism in the North and waged cruel and barbarous war upon Southern civilians. His Emancipation Proclamation was a criminal act, and because of it Lincoln was "the true parent of reconstruction, legislative robbery, negro supremacy, cheating at the polls, rapes of white women, lynching, and the acts of the Ku Klux Klan." Vulgar in his personal habits, Lincoln was weak and deceitful in character and was dominated by the radicals in his party. He vacillated on the question of surrendering Fort Sumter, and then having been pressured to a decision,

67. William E. Barton, "Abraham Lincoln was a Lee," *Good Housekeeping*, 88 (Jan., 1929), 20–21. Tyler's response may be found in his *Barton and the Lineage of Lincoln. Claim that Lincoln was Related to Lee Refuted* (n.p., [1930]). See also Thomas, *Portrait for Posterity*, 237. L. G. Tyler, *Criticism . . . of "History of the American People" by David S. Muzzey*, 2nd. ed., revised (Richmond, Va., 1932). Giles B. Cook, G. W. B. Hale, and Lyon G. Tyler, *Confederate Leaders and Other Citizens Request the House of Delegates to Repeal the Resolution of Respect to Abraham Lincoln, the Barbarian* (n.p., 1928).

he deliberately deceived the Confederate commissioners in Washington. Faced with cabinet opposition, he withdrew his plan to compensate slaveholders for their lost property. He backed down on his decision to reconvene the Virginia legislature after the fall of Richmond. Such a weak character, Tyler asserted, hardly could have held off the radicals and spared the South the horrors of Reconstruction. "The claim that Lincoln was a democrat, that he restored the Union, that he was a friend of the South, is the purest fiction imaginable."[68]

Given the reality of Lincoln's character and deeds, Tyler found it appalling that such a man could be elevated to the stature of a moral hero. The North, he surmised, having defeated the Southern nation by force of arms, now sought to deprive the South of its heritage, its heroes, and its self-respect by establishing Lincoln as the nation's demigod to whom all must bow. Let Southern children look to Southern heroes like Washington, Jefferson, Madison, Lee, and Davis, Tyler urged; that the North could canonize men like Lincoln and John Brown demonstrates its inferior character.[69]

One can sympathize to a degree with Tyler's reaction to the Lincoln cult which had captured most of the American people. Too many particulars in the Lincoln legend had been uncritically accepted. For example, Tyler rightly challenged the assumption, held as an article of faith by many on both sides of the Mason-Dixon line, that had Lincoln lived he would have been able to carry out his reconstruction plan. But Tyler went beyond criticism; like Charles L. C. Minor, Tyler did not seek to balance Lincoln's reputation but to destroy it. Tyler used history as a tool to chip away at the Lincoln monument. For this Bourbon historian, verification consisted of doubting every ascription favorable to Lincoln and accepting as true every deprecating reference, however scurrilous.

The intensity of Tyler's long-sustained attack upon Lincoln suggests that its author was moved by more than the love of a way of life which, if it had existed at all, had vanished during his childhood. Tyler's strong family loyalties provide a clue. His father, along with Robert E. Lee, was Tyler's great hero. As a young man he published his massive *The Letters and Times of the Tylers*, a labor of filiopietism which the family

68. Tyler, *John Tyler and Abraham Lincoln. Confederate Catechism*, 16, 19–20, 24–42. *Letters and Times of the Tylers* II, 632–39. *Propaganda in History*, 2nd ed., revised (Richmond, Va., 1921), 10–19. *Tyler's Quarterly*, 10 (July, 1928), 69.

69. Tyler, *General Lee's Birthday*, 15. *Richmond Dispatch*, Feb. 11, 1900.

biographer has called "a detailed defense and justification of his father's political career in every regard."[70] When *Time* magazine dared to call John Tyler a "dwarf" when compared to Lincoln, the son leaped to his father's defense with a detailed treatise declaring Tyler by far the superior man and president.[71]

The lives of the two presidents had crossed at a critical moment in the nation's history. John Tyler, it is recalled, was chairman of the Washington Peace Conference—"the Old Gentlemen's Convention"—which had tried to head off war in the spring of 1861. John Tyler blamed Lincoln and the Republicans for the failure of the conference. An interview with Lincoln on February 23, 1861, convinced him that the Republicans meant to coerce the South, and he returned to Virginia to work for secession.[72] Lyon Gardiner Tyler, overestimating his father's importance in these events, believed that the hopes of Virginia and the South were fixed on the ill and aged ex-president's efforts to strike a compromise peace.[73] In declining to accept a compromise based on the proposals of Tyler and John Crittenden, Lincoln not only doomed the peace conference but denied John Tyler his last chance to be a great man. In choosing war over a compromise peace, Lincoln also destroyed the culture in which the patrician Tylers could play a great role.

"I accept the results of the war and have tried to make the best of conditions," Tyler wrote in 1929. "I am commercialized, industrialized, and Northernized."[74] He was, of course, none of these things. Grandson

70. Seager, *And Tyler Too*, 552.

71. *Time*, 11 (April 9, 1928), 11–12. Tyler, *John Tyler and Abraham Lincoln*. The opinions of most scholars, in comparing the two presidents, pretty much concur with that of *Time*. Two informal polls among historians and political scientists conducted by Arthur M. Schlesinger rated Lincoln as the greatest president and Tyler "below average." *Life*, 25 (Nov. 1, 1948), and *New York Times*, July 29, 1962. A recent poll conducted by a sociologist asked about a thousand historians to rate presidents according to seven different criteria. In every category save one, Lincoln was ranked far ahead of Tyler. The historians, however, considered Tyler more "idealistic" than Lincoln. For Lyon Gardiner Tyler, this was the criterion which counted most; knowledge of the result of this poll has no doubt consoled his suffering shade. Gary M. Maranell, "The Evaluation of Presidents: An Extension of the Schlesinger Polls," *Journal of American History*, 57 (June, 1970), 104–13.

72. Seager, *And Tyler Too*, 458–60. Tyler, *Letters and Times of the Tylers* II, 616.

73. Tyler, *Letters* II, 574.

74. Tyler, *General Lee's Birthday*, 19.

of a Revolutionary War patriot, son of an ante bellum president, and himself a deposed patrician, Lyon Gardiner Tyler was never quite comfortable with the twentieth century. There was something musty and atavistic about his consuming hatred of Lincoln, his devotion to a dead culture, his family loyalties, and his manner of doing "history." He lived long out of his time. In death, fate played its last cruel trick on Lyon Gardiner Tyler. He breathed his last on February 12, 1935, as the "great Northern Nation" celebrated the 126th birthday of Abraham Lincoln.

5.

Southerner and American: The Images of Lincoln in the New South

After the restoration of home rule a growing number of Southerners became better disposed toward Lincoln's conduct and character. Most of these men identified themselves with ideals of the New South. Ex-Confederates, or sons of men who wore the gray, they revered the memory of heroic Southerners in arms and affirmed that those who cast their fortunes with the Confederacy did so in fidelity to the highest principles as they understood them. But unlike their unreconstructed brethren, these men of the New South looked to a future bright with promise. They rejoiced that the South was freed of the shackles of slavery and uncompromising sectionalism. Appreciating the great potential of Southern soil, labor, and unexploited mineral wealth, they envisioned a South of prosperous small freeholds and booming industries, an urban, progressive South, in which whites and blacks—in their proper and separate spheres—could share in the American heritage of success and abundance. From this New South prospective, one could reconcile being a good Southerner with being a good American.[1]

1. Woodward, *Origins of the New South*, ch. 6. An excellent recent study which analyzes the programs of the New South leadership is Paul M. Gaston, *The New South Creed: A Study in Southern Mythmaking* (New York, 1970).

Southerners of this disposition tended to think of Lincoln in terms that narrowed the differences between North and South. Certain aspects of Lincoln's career—his goodwill toward the South, humanitarianism, dislike of slave labor, and his rise from poverty to success—appealed to Southerners who sought to share in the new American nationalism which found in Lincoln an important symbol. These Southerners hailed Lincoln as a great American and, because of his Southern ancestry and views upon the Negro, even claimed him as a great Southerner. Because the Lincoln legend offered variations which could be appreciated by both Northerners and progressive Southerners, it grew to become one of the many links binding together the old sections in a new American nationalism.

Most Southerners came to believe that Lincoln's untimely death was a disaster to the South.[2] The harsh realities of Radical Reconstruction, fresh in Southern memories, contrasted vividly with Lincoln's plan, as he expressed it, to put the seceded states back into "proper practical relation" with the Union.[3] In working out a design for reconstruction, Lincoln had proceeded on the premise that the states of the Confederacy legally had never left the Union. As states they were not to be punished for the actions of a faction of their citizenry. Lincoln desired that the states reconstruct themselves through constitutional conventions and legislatures elected by citizens who had taken the oath of allegiance to the United States. These states, under home rule, would be fully restored to the Union when they repealed their secession acts and abolished slavery. Southerners had faith that Lincoln never would have permitted the Radicals to impose military-carpetbag rule upon the South. "Had Lincoln lived," ran the popular sentiment, the South would have been spared most of her postwar woes. Few Southerners questioned Lincoln's ability to withstand the avenging Radicals. "My admiration for the man is so great," said Virginia's William P. Trent, "that I can hardly conceive of his succumbing to Stevens and Sumner."[4]

This sympathy for presidential reconstruction represented a consti-

2. A few Southerners were so convinced of this that they forgot or overlooked the spontaneous expressions of joy with which many defeated rebels greeted the news of Lincoln's assassination. See, for example, W. S. Oldham, "Last Days of the Confederacy," *DeBow's Review*, After the War Ser. 7 (Dec., 1869), 1055–56.

3. April 11, 1865, in Lincoln, *Works* VIII, 403.

4. William P. Trent, "A New South View of Reconstruction," *Sewanee Review*, 9 (Jan., 1901), 18.

tutional about-face for the South. If secession were legal, as nearly all Southerners believed, then Lincoln's plan of reconstruction was grounded on the incorrect premise that the states had never been out of the Union. The Radical plan of treating the Southern states as conquered provinces seemed more consistent with the South's own logic. Moreover, the Constitution granted the President no such sweeping power to declare and execute a policy of reconstruction. Yet, after Appomattox, Southerners condemned the congressional Radicals' program as an invasion of the prerogatives of the executive; during the war the exercise of analogous power by the President had been denounced as tyrannous and unconstitutional. But these legal abstractions were swept away by the universal longing for home rule. Tucker C. DeLeon spoke for most Southerners when he wrote: "Reconstruction may be summed up: Abraham Lincoln died too early."[5]

Stories illustrating Lincoln's humanitarianism and acts of kindness toward Confederates were popular in the South after the war. It was said that Lincoln showed "uncontrollable grief" over the death of his rebel brother-in-law, Ben Hardin Helm, and that he secured the release or reprieved the death sentence of many a Confederate prisoner. The wife of General George Pickett told of Lincoln's visit to her home in occupied Richmond in search of his old friend Pickett. Southerners told each other that Lincoln was fond of "Dixie" and that he spoke well of General Lee at his last cabinet meeting.[6] Many of the excesses charged to Lincoln during the fighting were now blamed on Edwin M. Stanton, Lincoln's secretary of war, who seemed to many Southerners a kind of cruel and daemonic spirit whose evil designs upon the South were frustrated until assassination removed the President's staying hand.[7]

Some of these anecdotes were true, others exaggerated or apocryphal.

5. Tucker C. DeLeon, *Belles, Beaux and Brains of the 60's* (New York, 1909), 455–56.

6. *Confederate Veteran*, 4 (March, 1896), 72–73; 17 (March, 1909), 138. John M. Bullock, "President Lincoln's Visiting Card," *Century*, 55 (Feb., 1898), 565–71. G. L. Mordecai, *A Tribute to Lincoln. "Happy to Serve an Enemy." An Ex-Confederate Writes in Praise of the Late President* (New York, 1910). [Mary Neilson Jackson], *A Fair Rebel's Interviews with Abraham Lincoln* (n.p., 1917). Avary, "A Lincoln Souvenir in the South," pp. 506–508. M. L. Avary, *Dixie After the War* (New York, 1906), 43, 80. *Southern Historical Society Papers*, 30 (1902), 129–34; 33 (1905), 109. LaSalle Corbell Pickett, *What Happened to Me* (New York, 1917), 167–74, and "President Lincoln: Intimate Personal Recollections," p. 560.

7. H. S. Fulkerson, *A Civilian's Recollections of the War Between the States*,

But their popularity testified to the growth of a more generous estimate of Lincoln's character and to the spirit of reconciliation which these individual acts of humanitarianism symbolized. An Alabama-born authoress, Mary Raymond Shipman Andrews, found literary inspiration in this spirit. She wrote a short story, *The Perfect Tribute* (1907), about Lincoln's kindness to a dying Confederate prisoner and the young man's love for the sentiments expressed in the Gettysburg Address, a speech Lincoln thought a failure. The rebel captain (who does not know that his benefactor is the President) says:

> It's a wonderful speech. There's nothing finer. Other men have spoken stirring words, for the North and for the South, but never before, I think, with the love of both breathing through them. It is only the greatest who can be a partisan without bitterness, and only such today may call himself not Northern or Southern, but American. To feel that your enemy can fight you to death without malice, with charity—it lifts country, it lifts humanity to something worth dying for. They are beautiful, broad words and the sting of war would be drawn if the Soul of Lincoln could be breathed into the armies.

In death, the young Confederate reaches out and takes Lincoln's big hand. Mrs. Andrews' simple story of love and reconciliation was immensely popular on both sides of the Mason-Dixon line; it sold a million copies in book form alone and was made into a film. Thousands of Americans accepted it as a true incident.[8]

Southern public men frequently reached out their hands to the North by praising Lincoln in speech and print. That Southern politicians, ever sensitive to the tides of public opinion, could do this and not suffer at the polls testified to the mellowing sentiment for Lincoln throughout the South. Congressman Jesse J. Yeates, a North Carolina Democrat, praised

---

ed. P. L. Rainwater (Baton Rouge, La., 1939), 38. *Confederate Veteran*, 17 (April, 1909), 154–55.

8. Mary Raymond Shipman Andrews, *The Perfect Tribute* (New York, 1907). The story originally appeared in *Scribner's*, 40 (July, 1906), 17–24. Mrs. Andrews' Lincoln scribbles the Gettysburg Address on a scrap of brown wrapping paper while traveling by train to the battlefield dedication. According to Victor Searcher, her story may have been the origin of this popular myth. Victor Searcher, *Lincoln Today. An Introduction to Modern Lincolniana* (New York, 1969), 208, 304. Mrs. Andrews incorporated a beneficent Lincoln in two other popular stories, *The Counsel Assigned* (New York, 1912) and *The White Satin Dress* (New York, 1930).

Lincoln on the floor of the House of Representatives and declared that had Lincoln lived, he never would have permitted the gross corruption wrought by the Republican party in the South.[9] A Texas Democrat, Representative Morris Sheppard, said that Lincoln was "a constant student" of the Bible and a champion of prohibition. Had Lincoln lived, Sheppard believed, he would have waged war upon alcohol as fiercely as he did upon slavery.[10] In 1886, when the *Memphis Appeal* sought to pay tribute to Lucius Q. C. Lamar, Mississippi Redeemer and secretary of the interior under Cleveland, it praised Lamar's "wisdom, patriotism and statesmanship" as comparable to that of the merciful and just Lincoln.[11]

One of the most affectionate and poignant public tributes to the memory of Abraham Lincoln came from old Alexander H. Stephens. Broken in health but unbowed in spirit, Stephens was little more than a political atavism after the war. Yet he never stood higher in the hearts of his people, and Georgia returned him to Congress for four terms beginning in 1874 and elected him governor just before his death in 1883. In Congress, Stephens argued against the Civil Rights bill, lobbied for the Texas & Pacific railway project, and, predictably, defended states' rights. On Lincoln's birthday in 1878, the House accepted a gift of Francis Carpenter's monumental painting, "The Signing of the Emancipation Proclamation." Stephens, who had turned sixty-six the day before, was asked to speak. The painting depicted an event which had stirred Stephens' wrath in 1862, but time had worn away all but the core of affection in his memory of Lincoln. From his wheel chair, Stephens recalled his friendship with Lincoln in the Thirtieth Congress and spoke of the President's liberal spirit during the war: "Mr. Lincoln was warm-hearted; he was generous; he was magnanimous; he was most truly 'with malice toward none, with charity for all.' Every fountain of his heart was ever overflowing with the 'milk of human kindness.' From my attachment to him, so much to deeper was the pang in my breast at the horrible manner of his taking off. . . ."[12]

Stephens rambled on to say that slavery had not been without its

9. *Congressional Record*, 44th Cong., 1st sess., IV, March 23, 1876, p. 1922.

10. Morris Sheppard, *Abraham Lincoln. Speech of Congressman Morris Sheppard of Texas. Republican Club Banquet, New York, February 12, 1908* (n.p., [1908]).

11. Nov. 7, 1886, quoted in Edward Mayes, *Lucius Q. C. Lamar: His Life, Times and Speeches, 1825–1893*, 2nd ed. (Nashville. Tenn., 1896), 532.

12. *Congressional Record*, 45th Cong., 2nd sess., VII, Part I, 970.

virtues, although no Southerner wanted it restored, and he warned against a renewal of sectional excitement. But the public remembered the warm praise of Lincoln by the former Confederate vice president, and the gesture was well received in the North. The president of Columbia University wrote Stephens and said that he saw the old man's speech as in the very character of Lincoln himself.[13] Some of Stephens' fellow Southerners, however, were less generous. General Jubal A. Early, who considered Lincoln a traitor and despot, called Stephens' speech a "spectacle." Disturbed about the growing number of prominent ex-Confederates who praised things Yankee, Early asked Jefferson Davis, "Are our leading Southern representatives, and bitterest revilers of the North, about to resolve themselves into a mutual admiration society, leaving such 'irreconcilables' as you and myself out in the cold?"[14]

If "irreconcilable" in life, Davis in death was frequently compared to Lincoln in a manner to do credit to the memories of both presidents. During the war few Southerners doubted that the Mississippi aristocrat was superior in every detail to the lanky railsplitter from Illinois. After Appomattox, many Southerners continued to disparage Lincoln and praise Davis by comparison.[15] Critics of Davis' handling of the war, on the other hand, suggested that had the South possessed a man of Lincoln's abilities at the helm of affairs the cause might not have been lost.[16] But many Southerners did not fail to notice the many remarkable parallels in the lives of the two presidents:

> Jefferson Davis and Abraham Lincoln were born in Kentucky, in 1808 and 1809 respectively; both left their native State in childhood days; one emigrated North, the other South; both served in the Indian wars of the West; both commenced their political life about the same time, being Presidential Electors in the election of 1844, Davis for Polk and Lincoln for Clay; both were elected to Congress about the same time, 1845 or 1846; and were in the same year, and on almost the same day, elected to

13. Johnston and Browne, *Life of Stephens*, 537–38.

14. Feb. 16, 1878, in Rowland, ed., *Jefferson Davis* VIII, 82. See also Jubal A. Early, *A Memoir of the Last Year of the War for Independence. . . .* (Lynchburg, Va., 1867), iii–iv.

15. See, for example, *Land We Love*, 4 (March, 1868), 391–92.

16. R. Barnwell Rhett, "The Confederate Government at Montgomery," in Johnson and Buel, eds., *Battles and Leaders* I, 99–110. Blackford, *War Years with Jeb Stuart*, 258.

preside over their respective governments—one as President of the United States, the other as President of the Confederate States of America.[17]

A twist of fate, it was said, or perhaps Providential design, inspired Sam Davis to take his family to Mississippi and Tom Lincoln to move to the free soil of Indiana. The environments in which Lincoln and Davis matured shaped their ideas about slavery and the Union and made them spokesmen of their respective sections. In the careers of the two presidents, many Southerners saw in microcosm the tragedy of sectionalism and civil war. "Both of them . . . were the foremost champions of American principles," said John W. Daniel, of Virginia; "both of them were revolutionaries and as such must be judged."[18] This new perspective on Davis and Lincoln reflected a growing appreciation by Southerners of the common virtues and dedication to duty not only of the two presidents but of the sections which they represented.

"A strangely persistent rumor" during and after the war suggested that Lincoln and Davis had more in common than the purity of their characters. The slight physical resemblance between the two men and the proximities of their births in time and place gave rise to the legend that they were half-brothers, sons of virile Sam Davis.[19] Stories of Lincoln's irregular ancestry were widely told in the South. The uncertain origins and alleged sexual promiscuity of Nancy Hanks, Lincoln's mother, and the absence of certain records regarding her marriage to Tom Lincoln left a margin of doubt on which fertile imaginations could play. Old men in the North Carolina mountains swore that Lincoln was the illegitimate son of Abraham Enloe, a man of some distinction in Buncombe County, and that Enloe's angry wife had driven Nancy and her infant into the wilderness of Kentucky.[20] A reputed physical likeness

17. *Confederate War Journal*, 2 (Feb., 1895), 166.

18. "Life, Services, and Character of Jefferson Davis. An Oration by Hon. John W. Daniel. . . . January 25, 1890," in *Southern Historical Society Papers*, 17 (1889), 113–59. For similar sentiments about Lincoln and Davis, see T. C. DeLeon, "The Real Jefferson Davis," *Southern Historical Society Papers*, 36 (1908), 74–85; Gordon, *Reminiscences*, 16; S. C. Mercer, *The Two Kentuckians, Read by Mrs. Irwin Dugan Before the Filson Club, Louisville, Ky.* (poem) (Louisville, Ky., 1901).

19. Eliza Andrews, *War-Time Journal*, 237–39.

20. J. C. Coggins, *Abraham Lincoln. A North Carolinian with Proof*, 2nd ed., revised (Gastonia, N. C., 1927). William Macon Coleman, *The Evidence that Abraham Lincoln Was Not Born in Lawful Wedlock, or, the Sad Story of Nancy*

between Lincoln and John Marshall moved Lucinda Boyd to speculate that her fellow Virginian had a place in Lincoln's lineage. In *The Sorrows of Nancy*, she wove a romance in which Nancy Hanks is the illegitimate daughter of Marshall and Lincoln is the product of a liaison between Nancy and Marshall's adopted son.[21] In other tales Lincoln was the bastard son of Henry Clay, John C. Calhoun, Patrick Henry (who died ten years before Lincoln's birth), and was an unrecognized twig on the family tree of Robert E. Lee. The yarns all described the abused Nancy and her infant as being passed along in some fashion to the accommodating Tom Lincoln.[22]

These stories of Lincoln's origins, unlike those recounted by Bledsoe and Minor, are without malice. They do not attempt to discredit the man and his career because of his illegitimate birth. William Coleman, the chronicler of one of these tales, placed Lincoln above all Presidents "in the profound depth of his human sympathy and his Christ like spirit," adding that "the unfortunate circumstances of his parentage and birth can not affect his character or the esteem and reverence in which this memory is justly held."[23] Lucinda Boyd found the source of Lincoln's greatness in his irregular pedigree, for did not "the best blood of Virginia run in his veins"?

Walt Whitman had asked an audience in 1879: "Have you never realized it, my friends, that Lincoln, though grafted on the West, is essentially, in personnel and character, a Southern contribution?"[24] Long before Whitman made this observation, Southerners had speculated upon the irony of the great captain of their enemies being a man of their very own kith and kin. The yarns told of Lincoln's paternity fixed Lincoln as a Southern product; indeed, many in Virginia and North Caro-

---

Hanks (Dallas, Texas, 1899?). For a slightly different version of the "North Carolina tradition" of Lincoln's birth, see James H. Cathey, *Truth is Stranger Than Fiction; or, The True Genesis of a Wonderful Man* (n.p., 1899). Coggins argued that his account was strengthened by Biblical analogy. Like Abraham of Genesis 16 and 21, Enloe was forced to send his bondswoman and her son by him into the wilderness (pp. 156–57). Fortunately, Coggins did not carry the comparison of Ishmael and Lincoln further.

21. Lucinda Boyd, *The Sorrows of Nancy* (Richmond, Va., 1899).

22. J. G. deRoulhac Hamilton wittily disposed of all this foolishness in his article, "The Many-Sired Lincoln," *American Mercury*, 5 (June, 1925), 129–35.

23. Coleman, *Evidence*, 1.

24. Walt Whitman, *The Complete Poetry and Prose of Walt Whitman as Prepared by Him for the Deathbed Edition* (New York, 1948) II, 315.

lina were anxious to claim him as their own. Confederate General D. H. Hill enjoyed the thought that Southern leaders made the greatest contributions to both sides in the late war. George Thomas and David Farragut were the North's stoutest fighters, Hill pointed out, and they were Southern born; Lincoln was a Southerner "from first to last."[25] Congressman John Sharp Williams of Mississippi said that not only was Lincoln Southern in origin, but a Southern poor white at that—the class that gave America Henry Clay, Andrew Jackson, and Patrick Henry. "Bone of our bone and sinew of our sinew," Williams declared, Lincoln "received from a Southern ancestry on both sides—and especially upon his mother's side—his patient courage, his imperturbable perseverances, his loyalty to his ideals, and, above all, the characteristic common sense and sense of humor of the Southerner."[26]

The idea that Lincoln essentially was a Southern man offered attractive possibilities for Southern fiction, and Joel Chandler Harris successfully developed this theme in one of his most popular short stories, "The Kidnapping of President Lincoln" (1909). Harris' literary horizons were not broad—he once wrote that "no novel or story can be genuinely American unless it deals with the *common* people, that is, *country* people"—but he was a skilled craftsman within his chosen sphere of sketching Georgia scenes and attitudes in the dialect of Negroes and white crackers.[27] He is remembered best, of course, for his "Uncle Remus" stories.

Always embarrassed by praise of his works, Harris was a painfully shy man who could not endure crowds and who once escaped through a window rather than meet a stranger whom a friend wanted to introduce. But in print Harris could be direct and forceful (or sly and subtle, as in the Uncle Remus tales). In his fiction, articles, and hundreds of editorials for the *Atlanta Constitution*, he worked for a reconciliation between North and South.[28]

As a boy during the war Harris worked as a printer's devil on a Georgia plantation newspaper, *The Countryman*. He was filled with boyhood zeal for the Cause and with antipathy for Lincoln. In the columns of the little weekly, young Harris, behind the pseudonym "Oba-

25. *Southern Historical Society Papers*, 1 (May, 1876), 393, and 16 (1888), 443.
26. *Confederate Veteran*, 12 (Nov., 1904), 517–21.
27. Julia Collier Harris, ed., *The Life and Letters of Joel Chandler Harris* (Boston, 1918), 204.
28. *Ibid.*, 141.

diah Skinflint," published a letter in country dialect warning Old Abe to evacuate Washington before Jeff Davis gets there. Skinflint threatens to draw Lincoln's "blood with a lead pill the first time he sets his peepers on him."[29] But the mature Harris respected Lincoln and frequently said that, save for the war itself, the President's death was the South's greatest tragedy.[30]

In "The Kidnapping of President Lincoln" Harris introduced the character of Billy Sanders, a shrewd Georgia cracker with a talent for quickly getting to the essence of things. Sanders was Harris himself, although the fictional countryman, an easy talker and always in command of the situation, really enlarged the personality of the shy and reticent "Sage of Snap Bean Farm." Sanders falls in with Francis Bethune, a gallant young aristocrat who had been forced to resign from the Confederate army after an altercation with his colonel. The two men plan to pass through Union lines to Washington, kidnap the President, and return him South, thus ending the war and rescuing Bethune's reputation. The machinations of the plot are unimportant; the burden of the tale lies in the meeting of the Georgia cracker and the Illinois railsplitter.

Billy Sanders had "a secret admiration" for Lincoln before they ever met:

> He had read in the papers about the President's humble beginnings, how he studied his books by a lightwood knot fire, and how he had split rails for a livelihood at one period of his career. A hundred times he had remarked to thoughtless persons who were abusing Mr. Lincoln, "He may be wrong in his idees, but I'll bet you a thrip to a gingercake that his heart's in the right place."

Harris' Lincoln is guided by a powerful love for the Union, wearied with the great cares of office, chivalrous to a captured lady spy (Bethune's aunt), and magnanimous to a young Union soldier whom Stanton had ordered shot for desertion. Lincoln and Sanders relax in each other's company and swap yarns. The two are obviously of a kind, and Sanders tells the President, "Down our way they say you're a Yankee, but if that's so, the woods are full of Yankees in Georgia, all born an' raised right there." Lincoln laughs, "You're paying me the highest compliment I've had in many a day." Later, Sanders tells Mrs. Lincoln that he hasn't

29. *Ibid.*, 46–47.
30. *Ibid.*, 47.

felt so much at home since he left Georgia: "But I hear you're a Southerner, an' Mr. Lincoln is Georgy all over, and that accounts for it." In the end, the two Confederates decline to go through with the abduction scheme, Bethune explaining, "I would as soon kidnap my grandfather, or some one else equally dear to me." The essential fraternity of Georgia and Illinois has bridged the chasm of civil war.[31]

The seal was placed upon the South's claim to Lincoln when a biographical essay of the late President was included in the multivolume panegyric, *The South in the Building of the Nation* (1909–1913). The purpose of this massive work, written and compiled by many of the South's outstanding scholars and public men, is suggested in its subtitle: "A History of the Southern States Designed to Record the South's Part in the Making of the American Nation; to Portray the Character and Genius, to Chronicle the Achievement and Progress and Illustrate the Life and Traditions of the Southern People." In the biographical sketch by young Walter Lynwood Fleming, Lincoln's life and thought is described as profoundly shaped by Southern influences:

> Though in the supreme work of his life, Lincoln was opposed by the great mass of the Southerners, yet by birth and early training he was Southern; in his views relating to slavery and the negro he was very close to the large body of non-slaveholding Southerners; and in his attitude toward reconstruction he showed an appreciation of Southern conditions superior to those who had no actual knowledge of or connection with the South.[32]

31. Joel Chandler Harris, *On the Wing of Occasions. Being the Authorised Version of Certain Curious Episodes of the Late Civil War, Including the Hitherto Suppressed Narrative of the Kidnapping of President Lincoln* (New York, 1900), 149, 190, 193, 239. Billy Sanders turns up again in Harris' novel of Reconstruction, *Gabriel Tolliver* (New York, 1902), where he tells Alexander Stephens that Lincoln was "the best all-'round man I ever laid eyes on" (p. 120). Paul M. Cousins, a recent biographer of Harris, says the story of the kidnapping of Lincoln was an invention and that Harris did no historical research on it. *Joel Chandler Harris: A Biography* (Baton Rouge, La., 1968), 176. However, Walker Taylor, a Confederate officer, told of a plan to kidnap Lincoln in Washington in 1862 which was turned down by Jefferson Davis, in *Confederate Veteran*, 11 (April, 1903), 157–58.

32. *The South in the Building of the Nation* . . . (Richmond, Va., 1909–1913), X, 97–102. For what it is worth, Lincoln's sketch runs more than five pages, almost as much as Lee's and Jefferson's and much more than those of Davis, Jackson, and Madison.

Lincoln never could have been welcomed into the Southern fraternity unless it could be demonstrated, as Fleming suggested, that he was "right" on the Negro question. With their traditional racism reinforced by Darwinian theories and the conventional anthropological wisdom of the day, few Americans North or South doubted the innate inferiority of the Negro. A careful selection of Lincoln's words on the subject convinced many Southerners that the heart of the Great Emancipator actually had beat in time with his Southern brethren on most matters concerning the Negro. George Washington Cable, one of the New South's few advocates of equal rights, observed: "The early admissions and confessions of Abraham Lincoln have been much used in this debate by excellent men, who still repudiate and antagonize the conclusions of his latest wisdom as they did his earlier."[33]

Cable was talking about the question of deporting the American Negro population abroad, an idea once favored by Lincoln and revived around the turn of the century.[34] But his remarks could apply equally to the whole phenomenon of Southern racists finding aid and comfort in Abraham's bosom. Southern writers pointed out that Lincoln, although he hated slavery, was no abolitionist, that he asserted he had no right nor inclination to interfere with slavery in the states, that he rescinded the unauthorized emancipation orders of his generals, and that he proclaimed emancipation only when public pressure and the exigencies of war left him no alternatives. Lincoln's famous letter to Horace Greeley was quoted to prove that his primary interest was to save the Union and not to free the slaves. To illustrate Lincoln's antipathy for the Negro,

33. "The Southern Struggle for Pure Government" (1890) in *The Negro Question: A Selection of Writings on Civil Rights in the South*, ed. Arlin Turner (Garden City, N. J., 1958), 236.

34. I. A. Newby, *Jim Crow's Defense. Anti-Negro Thought in America, 1900–1930* (Baton Rouge, La., 1965), 179–84. On the one-hundredth anniversary of Lincoln's birth, William P. Pickett published *The Negro Problem: Abraham Lincoln's Solution* (New York. 1909). Pickett, a New Yorker, urged a "final solution" to the Negro problem by deporting and colonizing Negroes in Africa and the Caribbean. Negroes unwilling to leave the country would be placed on government reservations like the Indians. Such a solution would be consistent with Lincoln's aims and principles, argued Pickett, and he asked his readers in closing: "Are our professions of devotion to his memory, after all, anything more than hollow lip service, and have we in our hearts the courage and in our minds the intelligence and resolution to solve the negro problem as Lincoln would have had it solved?" (p. 564).

Southern propagandists cited his address in Charleston, Illinois, in 1858, in which Lincoln stated unequivocally that he believed blacks inferior to whites and that he did not favor Negroes voting, serving on juries, holding office, or intermarrying with whites. Evidence was offered confirming the fact that Lincoln contributed money and much thought to colonizing freed slaves abroad.[35]

Southerners could conclude, on the basis of this select testimony, that Lincoln was a most reluctant emancipator, and that had he lived he would have permitted the South to work out its racial problem consistent with the principles of white supremacy. Mississippi's archsegregationist James K. Vardaman thus expressed a popular sentiment when he declared that he and Lincoln shared "substantially identical" views on the race question.[36] Just what Lincoln's policy toward the Negro would have been had he lived is, of course, an unanswerable conundrum. But the Southern interpretation ignored the evolution in Lincoln's thinking about Negroes during the war years. Before his death he discarded any idea of colonizing the freedmen, and he spoke in favor of suffrage of the "very intelligent" and for black veterans of the Union army.[37]

35. Lincoln, *Works* III, 145–46. For Southern arguments in this vein, see *Southern Historical Society Papers*, 5 (Jan.–Feb., 1878), 16; 16 (1888), 319–39; 25 (1897), 380–81; and 27 (1899), 60–84. Also, George L. Christian, "Report of the History Committee of the United Confederate Veterans, held at Richmond, Va., May 30th–June 3d, 1907," in McGuire and Christian, *Confederate Cause and Conduct*, 180–81; *Land We Love*, 3 (June, 1867), 176; *Southern Bivouac*, 3 (Dec., 1884), 181–84; and Thomas Nelson Page, *The Negro: The Southerner's Problem* (New York, 1904), 16–18, 130–31. White segregationists continue to evoke Lincoln's name and words in support of white supremacy. See, for example, *New York Times*, Feb. 12, 1968, and *The Citizen: Official Journal of the White Citizens' Council of America* (Jackson, Miss., Feb., 1964).

36. *Congressional Record*, 51, 62nd Cong., 2nd sess., Senate, Feb. 6, 1914, p. 3040.

37. Lincoln to Michael Hahn, March 13, 1864, in Lincoln, *Works* VII, 243. In Lincoln's last public speech, on April 11, 1865, he announced publicly what heretofore had been private thoughts: "I would myself prefer that it [the elective franchise] were now conferred on the very intelligent, and on those who served our cause as soldiers." *Works* VIII, 403. Lincoln was speaking about the reconstruction government of Louisiana, which had failed to grant the franchise to blacks. Since the Louisiana experience was looked to as a model for reconstructing the South after the war, it may be inferred that Lincoln wished, if he was not ready to demand, that the vote be extended to selected blacks throughout the South.

A number of factors suggest that before his death Lincoln had given up any serious thoughts of settling blacks abroad: the failure of two small-scale attempts to colonize blacks, the opposition of most black leaders, Lincoln's expressed ad-

Thomas Dixon, Jr., went furthest of all Southern writers in attempting to bind Lincoln firmly to the Southern position on race. In his novels and plays Dixon championed the cause of white supremacy and presented Lincoln as a Southerner fully in sympathy with that cause. Born in 1864 of an old North Carolina family, Dixon grew up during Reconstruction, and the memories of those exciting and uncertain years later would be worked into his fiction. Dixon studied law and history and was elected to the North Carolina legislature before he was old enough to vote. He later entered the Baptist ministry and held pulpits in North Carolina, Boston, and New York. Tall, dark and gaunt, Dixon was remarkably Lincolnesque in appearance. His sensationalist sermons attracted large audiences, and he was a popular lyceum lecturer. Apparently he found it difficult to restrain his rhetoric, for a grand jury once indicted the young minister for slander. Dixon eventually left the ministry and devoted his full time to writing. He was a prolific author and through his works condemned modern heresies such as socialism, communism, women's emancipation, and pacifism. Fear of the Negro characterized most of his works. In his last, pessimistic novel, *The Flaming Sword* (1939), Negro communists take over the nation by force and establish a Soviet Republic of the United States.[38]

---

miration for the contributions made by Negro troops, his wish that the freedmen be given land and votes. However, there is an account by Benjamin Butler which is often cited by those who claim Lincoln continued to cherish colonization schemes. According to Butler, Lincoln just before he died expressed fear of a race war if the Negro troops were not disarmed and disposed of, and he told Butler he would like to colonize them—and all blacks, if possible—abroad. Butler replied that it would be impossible to resettle all blacks, but he urged Lincoln to give him command of the black troops to settle Panama and dig the isthmian canal. Lincoln is supposed to have replied, "There is meat in that," and urged Butler to speak to Seward on the matter. This account, written long after the event, doesn't quite ring true. Butler, given to self-advertisement, has Lincoln heaping praise upon him for his James River campaign; this was just after Lincoln removed the bumbling political general from command. Butler's story of Lincoln's fear of a race war initiated by armed blacks is hardly consistent with his remarks of about the same time (April 11, for example). Lincoln may have listened to Butler's plan, but that he initiated the conversation or responded to the Panama idea in the way Butler described may be doubted. *Autobiography of Major-General Benjamin F. Butler. Butler's Book* (Boston, 1892), 903–908.

38. Biographical details on Dixon have been gleaned from Raymond Allen Cook, *Fire from the Flint: The Amazing Careers of Thomas Dixon* (Winston-Salem, N. C., 1968); *The National Cyclopedia of American Biography* (New York, 1906), XIII, 189; *Bookman*, 20 (Feb., 1905), 498–500; and Stanley J. Kunitz and

Dixon published his first story (about the Ku Klux Klan) as a teenager, and his critics claimed his literary talent improved little over the next several decades. *The Leopard's Spots,* his first novel and the first volume in a trilogy about the Klan, appeared in 1902. It betrayed little in the way of literary art. William E. Dodd, lamenting the lack of interest in serious books in the South, observed that his fellow Southerners read only novels like *The Leopard's Spots* and "a few others which belong to the invertebrate kingdom."[39]

A reviewer of *The Clansman* (1905), Dixon's second novel, threw up his hands: "Of the stories of Mr. Dixon's books the less said the better. The one tribute that can be paid them is that it must take a mind somewhat out of the ordinary to construct such superlatively bad ones." But the same critic confessed that "*The Clansman* may be summed up as a very poor novel, a very ridiculous novel, not a novel at all, yet a novel with a great deal to it."[40]

Dixon's plots are crude and his characters often wooden and stereotyped. But there is a certain power in these works; one feels radiating from the pages Dixon's passionate commitment to his theme of white supremacy. Dixon had given up the ministry but not the pulpit, and his novels are racist sermons in the guise of fiction. Widely read if not praised, *The Leopard's Spots* and *The Clansman* each sold more than a million copies. *The Clansman* toured the nation as a play and later was wrought by D. W. Griffith into the epic motion picture *The Birth of a Nation* (1915), which exposed millions to Dixon's version of Reconstruction.

Dixon portrays the Ku Klux Klan as a heroic band of white knights which rescues white civilization from the threat of mongrelization. Race-mixing is the most heinous of crimes, and Dixon dwells frequently upon what he deems the repulsiveness of Negroid features: "Amalgamization simply meant Africanization. The big nostrils, flat nose, massive

---

Howard Haycraft, eds., *American Authors, 1600–1900: A Biographical Dictionary of American Literature* (New York, 1938), 387.

39. Dodd, "Some Difficulties of the History Teacher in the South," 119. Dixon did not claim literary distinction but candidly admitted he was a propagandist: "I have made no effort to write literature. . . . My sole purpose in writing was to reach and influence with my argument the mind of millions. I had a message and I wrote it as vividly and as simple as I know how." Quoted in Cook, *Fire from the Flint,* 199.

40. *Bookman,* 20 (Feb., 1905), 560.

jaw, protruding lips and kinky hair will register their animal marks over the proudest intellect and the rarest beauty of any other race. The rule that had no exception was that one drop of negro blood makes a negro."[41] According to Dixon the only solution to the race problem, short of exterminating or deporting all Negroes, is the absolute subjection of black to white. "In a Democracy," says Dixon's protagonist in *The Leopard's Spots*, "you can not build a nation inside of a nation of two antagonistic races, and therefore the future American must either be an Anglo-Saxon or a Mulatto. It is my work to maintain the racial absolutism of the Anglo-Saxon in the South, politically, socially, economically."[42]

Lincoln's magnanimous plans for peace are mentioned in *The Leopard's Spots*, and his Charleston speech is cited to show that he stood with the South for white supremacy.[43] But it is in *The Clansman* that Dixon begins to develop Lincoln as a character for historical fiction. The first quarter of the book is dominated by "The Great Heart," Lincoln, whose essentially Southern character is revealed in a dialogue with a South Carolina lady:

> "I must tell you, Mr. President," she said, "how surprised and how pleased I am to find you are a Southern man."
>
> "Why, didn't you know that my parents were Virginians, and that I was born in Kentucky?"
>
> "Very few people in the South know it. I am ashamed to say I did not."
>
> "Then, how did you know I am a Southerner?"
>
> "By your looks, your manner of speech, your easy, kindly ways, your tenderness and humour, your firmness in the right as you see it, and, above all, the way you rose and bowed to a woman in an old, faded black dress, who you knew to be an enemy."
>
> "No, Madam, not an enemy now," he said, softly. "That word is out of date."
>
> "If we had only known you in time—"[44]

41. Thomas Dixon, *The Leopard's Spots: A Romance of the White Man's Burden—1865–1900* (New York, 1902), 382.

42. *Ibid.*, 333.

43. *Ibid.*, 35, 67–68.

44. Thomas Dixon, *The Clansman: An Historical Romance of the Ku Klux Klan* (New York, 1905), 31–32.

There follows a duel of wills between Lincoln and evil Austin Stoneman (representing Thaddeus Stevens) over the fate of the prostrate South: "The two men were face to face at last, — the two men above all others who had built and were to build the foundations of the New Nation, — Lincoln's in love and wisdom to endure forever, the Great Commoner's in hate and madness, to bear its harvest of tragedy and death for generations yet unborn."[45] Lincoln venerates the Constitution; Stoneman dismisses it as "a worn rag." Lincoln wants to restore the rights of the Southern states; Stoneman demands they be treated as conquered provinces. The real clash between the two giants comes over the status of the emancipated slave in the South. Stoneman wants to elevate the freedman to power in order to chastise and humble the traitors. Lincoln replies by suggesting the Negroes be colonized in the tropics: "We can never attain the ideal Union our fathers dreamed, with millions of an alien, inferior race among us, whose assimilation is neither possible nor desirable. The Nation cannot now exist half white and half black, any more than it could exist half slave and half free."[46]

Dixon further developed his image of Lincoln in another novel, *The Southerner* (1913), and in *A Man of the People* (1920), a short-lived Broadway play about Lincoln in the election of 1864. The book is encumbered with the usual romances and elaborate subplots, but the commanding figure is Lincoln. The President's Southern perspective is emphasized when the abolitionist Senator Winter curses Lincoln: "Bah! The trouble is Lincoln's a Southerner-born in the poisonous slave atmosphere of the South. He grew up in Southern Indiana and Illinois. His neighbors there were settlers from the South. He has never breathed anything but Southern air and ideals. It's in his blood."[47] The idea that Lincoln's Southern credentials rest ultimately upon his orthodoxy on the racial question is reinforced when Dixon's Lincoln, as a Hoosier lad, meets his first Negro and the impression is set for life:

> The Boy stood rooted to the spot and watched until the negro disappeared. It was the first black man he had ever seen. He had heard of negroes and that they were slaves. But he had no idea that one human being could be so different from another.

45. *Ibid.*, 41.
46. *Ibid.*, 46.
47. Thomas Dixon, *The Southerner: A Romance of the Real Lincoln* (New York, 1913), 265–66.

> The thing that puzzled him beyond all comprehension was why a big strong man like that, if he were a man, would submit. Why didn't he fight and die? A curious feeling of contempt filled his mind. This black thing that looked like a man and talked like a man couldn't be one. No real man would grin and laugh and be a slave.[48]

In *The Southerner* Dixon goes beyond portraying Lincoln as a wise and great-souled statesman and elevates him to a Christ-like folk hero. Tom Lincoln is no shiftless cracker, but a sturdy frontiersman; Lincoln's mother radiates a Madonna-like beauty and experiences a vision of her unborn son's future greatness. Lincoln's boyhood—Dixon calls the young Lincoln "Boy," with the B faithfully capitalized—is as exemplary as Parson Weems would desire. The lad respects his parents and cannot lie to his mother, believes in God, is generous to others and kind to animals. After destroying slavery and restoring the Union, Lincoln, enshrined in the hearts of his people and confident of his power, sets his soul "to heal the bitterness of the war and remove the negro race from physical contact with the white." But a madman intervenes: "The curtains in the box at Ford's theatre were softly drawn apart by an unseen hand. The Angel of Death entered, paused at the sight of the smile on his rugged, kindly face, touched the drooping shoulders, called him to take the place he had won among earth's immortals and left to us 'the gentlest memory of our world.' "[49]

Thomas Dixon's admiration of Lincoln approached that of the diviners in the North who saw Lincoln as God's chosen instrument. But, for Dixon, it was not Lincoln's humanitarianism, humility, or democracy which elevated the late President to greatness; it was Lincoln's racism which ennobled the man and made him a Southerner. Dixon did not wholly distort Lincoln's expressed views on race, but he did neglect the great compassion which tempered Lincoln's attitude toward the Negro and which subjected that attitude to the changes which were already evident before his death. True greatness must rest upon more permanent and honorable qualities than discredited racism. Lincoln possessed such qualities in abundance, but they were diminished before the one Lincolnian attitude with which Dixon could be empathic.

Dixon's Lincoln contrasted sharply with the image of Lincoln held

48. *Ibid.*, 18–19.
49. *Ibid.*, 543.

by most contemporary Negroes. During the war, slaves associated Lincoln's name with freedom, and this respect was little diminished by the imperfect emancipation which followed Appomattox. Northern teachers who ventured South to instruct the freedman observed this reverence of Lincoln's memory and reinforced it with lessons about the Great Emancipator. A Yankee teacher in Georgia wrote:

> The spirit of veneration of Lincoln which was common in the schools is well illustrated in the story of the Negro child who stood in the hallway of a school, and gazed with wonder at the portrait of Lincoln. His teacher said, "That is the man who made you free!" "The homely round face was all aglow with the most pathetic wonder, awe and delight, the latter breaking out in as lovely a smile as I ever saw," wrote the teacher. "Is it God?" the child asked. "No," replied the teacher, "it's Lincoln." "The unsophisticated" country lad stood quietly, gazing at the portrait. "It was a perfect triumph of soul over body," a veritable "glory!"[50]

The tale, certain to delight Northern readers, may have been embellished in the telling, but it represented the almost universal admiration for Lincoln among blacks. Most Negroes agreed with Booker T. Washington, the most respected black leader of his time, in his estimation of Lincoln. Born a slave, Washington remembered his mother praying for Lincoln's success. He was "our hero and benefactor," Washington said in 1899; "the name of Abraham Lincoln" should be "permanently linked with the highest interests of the Negro race." Lincoln was "the Emancipator of America" who liberated blacks from slavery and whites from fear. In his upward struggle from poverty and ignorance to greatness he was an example for youth of both races and for the ascending Negro people as a whole.[51]

Lincoln was not without his Negro critics. Some Northern blacks opposed him in 1860 as insufficiently radical on the slavery question. During the war he was censured for his ideas of colonizing blacks abroad and for his reluctance to declare immediate emancipation and employ black troops. Most of this criticism turned to praise after the

50. *Freedmen's Journal* (Boston) V, no. 6 (June, 1869), 12. Quoted in Henry Lee Swint, *The Northern Teacher in the South, 1862–1870* (Nashville, Tenn., 1941), 90.

51. Booker T. Washington, *An Address . . . For Delivery at a Dinner Given by Members of the Union League Club on February 12, 1899. . . .* (n.p., [1899]). B. T. Washington, "Lincoln and the Black Man," *Alexander's Magazine*, 7 (Feb., 1909), 147–48.

Emancipation Proclamation was promulgated.[52] Chief among these black critics of Lincoln was Frederick Douglass. Like Washington, Douglass was born a slave. Escaping to the North as a young man, he became an outstanding abolitionist orator, editor, and author and the leading Negro spokesman of the Civil War period. He continued the fight for equal rights until his death in 1895. Douglass' praise of Lincoln was measured. He acknowledged the good work done by the Emancipation Proclamation, but, in an oration at the unveiling of the Freedmen's Monument in Washington eleven years after Lincoln's death, he reminded fellow blacks that "Abraham Lincoln was not, in the fullest sense of the word, either our man or our model. In his interests, in his associations, in his habits of thought, and in his prejudices, he was a white man."[53] But Douglass respected Lincoln's memory. Lincoln had called him friend, welcomed him to the White House, and solicited his advice on public policy. "I was impressed with his entire freedom from popular prejudice," Douglass wrote in 1886. "He was the first white man I talked with in the United States freely, who in no single instance reminded me of the difference between himself and myself, of the difference in color, and I thought that all the more remarkable because he came from a State where there were black laws."[54]

In recent years, Lincoln's reputation among blacks has been in eclipse. In their search for black identity and pride and in their haste to challenge white standards and white heroes, many Negroes have applied a harsh standard which discredits any historical figure who was not unequivocally for full social and political equality regardless of the social context in which he lived. By such standards Lincoln has been found wanting. For Malcolm X, Lincoln "did more to trick Negroes than any other man in history."[55] Writer Julius Lester condemns Lincoln as a colonizationist and hesitant emancipator, concluding, "blacks have no reason to feel grateful to Abraham Lincoln. Rather, they should be angry

52. McPherson, *The Negro's Civil War*, 48–53, 89–97, 302–304.

53. Frederick Douglass, *Oration of Frederick Douglass Delivered on the Occasion of the Unveiling of the Freedmen's Monument in Memory of Abraham Lincoln in Lincoln Park, Washington, D.C., April 14th, 1876* (Washington, D.C., 1876).

54. Allen Thorndike Rice, ed., *Reminiscences of Abraham Lincoln by Distinguished Men of His Time* (New York, 1886), 193.

55. Quoted by Robert Penn Warren, *Who Speaks for the Negro?* (New York, 1965), 262.

at him."[56] Evanescent impressions of this disrespect for Lincoln are abundant. In the recently released film *Putney Swope*, blacks idle away the time by throwing darts at Lincoln's picture. In the phenomenally successful rock-musical *Hair*, "Abie-Baby's" reputation as an emancipator is ridiculed.

One of the most detailed attacks upon Lincoln by a Negro came from the pen of Lerone Bennett, Jr., an editor of *Ebony*. In a widely read and much discussed recent article, Bennett asked the question "Was Abe Lincoln a White Supremacist?" and answered it with a strong affirmative. On the basis of highly selective testimony, Bennett argues that Lincoln was a most reluctant emancipator who believed that blacks were inferior and ought to be kept separate from whites, if possible by colonizing them abroad. At best, Lincoln "was the very essence of the white supremacist with good intentions," Bennett concludes. "Lincoln must be seen as the embodiment, not the transcendence, of the American tradition, which is, as we all know, a racist tradition."[57]

Bennett commits the same error as did Dixon and others who wrote with approval of Lincoln's alleged views on race. He let his preconceived ideas govern his selection of evidence. Thus, Lincoln's Charleston, Illinois, speech of 1858 is quoted to prove Lincoln's racism, but later evidence that Lincoln tempered these early views is ignored. Frederick Douglass' criticism of Lincoln is cited, but not his opinion that Lincoln was without prejudice. Some dubious testimony is offered, such as Benjamin Butler's account of his visit with Lincoln in 1865 wherein Lincoln allegedly said he still desired to colonize Negroes. Through ignorance or malice, Bennett distorts Lincoln's views. When Bennett writes, "Lincoln was not opposed to slavery; he was opposed to the *extension* of slavery," he ignores the fact that for Lincoln, restricting the expansion of slavery was a means to destroy it gradually and without war, to place it, in Lincoln's words, "in course of ultimate extinction."[58] Lincoln and the abolitionists did not differ in their desire to rid the nation of slavery, but only in the proper method to do so. Bennett and many other writers, white and black, underestimated the dynamism in Lincoln's thoughts about race. "The Civil War . . . was a revolution and radically changed men," ob-

56. *Look Out, Whitey! Black Power's Gon' Get Your Mama!* (New York, 1968), 58.

57. 23 (Feb., 1968), 35–42.

58. June 16, 1858, in Lincoln, *Works* II, 461.

served historian Carter G. Woodson.[59] War was the crucible in which the Southern-born, frontier-bred Lincoln grew to entertain a larger and more generous estimate of the black man and his potential.

Blacks as well as whites have found in Lincoln a usable symbol to invoke according to their several purposes. Booker T. Washington believed Lincoln a great and worthy hero. Frederick Douglass offered qualified praise. Followers of the black nationalism ideas of Bishop Henry McNeal Turner and Marcus Garvey might quote with approval Lincoln's support of black colonization. For many of today's black militants Lincoln was just another honky racist. There is something sadly ironic in seeing black extremists and Ku Kluxers clasping hands over the grave of the Great Emancipator's reputation.

More appealing than the image of Lincoln as white racist is that of Lincoln the symbolic ideal American. The qualities of this "American" Lincoln are difficult to isolate and define and are perhaps best expressed poetically, as in James Russell Lowell's description of Lincoln as "New birth of our new soil, the first American."[60] This theme represents Lincoln as the product of uniquely American conditions, especially those of the Ohio River frontier, the "valley of democracy," to which both North and South contributed. Like the brave new nation which Northern intellectuals and poets hoped would emerge from the purifying fires of civil war, this symbolic Lincoln expressed a democratic and beneficent American nationalism purged of the old sins of slavery and sectionalism.[61]

The "self-made man" tradition was an element in the American national faith which appealed to many New Southerners and which found in Lincoln an important symbol. This tradition, with its Biblical sanctions of hard work and success in this world, entered America with the first English settlers, prospered, and found powerful expression in the life and writings of Benjamin Franklin. At no time, however, was the cult of the self-made man more popular than in Gilded Age America with its widened fields of enterprise and new millionaires. The life of Abraham Lincoln seemed a perfect model to demonstrate the truth that by luck and pluck one could overcome humble beginnings and achieve

59. *Journal of Negro History*, 31 (July, 1946), 357–60.

60. Horace E. Scudder, ed., *The Complete Poetical Works of James Russell Lowell* (Boston, 1925), 344.

61. Basler, *The Lincoln Legend*, 228–37.

greatness. William H. Thayer, O. J. Victor, Horatio Alger, Jr., and the McGuffey readers preached the lessons of Lincoln's life to America's schoolchildren.[62]

The South, with its aristocratic and agrarian values, had remained somewhat aloof from praising this tradition, insofar as it celebrated mere neolatry and main-chance moneygrubbing. Yet, however much patricians like Lyon G. Tyler deplored the rise of the self-made man, he had been well represented in the ante bellum South. Agrarian capitalism, based on the manipulation of land, cotton, and slaves, had produced first-generation wealth and fame; Andrew Jackson, Henry Clay, and Patrick Henry were among the many Southerners who had risen from poverty to greatness. After the war, these virtues of success and self-help were increasingly praised. The New South was full of young men on the make, and some of the emerging leadership had come from humble backgrounds.[63] The New South itself, rising from defeat, humiliation, and impoverishment, could be imagined as a kind of Horatio Alger success story. Furthermore, when Southerners praised the self-made man and Lincoln as the very model of him, they were laying another plank on the bridge of reconciliation between the sections. When Senator John Sharp Williams of Mississippi said that Lincoln's career illustrated "the fact that those of humblest origin in a free democracy of equal opportunities can and often do reach the very highest station," he knew his remarks would be warmly received in the North.[64] Northern parents who read the published verse of a twelve-year-old Richmond schoolboy—"Though born in a cabin, you still will be lucky / If your life is like Lincoln of old Kentucky"—could take comfort in the knowledge that

62. Horatio Alger, Jr., *Abraham Lincoln, The Backwoods Boy* (New York, 1883). William M. Thayer, *The Pioneer Boy and How He Became President* (Boston, 1863). O. J. Victor, *The Private and Public Life of Abraham Lincoln* (New York, 1864). The common theme in these biographies, according to Roy Basler, is that "Lincoln furnished an ideal figure for the vindication of the honesty, industry, and grit that was 'bound to rise.' He was a model of purity and a stainless example." *The Lincoln Legend*, 106.

63. Buck, *Road to Reunion*, 181.

64. John Sharp Williams, *Lincoln Birthplace Farm at Hodgenville, Ky. Address Delivered on the Occasion of the Acceptance of a Deed of Gift to the Nation by the Lincoln Farm Association of the Lincoln Birthplace Farm at Hodgenville, Ky. . . . September 4, 1916*, 64th Cong., 1st sess., Senate Doc. No. 345 (Washington, D.C., 1916).

children on both sides of the Mason-Dixon line were learning the same values and admiring the same heroes.[65]

The most concrete expression of these intertwined themes of Lincoln, reconciliation, and self-help was in the founding of a college bearing Lincoln's name in one of the states of the Old Confederacy. General Oliver Otis Howard chanced to be in the Cumberland Gap area of Tennessee in 1895 while on a lecture tour. Impressed by the vision of some local people and perhaps remembering Lincoln's affection for the loyal mountain folk of East Tennessee, Howard helped found and promote Lincoln Memorial University two years later. The purpose of the little college, according to one of its brochures, was and is "to spread the gospel for self-control, the gospel of clear-thinking and clean living, the gospel of honest toil and neighborliness among the people of America; to be the embodiment of the life and spirit of Abraham Lincoln . . . ."[66] The theme of reconciliation was carried down to the smallest detail. Howard was chairman of the board; a Confederate veteran was vice-chairman. The school's colors were blue and gray, and its major building was named Grant-Lee Hall. Students, mostly poor mountain people, were offered courses in the liberal, agricultural, and mechanical arts and were required to take a course about Lincoln.[67]

Many men of the New South paid honest tribute to the "American" Lincoln whose spirit inspired Lincoln Memorial University. They wanted to destroy forever the sectional strictures that had bound the South before the war. As conscious conciliators, they discovered in Lincoln a usable symbol representing the kind of nationalism which they hoped to share with their Northern brethren. Northern and Southern men could unite in fraternal love for the Lincoln described by Maurice Thompson, Hoosier poet and Confederate veteran:

> He was the North, the South, the East, the West,
> The thrall, the master, all of us;

65. Robert Morris, "The Cabin Where Lincoln was Born," in A. Dallas Williams, ed., *The Praise of Lincoln: An Anthology* (Indianapolis, Ind., 1911), 53, 228.

66. John L. Dickinson, ed., *Lincoln Memorial University. Living Tribute to a Big Brother of Humanity* (Harrogate, Tenn., 1928).

67. Robert L. Kincaid, *The Lincoln Heritage in the Cumberlands. An Address Delivered Before the Lincoln Fellowship of Southern California, October 20, 1950* (Los Angeles, 1951). R. L. Kincaid, *The Wilderness Road* (Indianapolis, Ind., 1947), 339–45. O. O. Howard, *The Autobiography of Oliver Otis Howard, Major General United States Army* (New York, 1907) II, 568–69.

> There was no section that he held the best;
> His love shone as impartial as the sun.[68]

Henry W. Grady was among those Southerners for whom the symbolic "American" Lincoln had powerful appeal. As editor of the *Atlanta Constitution*, Grady was a persuasive spokesman for the New South credo of industrialism, urbanization, education, and democracy. He was also a tireless and eloquent pleader for sectional reconciliation; upon his untimely death in 1889, a eulogist remarked that Grady died "literally loving a Nation into peace."[69] In Grady's famous "New South" speech before the New England Society in New York in 1886, he evoked the spirit of Lincoln to seal the bond of new-found brotherhood between North and South:

> My friends, Dr. Talmage has told you that the typical American has yet to come. Let me tell you that he has already come. Great types, like valuable plants, are slow to flower and fruit. But from the union of these colonists, Puritans and Cavaliers, from the straightening of their purposes and the crossing of their blood, slow perfecting through a century, came he who stands as the first typical American, the first who comprehended within himself all the strength and gentleness, all the majesty and grace of this Republic—Abraham Lincoln. He was the sum of Puritan and Cavalier, for in his ardent nature were fused the virtues of both, and in the depths of his great soul the faults of both were lost. He was greater than Puritan, greater than Cavalier, in that he was American, and that in his honest form were first gathered the vast and thrilling forces of his ideal government—charging it with such tremendous meaning and elevating it above human suffering that martyrdom, though infamously aimed, came as a fitting crown to a life consecrated from the cradle to human liberty. Let us, each cherishing the traditions and honoring his fathers, build with reverent hands to the type of this simple but sublime life, in which all types are honored, and in our common glory as Americans there will be plenty and to spare for your forefathers and for mine.[70]

Loud and sustained cheering greeted Grady's remarks.[71] In his tribute to Abraham Lincoln he had touched one of the most responsive emo-

68. Maurice Thompson, "At Lincoln's Grave," in Williams, ed., *The Praise of Lincoln*, 17.

69. "Speech of Hon. John Temple Graves," in Joel Chandler Harris, ed., *Life of Henry W. Grady, Including His Writings and Speeches* (New York, 1890), 380.

70. *Ibid.*, 85–86.

71. Raymond B. Nixon, *Henry W. Grady, Spokesman of the New South* (New York, 1943), 342–43.

tional chords of the North and thereby attuned his Yankee audience to the New South's message of economic progress and sectional goodwill.

Woodrow Wilson was another young man of the New South who admired Lincoln, the American. Because of his career as university professor and administrator, governor of New Jersey, and President of the United States, Wilson usually is considered from a national perspective. But, as his biographer, Arthur Link, reminds us, Wilson's roots were thoroughly Southern.[72] Born in Virginia, he grew up in war-time and Reconstruction Georgia; Tommy Wilson's earliest recollection, he later wrote, was hearing "that Mr. Lincoln was elected and there was to be war."[73] Wilson received much of his schooling in the South, at Davidson, University of Virginia, and Johns Hopkins (where he was a classmate of Thomas Dixon). His father was an ardent Confederate, and although Wilson himself was no great enthusiast for the Lost Cause, he believed that the men of 1860–1861 did what they thought was right. As an undergraduate at Princeton, Wilson defended his native South; in a student argument on Reconstruction, an enraged Wilson stalked from the room.[74] He married a Georgia girl, practiced law in Atlanta, and lived in the South twenty-four years.

Young Wilson was interested in the rebuilding of the South, and as a student he wrote articles on industrialism, education, and the Negro in Southern politics.[75] He echoed the sentiments of Grady and other New South statesmen when he said: "I yield to no one precedence in love for the South. But *because* I love the South I rejoice in the failure of the Confederacy. . . ."[76] Wilson dreamed of political leadership—as an undergraduate he penned cards announcing Thomas Woodrow Wilson, Senator from Virginia—but he had little interest in the rough stump and

72. Arthur Stanley Link, *Wilson* (Princeton, N. J., 1947–) I, 1–35. In a recent article, Link notes that as a young man Wilson for a time "went far toward repudiating identification with the South." "Woodrow Wilson: The American as Southerner," *Journal of Southern History*, 26 (Feb., 1970), 3–17.

73. Woodrow Wilson, *The Public Papers of Woodrow Wilson*, ed. Ray Stannard Baker and William E. Dodd (New York, 1925–1927) II, 83.

74. Ray Stannard Baker, *Woodrow Wilson: His Life and Letters* (Garden City, N. Y., 1927–1940) I, 82.

75. Woodrow Wilson, *Papers of Woodrow Wilson*, ed. Arthur S. Link *et al.* (Princeton, N. J., 1966–) II, 19–25, 26–31, 49–55, 119–25, 326–32.

76. March 6, 1880, in *ibid.*, 618–19.

spindle politics of the New South and seemed destined for the career of a quiet academician.[77]

For Woodrow Wilson, Southerner, Lincoln was "the supreme American of our history," "one of the most singular and admirable figures in the history of modern times."[78] He admired Lincoln's remarkable rise from humble origins, his wise and restrained use of enormous executive power, and his generous policy toward the defeated South.[79] Wilson saw in Lincoln the genius not of sections or classes but of "the common product of the nation." Lincoln was a man of the people, "a very normal man, but normal in gigantic proportions." In a very few years, Woodrow Wilson would lead his people in great crusades in war and peace; in 1909, he found inspiration in Lincoln's example:

> The lesson of this day is the future as well as the past leadership of men, wise men, who have come from the people. We should not be Americans deserving to call ourselves the fellow-countrymen of Lincoln if we did not feel the compulsion that his example lays upon us—the compulsion, not to heed him merely but to look to our own duty, to live every day as if that were the day upon which America was to be reborn and remade. . . .[80]

Henry Watterson, the Kentucky editor, went furthest of all Southerners in identifying the new American nationalism with the image of Lincoln. Watterson was born and raised in Tennessee and lived most of his life in Kentucky. He was a border statesman in the Clay-Crittenden tradition who labored to bind up the wounds of the nation sundered despite the best efforts of his predecessors.

Watterson met Lincoln in March, 1861, when he was a twenty-one-year-old reporter helping in the coverage of the inauguration. Lincoln was kind to the young cub and personally assisted him in securing a copy of the inaugural address.[81] Watterson soon returned to Tennessee. No

77. Link, *Wilson* I, 6, 10.

78. Woodrow Wilson, "A Calendar of Great Americans," *Forum*, 16 (Feb., 1894), 724. Woodrow Wilson, *Division and Reunion. With Additional Chapters Bringing the Narrative Down to the End of 1918, by Edward S. Corwin* (New York, 1925), 216. The first edition of *Division and Reunion* appeared in 1893.

79. *Division and Reunion*, 216, 238, 256–57. Woodrow Wilson, *A History of the American People* (New York, 1903) IV, 206–207, 261. Woodrow Wilson, "Reconstruction of the Southern States," *Atlantic Monthly*, 87 (Jan., 1901), 1–15.

80. "Abraham Lincoln: A Man of the People," Feb. 12, 1909, in *Public Papers of Woodrow Wilson* II, 100.

81. Henry Watterson, *The Editorials of Henry Watterson*, comp. with an intro-

friend of slavery nor a believer in secession, he nevertheless was caught up in the local excitement and cast his lot with his neighbors and the Confederacy. During the war he saw irregular service with various commands, punctuated by editorial duties on several Confederate newspapers. War's end found him in Cincinnati as editor of the *Evening Times*.[82]

Years after the war, Watterson wrote of meeting Lincoln: "Somehow, I had a great impression of Mr. Lincoln from the first, and, during four succeeding years of War, though serving on the opposite side, this never left me."[83] Perhaps. But as editor of the *Rebel*, a Confederate army newspaper, Watterson had some pretty harsh things to say about the Yankee chieftain: Lincoln was "a man without mind or manners. . . . a rude, vulgar, obscure backwoods pettifogger," a "knock-kneed, shamble gaited, bow-legged. . . . pigeon toed, swob-sided. . . . shapeless skeleton in a very tough, very dirty, unwholesome skin . . . born and bred a rail-splitter . . . and a rail-splitter still."[84] But these war-time passions quickly cooled. Watterson was sincerely grieved by Lincoln's assassination, and in an angry editorial in the *Evening Times*, he accused Jefferson Davis of instigating the murder—a charge he soon regretted and rescinded.[85]

As editor of the *Louisville Courier-Journal*, beginning in 1868, Watterson devoted his career to promoting democratic nationalism and wiping out the last vestiges of sectionalism. He preached the gospel of reconciliation at veterans' reunions, to business groups, and through the editorial columns of his newspaper. "I can truly say," he told a gathering of Union veterans, "that each soldier who laid down his life for his opinions was my comrade, no matter in which army he fought."[86] The day of the nationalist has replaced that of the sectionalist, and the South, "I

duction and notes by Arthur Krock (New York, 1923), 186–202. The article originally appeared in *Cosmopolitan Magazine*, 46 (March, 1909), 363–75. See also Watterson's autobiography, "*Marse Henry*" (New York, 1919) I, 75–79.

82. "*Marse Henry*," I, 82–97. Joseph Frazier Wall, *Henry Watterson, Reconstructed Rebel* (New York, 1956), 31–50.

83. Feb. 7, 1905, in *Editorials of Henry Watterson*, 189.

84. *The Rebel* (Chattanooga, Tenn.), Aug. 6, 1863, quoted by Wall, *Henry Watterson*, 39.

85. *Ibid.*, 53.

86. Speech to Union veterans, National Cemetery, Nashville, Tenn., Decoration Day, 1877, in Henry Watterson, *The Compromises of Life, and Other Lectures and Addresses. . . .* (New York, 1903), 277.

thank God . . . is simply a geographic expression."[87] It was fortunate that the South lost the "War of the Sections"—Watterson disliked the term Civil War—because Confederate victory would have fragmented the continent into tiny, weak states which would have been easy prey to European despots. The real issue of the war, ran Watterson's message, was not the Negro, but the perpetuation of free government, which was inseparable from the maintenance of the Union; "if the Union failed, Freedom failed." The war was inevitable and necessary to purge the country of the old sins of slavery, secession, and sectionalism, and from it has come a mature American people.[88]

Watterson was certain that God interposed Himself between the South and victory. He saw a "mysterious agent" which checkmated the Confederates at critical moments in battle: Longstreet's failure to follow orders at Gettysburg, the timely arrival of the *Monitor* at Hampton Roads, the fall of Stonewall Jackson and Albert Sidney Johnston at the threshhold of victory. "The best that can be said of the South," Watterson concluded, "is that it stood so long against such odds."[89]

For Watterson, Abraham Lincoln was the towering figure in the war, and he had no doubt that Lincoln was an instrument chosen by God to fulfill His purposes on earth. How else could one understand Lincoln's marvelous career, except through realizing that he was guided by "unseen hands"? How else could one explain his remarkable rise from poverty and obscurity, his fortunate defeat by Douglas in 1858, and the Providential split in the Democratic party in 1860? Lincoln's commonsense genius, his mastery over the powerful men in his cabinet, and his kindness and understanding toward the South were certainly God-granted gifts. In Watterson's most popular oration, he asserted: "Surely, he [Lincoln] was one of God's own; not in any sense a creature of circumstance, or accident. Recurring to the doctrine of inspiration, I say, again and again, he was inspired of God, and I cannot see how anyone who believes in that doctrine can believe anything else."[90] Had Lincoln

87. *Ibid.*, 286. "The New South," speech to American Bankers' Association, Louisville, Oct. 11, 1883, in *ibid.*, 289.

88. "Let Us Have Peace," speech at the annual banquet of the Society of the Army of the Tennessee, Chicago, Oct. 9, 1891, in *ibid.*, 295. "Abraham Lincoln," in *Editorials of Henry Watterson*, 193–94. "Thank God for Gettysburg," July 4, 1913, in *ibid.*, 317–23.

89. *Editorials of Henry Watterson*, 317–18.

90. Henry Watterson, *Abraham Lincoln. An Oration Delivered Before the*

lived, Watterson was confident, there would have been no repressive reconstruction. Perhaps mad John Wilkes Booth was himself "an instrument in the hands of God to put a still deeper damnation upon the taking off of the Confederacy and to sink the Southern people yet lower in the abyss of affliction and humiliation which the living Lincoln would have spared us."[91]

One of Watterson's most controversial utterances was his oft-repeated assertion that Lincoln, at the Hampton Roads peace conference in 1865, took Alexander Stephens aside and said, "Let me write Union at the top of this page and you may write below it whatever else you please." "I have not cited this fact of history," Watterson explained, "to attack, or even to criticize the policy of the Confederate Government, but simply to illustrate the wise magnanimity and justice of the character of Abraham Lincoln."[92] He claimed that the story was confirmed by Stephens himself in private conversation with friends. Actually, the incident is almost certainly apocryphal. Stephens did not mention it in his memoirs, and a check of the abundant published accounts by the participants in the conference would have shown Watterson that emancipation certainly was a condition for peace. Nevertheless, the story passed into the popular mythology, and Watterson continued to repeat it.

Watterson's description of the alleged Hampton Roads incident set off a vigorous debate in the South. The account was usually dismissed as a veiled attack on Jefferson Davis. "The effect of the story as it is generally told," wrote Julian S. Carr in rebuttal, "is to make a good impression about President Lincoln and a bad impression of President Davis; the one big-souled and yielding, and the other blind and self destructive."[93] After much debate and searching of records, most interested Southerners were satisfied that no such exchange between Stephens and

---

Lincoln Union. . . . Chicago, February 12, 1895 (Louisville, Ky., 1899). This oration also appears in *Compromises of Life*, 137–80. For further development of this theme see *Editorials of Henry Watterson*, Feb. 12, 1909, pp. 202–206, and *Rail Splitter*, 1 (Feb., 1910), 31–32.

91. *Editorials of Henry Watterson*, 205. Response to toast to Abraham Lincoln, annual banquet of the Confederate Veterans Camp of New York, Jan. 26, 1903, in *Southern Historical Society Papers*, 30 (1902), 124, and also appearing in *Compromises of Life*, 363–69.

92. Watterson, *Abraham Lincoln* (Lincoln Union speech, 1895). Apparently, Watterson had frequently mentioned the anecdote before this occasion.

93. *The Hampton Roads Conference*, 3.

Lincoln had taken place. Critics of Davis, however, continued to use Watterson's story to support their contention that the Confederacy could and ought to have quit with honor before total defeat. Friends of Lincoln repeated the incident to document the President's high statesmanship and kindness to the South.[94]

Watterson believed that the South had as much reason to canonize Lincoln as did the North and that a true understanding of Lincoln's mission and works would bind Southerners closer to the Union. Not all of his fellow Southerners appreciated his crusade. Robert L. Preston accused Watterson of abandoning the South to worship the Lincoln idol: "Why have you done this thing? What evil genius inspired you . . . to tarnish the fair name of the land of your birth." In a barb aimed not only at Watterson but all the New South statesmen, he added: "The South is fully conscious that her sons that have forsaken her and sold their birthright for the savory pottage of materialism have been caught by the lure and glare of the dazzling cities of the plain."[95]

Watterson had not sold his Southern birthright. As a man of the New South he wished to expand that birthright into a greater American nationalism. Like Grady and Wilson, he found in Lincoln a usable symbol to represent the best of North and South melded into a common American consciousness. He lived to see much of his work fulfilled. During the centennial of Lincoln's birth, when hundreds of Southerners offered public tribute to the memory of their late enemy, Robert Todd Lincoln wrote Watterson: "The events of the birthday celebration seem to prove that the often repeated hopes and prayers of my father have been almost

94. Reagan, *Memoirs*, 166–79. *Southern Historical Society Papers*, 14 (1886), 499. *Confederate Veteran*, 3 (April, 1895), 109; 5 (July, 1897), 347–49; 9 (May, 1901), 228–29; 13 (June, 1905), 268, and (July, 1905), 325–26. *Richmond Dispatch*, Feb. 25, 1900. Among those Southerners who accepted the story as true were E. P. Alexander, *Military Memoirs of a Confederate* (New York, 1910), 587–88, and DeLeon, *Belles, Beaux and Brains of the 60's,* 102. Watterson also said that Lincoln was willing to pay up to $400 million to compensate Southerners for their slave property. This incident was also widely discussed in the South. As far as I can tell from his published writings and speeches, Watterson made it clear that Lincoln discussed this matter only informally at Hampton Roads and that Lincoln had no authorization to make a concrete offer of compensation. Watterson was more circumspect in this part of his account of the conference than with the alleged Lincoln-Stephens exchange.

95. Robert L. Preston, *Southern Miscellanies No.* 2 (Leesburg, Va., May, 1919), 9, 35.

perfectly realized—that this is so is, I think, due more to you than to any other living man."[96]

The one-hundredth anniversary of Lincoln's birth, on February 12, 1909, was celebrated as a great festival of patriotism throughout the country. Americans are fond of centennials—perhaps the passage of one hundred years in this young country suggests great permanency and tradition—and few public men failed to prepare appropriate remarks for the occasion. Fewer still were the magazines and newspapers which did not carry at least one Lincoln article that month. The great men of the nation made pilgrimages to the Lincoln shrines—President Theodore Roosevelt to Lincoln's birthplace at Hodgenville, Kentucky; William Jennings Bryan to Springfield (where Negroes were barred from the banquet honoring the memory of the Great Emancipator).[97] Congress moved to mark the day by declaring a special federal holiday and issuing 100 million two-cent Lincoln postage stamps. Lawmakers in Washington also fought over the location of the proposed Lincoln Memorial and debated the wisdom of a Lincoln Highway from Washington to Gettysburg (one irreverent Mississippi senator suggested that the road should run to Manassas).[98] Stock exchanges, banks, and schools closed the country over.

Private groups and citizens joined in the Lincoln day celebration in ways ranging from the sublime to the bizarre. The Grand Army of the Republic and almost all other patriotic and fraternal organizations recognized the centennial in some fashion. The Prohibition National Committee urged all temperance men to observe the birthday of a "lifelong total abstainer and one of the first prohibitionists in the United States."[99] Lincoln Memorial University seized the occasion to launch a half-million-dollar endowment drive. One Silas G. Pratt was moved to write a Lincoln symphony, and a Kentucky sportsman threw a big Lincoln day party in honor of his champion trotter, Nancy Hanks.[100]

96. Quoted by Wall, *Henry Watterson*, 293.

97. *Cleveland* (Ohio) *Leader*, Feb. 13, 1909. Southerners did not fail to note that Negroes would be barred from attending the banquet; see *Athens* (Ga.) *Banner*, Feb. 6, 1909.

98. *Washington* (D. C.,) *Star*, Jan. 21, 1909. *Charlotte* (N. C.) *Observer*, Jan. 22, 1909. *Winston-Salem* (N. C.) *Journal*, Jan. 1, 1909.

99. *Chicago Post*, Nov. 21, 1908.

100. *Chicago Tribune*, Dec. 27, 1908. *Atlanta Journal*, Feb. 12, 1909. *Louisville Courier-Journal*, Feb. 13, 1909.

Southerners played a conspicuous role in the Lincoln centennial. Union and Confederate veterans often were paired as orators in Lincoln day celebrations. Prominent Southerners spoke in praise of Lincoln across the North: Woodrow Wilson in Chicago; Emory Speer, the Georgia jurist, in New York; Virginia novelist Thomas Nelson Page in Washington; Secretary of War Luke Wright, a Tennessean, at Hodgenville, Kentucky; and Mississippian J. M. Dickinson, who would succeed to Wright's portfolio in William Howard Taft's cabinet, in Chicago.[101]

Praise of Lincoln was not confined to the North. Lincoln's centennial was observed in hundreds of communities of the old Confederacy. Exercises were held in many schools, and Southern youths pored over Lincoln's words. Arkansas declared a half-day holiday; New Orleans dismissed school for two days. Most federal offices and many banks, courts, and businesses were closed. Several state legislatures adjourned or paused to pay respects to the memory of Lincoln.[102] The centennial was observed at innumerable banquets and public meetings with Union and Confederate veterans joining in the tribute.

Speeches by Southerners in praise of Lincoln touched on almost all the manifold themes of the Lincoln legend and echoed the sentiments of men in the North and West. There was a certain reserve in most of these tributes—few Southerners rejoiced over the fall of the Confederacy quite so openly as Henry Watterson—but generally praise of Lincoln in the South was honest and widespread. Southerners (especially children in school exercises) lauded the pioneer boy who grew up to become President; the preserver of the Union; the wise and kind-hearted leader; the Southerner; and, most of all, the American, the one in whom was realized all the great and latent virtues of the common man.[103]

101. Wilson, "Abraham Lincoln: A Man of the People." Emory Speer, *Lincoln, Lee, Grant, and Other Biographical Addresses* (New York, 1909), 19–44. Thomas Nelson Page, "A Southerner's View of Abraham Lincoln, February 12, 1909," in *Proceedings of the Massachusetts Historical Society*, 69 (Oct., 1947–May, 1950), 308–30. Luke Wright, "Lincoln and the Lost Cause" in Nathan William MacChesney, ed., *Abraham Lincoln: The Tribute of a Century, 1809–1909* (Chicago, 1910), 261–66. J. M. Dickinson, *A Voice From the South* (n.p., [1909]).

102. *Raleigh* (N.C.) *Observer*, Feb. 13, 1909. *Nashville* (Tenn.) *American*, Feb. 14, 1909.

103. In addition to the comments cited in n. 100, above, the following are more or less representative of opinions expressed in the Southern press: *Chattanooga News*, Feb. 6, 1909; *Mobile Register*, Feb. 12, 1909; *Jacksonville Times-Union-Citizen*, Feb. 12, 1909; *Memphis Commercial-Appeal* (quoted in *Birmingham Age-*

Probably the most elaborate Lincoln commemoration in the South was held in Atlanta on February 14, and the spirit of its services may be taken as representative of such occasions.[104] Union and Confederate veterans joined in arranging the services in Trinity Methodist Episcopal Church, South. The sanctuary was filled to overflowing with the great and small of the city, and hundreds were turned away. The chaplain of the Grand Army of the Republic post in Atlanta presided, prayers were offered by the commander-in-chief of the United Confederate Veterans, Lincoln's favorite poem was read by a former Confederate cavalry colonel, and a retired Union general recited the Gettysburg Address. Dr. James W. Lee, pastor at Trinity, son of a Confederate veteran, and, according to the *Atlanta Constitution*, "a true son of the South," delivered the principal address.

The Reverend Lee was at one with Henry Watterson in believing Lincoln to be inspired by God. Lincoln, said Lee, discerned and merged himself with the "divine idea" unfolding itself in history. Lee never explained the exact nature of this "divine idea"—even men of God cannot be too certain about such things—but he was confident that it was identified with "the central purpose of this nation." It was Lincoln's conjunction with these eternal designs that permitted him to prevail over a great man like Jefferson Davis and over a cause which, however just it appeared at the time, "was not moving in the track of events." It is in God's will that men find peace; in the story of Lincoln's mission, courage, and sacrifice, let men find inspiration and fraternity.

> Soldiers in blue, and soldiers in gray, more of whom now march amid the hills of day than drag their weary feet over the scenes of conflict, are able to see, by the light of a larger, sweeter time, territory sufficient in the heart of Lincoln for all brave men to stand and love, and the armies of Grant and the armies of Lee, now, thank God, united on earth and united in Heaven, will both regard the martyred president as their commander-in-chief to all eternity.

Herald, Feb. 12, 1909); and extracts in Lucian Lamar Knight, *Memorials in Dixieland* (Atlanta, 1919), 383–87.

104. *Services in Commemoration of the One Hundredth Anniversary of the Birth of Abraham Lincoln, Arranged by Union and Confederate Veterans, Under the Auspices of O.M. Mitchel Post No. 1, Grand Army of the Republic. . . .* (Atlanta, 1909).

These paeans of praise sung to the memory of Lincoln did not represent a unanimous Southern opinion. Public recognition of the centennial seems to have been confined to the cities and larger towns. In some Southern communities only Union veterans and Negroes took special note of the day; in many small towns and villages only the absence of regular postal services suggested that this Friday differed from any other. Certainly, in many cases silence masked feelings quite different from those expressed by Southern admirers of Lincoln.

Some decidedly discordant notes were heard. A writer in *Confederate Veteran* conceded that "Lincoln was a fairly good man," but not the equal of Jefferson Davis.[105] Nor, said the *Nashville Banner*, could Lincoln's character be compared with the unblemished reputations of Lee and Jackson.[106] The old charges of despotism, cruelty, infidelity, and responsibility for the war were raked out and hurled out at Lincoln's memory.[107] Some Southerners deplored the Lincoln myth as the conscious product of sentimentalism and self-serving interests. The whole Lincoln story, George L. Christian told a gathering of Confederate veterans in Richmond, "*amounts to a patent perversion of the truth, and a positive fraud on the public*."[108]

These harsh judgments were conspicuous because they were out of tune with what appeared to be a pouring forth of genuine Southern sentiment. Sectionalism persisted, and much anti-Lincoln spirit still flourished in the South. But that hundreds of Southerners were willing to go on record in praise of Lincoln suggests that an evolution of sincere fraternal spirit had done much to erode the old hatreds and prejudices in the South.

Looking backward from the perspective of 1909 it was clear that the South never had been immune from the Lincoln legend. Like their Northern brethren, Southerners responded to the manifold appeals of

105. 17 (April, 1909), 154.

106. *Nashville Banner*, Feb. 12, 1909.

107. *Confederate Veteran*, 17 (April, 1909), 153–54. *New Orleans Picayune*, Feb. 13, 1909. *Columbia* (S. C.) *State*, Feb. 14, 1909. Berkeley Minor, *Lincoln* (Staunton, Va., 1909). "Southern Press on Lincoln," *Literary Digest*, 38 (Feb. 27, 1909).

108. George L. Christian, *Abraham Lincoln: An Address Delivered Before R. E. Lee Camp No. 1, Confederate Veterans, at Richmond, Va., on October 29, 1909* (Richmond, Va., 1909), 7.

Lincoln's memory according to their own needs and purposes. Secessionists and Confederates saw in Lincoln the cause for revolution. For unreconstructed rebels such as Bledsoe, Minor, and Tyler, Lincoln remained the Yankee villain and sworn enemy of all that was best and unique in Southern civilization. But for many who had experienced Reconstruction, Lincoln was "the South's best friend." Morris Sheppard's Lincoln was a champion of prohibition. The Lincoln of Thomas Dixon's imagination was an archsegregationist; Booker T. Washington's Lincoln was heroic and an inspiration to the black race. For Henry Watterson, Lincoln had been guided in every step by God; Southern schoolchildren were taught that Lincoln was the ideal self-made man. The Lincoln legend was broad enough to embrace many diverse, even contradictory, interpretations.

A more liberal estimate of Lincoln's character and deeds was bound to come as the South slowly merged into a broader American nationalism which found a symbolic expression in Lincoln. But the Lincoln legend also acted as a kind of force attracting Southerners back into the Union of their fathers. In the symbolic Lincoln were represented the finest human ideals of American nationalism—the spirit and potential of democracy and the love of country and countrymen which knew no sectional lines. These ideals appealed to Southerners emerging from war and defeat and yearning for a return to peace and a share of America. They were given additional force by being represented in what was, in part, a genuine Southern contribution to the national heritage. The conscious conciliators of the New South found in Lincoln a most usable symbol of reunion; in praising Lincoln they announced to the North their willingness to share in those very national virtues for which the North had canonized Lincoln as its martyr-hero. The appeals of Lincoln were universal, and the sectional demigod became the national hero.

There is a gentle irony in the story. The living President Lincoln was a cause for disunion, war, and fratricide. The dead Lincoln, incarnated in the living symbol based upon the character of the real man, was a powerful force for reunion and fraternity.

Bibliography

Scholars are both blessed and cursed with the enormous literature which surrounds Abraham Lincoln. More words have been written about Lincoln than about any other American. Considerable care must be taken in picking one's way through the relevant and the trivial. A good introduction to the needs and problems of Lincoln bibliography is James G. Randall's query, "Has the Lincoln Theme Been Exhausted?" *American Historical Review*, 41 (January, 1936), 270–94, and Clyde C. Walton's answer, "An Agonizing Reappraisal: 'Has the Lincoln Theme Been Exhausted?' " in O. Fritiof Ander, ed., *Lincoln Images: Augustana College Centennial Essays*. Augustana Library Publications, No. 29 (Rock Island, Ill., 1960), 99–105. Walton reviews the abundant Lincoln material published since Randall's article and warns against the danger of Lincoln scholarship's declining into mere antiquarianism. The most rewarding path of Lincoln studies today, he concludes, is the examination of Lincoln's greatness of character in order to determine "what made him the man he was. . . . And this may be the reason why the research goes on, and why the Lincoln theme will never be exhausted."

The best thing to happen to Lincoln bibliography was the compilation by Jay Monaghan, *Lincoln Bibliography, 1838–1939. Collections of the*

Illinois State Historical Library, Volumes XXXI–XXXII. Bibliographical Series, Volumes IV–V, 2 vols. (Springfield, Ill., 1945). Monaghan provides an annotated list of 3,958 books and pamphlets on Lincoln. His list is necessarily selective and excludes, among other things, articles on Lincoln published in periodicals. Victor Searcher, *Lincoln Today: An Introduction to Modern Lincolniana* (New York, 1969) "embraces all books on Lincoln now in print; and all those published during and after 1955 even if not now in print." Searcher's compilation also includes plays, films, tapes, sheet music, and phonodiscs. Monaghan and Searcher should be supplemented by Richard Booker's compilation, *Abraham Lincoln in Periodical Literature, 1860–1940* (Chicago, 1941), which lists 1,244 articles on Lincoln from selected journals and magazines. An earlier but still useful catalogue is *Abraham Lincoln: List of Books and Magazine Articles on Abraham Lincoln. . . . The Chicago Public Library Bulletin No. 7* (Chicago, 1909). "A Check List of Magazine Articles in All Languages About Abraham Lincoln. Compiled for Personal Use and Typed in Six Copies. New York, 1927" is a private list prepared by the Union Square Book Shop from the collection of an anonymous Californian; a copy may be found in the Henry Horner Collection, Illinois State Historical Library, Springfield, Illinois. *Lincoln Images*, cited above, includes a large bibliography of some of the fifteen to twenty thousand books, articles, and pamphlets on Lincoln which had appeared up to 1960. Other useful sources for Lincoln bibliography included W. R. Jillson, *Abraham Lincoln in Kentucky Literature, 1859–1949* (Frankfort, Ky., 1951); Oliver Hazelrigg, "Abraham Lincoln Memorials: Check List of Lincoln Sermons, Eulogies, Orations, Discourses, Addresses and Speeches in Commemoration of His Death, April 15, 1865," *Biblio*, 2 (May–August, 1923), 445–48, 469–71, 489–91, 509–11; and two sales catalogues: *Abraham Lincoln: Rare Pamphlets, Books, Autographs, Portraits and Prints, Fine Association Items From the Hart, Burton and Lambert Collections* (Chicago, 1933), and *Two Hundred and Fifty-Four Sermons, Eulogies, Orations, and Poems and Other Pamphlets Relating to Abraham Lincoln Sold at Auction February 11, 1914, at Heartman's Auction. . . .* (New York, 1914). *Americana: Catalogue of the Famous Abbatt Reprints* (New York, n.d.) is an index to "Extra Numbers"—200 reprints of rare Americana—of the *Magazine of History*, including the 48-piece "Rare Lincolniana" series.

A number of periodicals have been given exclusively to Lincoln subjects and bibliography and have proved useful sources for this study. *The Abraham Lincoln Quarterly* (Springfield, Ill., 1940–1952) was a scholarly journal published by the Abraham Lincoln Association. This journal superseded the *Bulletin of the Abraham Lincoln Association* (Springfield, Ill., 1923–1939), and *The Abraham Lincoln Association Papers* (Springfield, Ill., 1924–1940). The latter consisted of addresses delivered to the association on Lincoln's birthday and from 1924 to 1928 was known as *The Lincoln Centennial Association Papers.* Other periodicals devoted to Lincoln subjects included *The Lincoln Annex* (Providence, R. I., 1949–1953), published by the Friends of the Library of Brown University; *The Lincoln Family Magazine* (New York, 1916–1917), chiefly genealogical in orientation; and the short-lived *The Rail Splitter* (Chicago, 1910). The quarterly *Lincoln Herald* (Harrogate, Tenn., 1899–1933, 1937–), published by Lincoln Memorial University, continues to offer popular articles on Lincoln and kindred subjects and a regular review of current Lincoln literature.

The standard reference tools for research are also profitable for finding Lincoln material in American literature. These are: Lewis Leary, *Articles in American Literature, 1900–1950* (Durham, N. C., 1954); *Cumulated Magazine Subject Index, 1907–1949; A Cumulation of the F. W. Faxon Company's Annual Magazine Subject Index*, 2 vols. (Boston, 1964); *Readers' Guide to Periodical Literature* (New York, 1901–), and H. G. Cushing and A. V. Morris, eds., *Nineteenth Century Readers' Guide to Periodical Literature, 1890–1899 . . .*, 2 vols. (New York, 1944); and *Poole's Index to Periodical Literature*, 6 vols. (Boston, 1893–1908). For doctoral dissertations and masters' theses, see *Dissertation Abstracts* (Ann Arbor, Mich., 1938–); James Woodress, ed., *Dissertations in American Literature, 1891–1955, With Supplement, 1956–1961* (Durham, N. C., 1962); and Clyde H. Cantrell and Walton R. Patrick, eds., *Southern Literary Culture: A Bibliography of Masters' and Doctors' Theses* (University, Ala., 1955). Helpful in identifying obscure authors and supplying biographical information were Oscar Fay Adams, *A Dictionary of American Authors*, 4th ed. (Boston, 1901), and two compilations by Stanley J. Kunitz and Howard Haycraft, *American Authors, 1600–1900: A Biographical Dictionary of American Literature* (New York, 1938) and *Twentieth Century Authors: A Biographical Dictionary of Modern Literature* (New York, 1942).

There are hundreds of Lincoln biographies; for this study I found four especially valuable. Benjamin Thomas' *Abraham Lincoln, a Biography* (New York, 1952) is the best single-volume study of the President. John G. Nicolay and John Hay, *Abraham Lincoln, a History*, 10 vols. (New York, 1890), is an "authorized" biography written by Lincoln's secretaries, who profited not only from their personal experiences with the President but also from the use of many papers not open to other scholars of their day. *Herndon's Life of Lincoln; The History and Personal Recollections of Abraham Lincoln as Originally Written by William H. Herndon and Jesse W. Weik* (Cleveland, Ohio, 1942) was written by Lincoln's friend and law partner and originally appeared in 1889. It must be used with care, as not all Herndon's "personal recollections" of Lincoln are reliable. *Lincoln the President: Springfield to Gettysburg* 4 vols. (New York, 1945–1955) is a superb study of the war-time Lincoln written by James G. Randall and completed after his death by Richard N. Current. Benjamin Thomas' *Portrait for Posterity; Lincoln and His Biographers* (New Brunswick, N. J., 1947) is a scholarly examination of Lincoln biographies, chiefly through the correspondence of the men and women who wrote them. Lincoln's writings, so frequently used and misused by Southerners and Northerners alike, have been assembled and edited by Roy P. Basler in *Collected Works*, 8 vols. (New Brunswick, N. J., 1953).

STUDIES ON LINCOLN AS MYTH AND LEGEND

An increasing number of scholars have sought to explore the nature of the Lincoln legend and to explain why Lincoln has become an American hero. Dixon Wector, in *The Hero in America: A Chronicle of Hero-Worship* (New York, 1941), considers the nature of American heroes and finds the source of Lincoln's heroic appeal in his essential democracy. Lloyd Lewis, *Myths After Lincoln* (New York, 1941), discusses the quasi-religious myths surrounding Lincoln and suggests that Lincoln fulfills a deeply felt national need for a martyred folk-hero. Roy P. Basler, in *The Lincoln Legend: A Study in Changing Conceptions* (Boston, 1935), explores different aspects of the Lincoln legend as reflected in American literature. Basler examines the same problem in his "Lincoln and Literature," *Journal of the Illinois State Historical Society*, 52 (Spring, 1959), 33–44, and "Abraham Lincoln: An Immortal Sign," in Norman A. Graebner, ed., *The Enduring Lincoln: Lincoln Sesquicen-*

tennial Lectures at the University of Illinois (Urbana, Ill., 1959). Other works dealing with Lincoln as a subject in myth and folklore are David M. Potter, *The Lincoln Theme and American National Historiography* (London, 1948); David Donald, "The Folklore Lincoln," *Journal of the Illinois State Historical Society*, 40 (December, 1947), 377–96; Richard Hofstadter, "Abraham Lincoln and the Self-Made Myth," in his *American Political Tradition and the Men Who Made It* (New York, 1948), 92–134; and William C. Carleton, "Sources of the Lincoln Legend," *The Prairie Schooner*, 25 (1951), 184–90.

STUDIES ON LINCOLN AND THE SOUTH

Several writers have considered the relationship between Lincoln and the South. J. G. deRoulhac Hamilton, writing on the occasion of the Lincoln centennial, reviewed changing Southern attitudes toward Lincoln and concluded that Lincoln's appeal to the South lay in his humanitarianism and democracy; see his "Lincoln and the South," *Sewanee Review*, 17 (April, 1909), 128–38. Richard B. Harwell argues that Lincoln has become to most Southerners a hero to rank with Washington and Lee in his "Lincoln and the South," in Ralph G. Newman, ed., *Lincoln for the Ages* (Garden City, N.Y., 1960), 203–207. Robert L. Kincaid, former president of Lincoln Memorial University, has studied the mutual affection between Lincoln and the pro-Union area of the southern Appalachians; see his "Lincoln and the Loyal South," *Vital Speeches*, February 15, 1949, pp. 269–73, and "Lincoln Allegiance in the Southern Appalachians," *Journal of the Illinois State Historical Society*, 52 (Spring, 1959), 164–79. Lincoln's Southern background is discussed in Arthur Charles Cole, "Abraham Lincoln and the South," *Lincoln Centennial Association Papers* (Springfield, Ill., 1928), 43–78, and James G. Randall, *Lincoln and the South* (Baton Rouge, La., 1946). Archibald Rutledge, a South Carolinian, praised Lincoln for his qualities of heart but believed the war was a mistake and that Lincoln "destroyed a noble civilization, and established, as far as the race question is concerned, something like permanent chaos." See Rutledge's "A Southerner Views Lincoln," *Scribner's Magazine*, 83 (February, 1928), 204–13; "Lincoln: A Southern View," *The Reviewer*, January, 1925, pp. 1–16; and "Lincoln and the Theory of Secession," *South Atlantic Quarterly*, 41 (October, 1942), 270–83. For other comments on the South's views of Lincoln, see

V. M. Scanlan, "A Southerner's View of Abraham Lincoln," *Papers in Illinois History and Transactions for the Year 1942* (Springfield, Ill., 1944), and "Attitude of the South Toward Lincoln," in *Addresses Delivered at the Annual Dinners of the Lincoln Club of Los Angeles, 1921–1940* (n.p., 1940), 153–60.

GUIDES TO SOURCES FOR THE CONFEDERACY

Catton, Bruce, and E. B. Long. Research notes for Bruce Catton's *Centennial History of the Civil War*, made available by Doubleday & Co., Inc. Division of Manuscripts, Library of Congress, Washington, D. C.

Crandall, Marjorie Lyle. *Confederate Imprints: A Check List Based Principally on the Collection of the Boston Atheneum*. 2 vols. Boston, 1955. 5,302 titles from the Boston Atheneum and selected libraries.

Freeman, Douglas Southall, ed. *A Calendar of Confederate Papers, With a Bibliography of Some Confederate Publications*. Richmond, Va., 1908.

———. *The South to Posterity. An Introduction to the Writing of Confederate History*. New York, 1939. A description of some of the primary sources for Confederate history.

Harwell, Richard B. "Confederate Anti-Lincoln Literature," *Lincoln Herald*, 53 (Fall, 1951). A review of eight anti-Lincoln pieces found in the Huntington Library.

———. *Confederate Belles-Lettres: A Bibliography and a Finding List of the Fiction, Poetry, Drama, Songsters, and Miscellaneous Literature Published in the Confederate States of America*. Hattiesburg, Miss., 1941. 105 titles.

———. *The Confederate Hundred: A Bibliophilic Selection of Confederate Books*. Urbana, Ill., 1964. Description of 100 Confederate imprints.

———. *Confederate Music*. Chapel Hill, N. C., 1950. List of sheet music published in the Confederacy, with descriptions of some Confederate songs and composers.

———. *Cornerstones of Confederate Collecting*. 2nd ed. Charlottesville, Va., 1953. Reviews 20 Confederate imprints.

———. *More Confederate Imprints*. 2 vols. Richmond, Va., 1957. A supplement to Crandall, listing 1,773 imprints.

Rudolph, E. L. *Confederate Broadside Verse: A Bibliography and Finding List of Confederate Broadside Ballads and Songs.* New Braunfels, Texas, 1950.

OFFICIAL DOCUMENTS

"Proceedings of the Confederate Congresses." *Southern Historical Society Papers,* NS, 6–14 (Richmond, Va., 1923–1959). Taken mostly from the war-time *Richmond Examiner.*

Richardson, James D., comp. *A Compilation of the Messages and Papers of the Confederacy Including the Diplomatic Correspondence, 1861–1865.* 2 vols. Nashville, Tenn., 1905. Vol. I contains messages and letters of Jefferson Davis; Vol. II consists of diplomatic correspondence.

United States Congress. *Congressional Record.* Washington, D. C., 1874– .

———. *Journal of the Congress of the Confederate States of America, 1861–1865.* 58th Cong., 2nd sess. Senate Document No. 234. 7 vols. Washington, D. C., 1904–1905.

———. *Report of the Joint Committee on Reconstruction at the First Session, Thirty-Ninth Congress.* Washington, D. C., 1866.

———. *The Congressional Globe.* Washington, D. C., 1834–1873.

PERIODICALS AND NEWSPAPER COMPILATIONS

Bardolph, Richard. "Malice Toward One: Lincoln in the North Carolina Press." *Lincoln Herald,* 53 (Winter, 1951), 34–45. Cites numerous and extremely malicious extracts from North Carolina newspapers just before and during the war.

The Bugle Horn of Liberty, 1863.

Confederate Veteran, 1893–1932.

Confederate War Journal, 1893–1895.

DeBow's Review: Agricultural, Commercial, Industrial Progress & Resources, 1846–1880. Not published, 1864–1865, 1870–1879.

Dumond, Dwight Lowell, ed. *Southern Editorials on Secession.* New York, 1931.

Fetter's Southern Magazine, 1892–1895.

The Land We Love: A Monthly Magazine Devoted to Literature, Military History, and Agriculture, 1866–1869.

The Lincoln Centenary in Literature: Selections From The Principal Magazines of February and March, 1909, Together With a Few From 1907–1908. 2 vols. New York, 1909.

MacChesney, Nathan William, ed. The Lincoln Centenary, 1809–1909. Being a Collection in Forty-Two Volumes, Made Under the Auspices of the Lincoln Centennial Memorial Committee of One Hundred, of the Current Comment, in Prose and Poetry, in Picture and Cartoon, Appearing in the Newspapers and Magazines, at Home and Abroad, in Commemoration of the One Hundredth Anniversary of the Birth of Abraham Lincoln, on the Twelfth of February, A. D., 1909. Presented to the Chicago Historical Society, 1912.

The Magnolia Weekly: A Home Journal of Literature and General News, 1862–1864.

The New Eclectic: A Monthly Magazine of Select Literature, 1868–1870.

Publications of the Southern Historical Association, 1897–1907.

Scott's Monthly Magazine, 1865–1869.

The Sewanee Review, Quarterly, 1892– .

The South Atlantic Quarterly, 1902– .

Southern Bivouac: A Monthly Literary and Historical Magazine, 1882–1887.

Southern Field and Fireside, 1859–1864.

Southern Historical Society Papers, 1876–1890. NS, 1914–1954.

The Southern Illustrated News, 1862–1865.

Southern Literary Messenger, 1834–1865.

The Southern Magazine (Baltimore, Md.), 1871–1875. Absorbed *New Eclectic.*

The Southern Magazine (Manassas, Va.), 1899.

"Southern Press on Lincoln," *Literary Digest*, 28 (February 27, 1909).

Southern Punch, 1863–1865.

Southern Review, 1867–1879.

Steen, Ralph W. "Texas Newspapers and Lincoln," *Southwestern Historical Quarterly*, 51 (January, 1948), 199–212. Traces changing attitudes toward Lincoln in Texas press; many extracts.

Tyler's Quarterly Historical and Genealogical Magazine, 1919–1952.

The Weekly Register: Devoted to a Record of Important Documents and Events of the Times; With Essays on Subjects Connected With Arts, Science, and Literature, 1864.

PUBLISHED LETTERS, DIARIES, MEMOIRS, CONTEMPORARY COMMENTARY

ALEXANDER, E. P. *Military Memoirs of a Confederate: A Critical Narrative.* New York, 1910.

ANDERSON, JOHN Q., ed. *Brokenburn: A Diary of Kate Stone, 1881–1868.* Baton Rouge, La., 1955.

ANDREWS, ELIZA FRANCES. *The War-Time Journal of a Georgia Girl, 1864–1865*, ed. Spencer Bidwell King. Macon, Ga., 1960. Originally published, 1908. This diarist edited her own journal for publication and omitted a few passages from the original text.

ANDREWS, MATTHEW PAGE. *Women of the South in War Times.* Baltimore, Md., 1920. An anthology of writings by Confederate ladies, with much annotation by the editor.

AVERY, MYRTA LOCKETT. *Dixie After the War. An Exposition of Social Conditions Existing in the South, During the Twelve Years Succeeding the Fall of Richmond.* New York, 1906.

———. "A Lincoln Souvenir in the South. A Letter from Abraham Lincoln to Alexander H. Stephens, Which Hangs on the Walls of a Southern Home," *Century Magazine*, 73 (February, 1907), 506–508.

———, ed. *Recollections of Alexander H. Stephens: His Diary Kept When a Prisoner at Fort Warren, Boston Harbour, 1865, Giving Incidents and Reflections of His Prison Life and Some Letters and Reminiscences.* New York, 1910.

BARBEE, DAVID RANKIN. *An Excursion in Southern History, Briefly Set Forth in the Correspondence Between Senator A. J. Beveridge and David Rankin Barbee....* Asheville, N. C., 1928.

———, and Milledge L. Bonham, Jr., eds. "Fort Sumter Again," *Mississippi Valley Historical Review*, 28 (June, 1941), 63–78. A reproduction of Charles S. Morehead's account of his interview with Lincoln, April, 1861.

BARNWELL, ROBERT W. *The Lines and Nature of Lincoln's Greatness.* Columbia, S. C., 1931.

BLACKFORD, SUSAN LEIGH, comp. *Letters from Lee's Army; or, Memoirs of Life In and Out of the Army in Virginia During the War Between the States. Annotated by Her Husband Charles Minor Blackford. Edited and Abridged for Publication by Charles Minor Blackford III.* New York, 1947. Originally published, 1894–1896. Mostly letters to and from Susan Leigh Blackford and Charles Minor Blackford, with a diary of William M. Blackford.

BLACKFORD, WILLIAM WALLIS. *War Years with Jeb Stuart.* New York, 1945.

BLACKNALL, O. W. *Lincoln as the South Should Know Him.* 2nd ed. Raleigh, N. C., 1915.

BLEDSOE, ALBERT TAYLOR. *An Essay on Liberty and Slavery.* Philadelphia, 1856. This defense of slavery was later included in E. N. Elliot, ed., *Cotton is King and Pro-Slavery Argument.* Augusta, Ga., 1860.

———. *Is Davis a Traitor; or, Was Secession a Constitutional Right Previous to the War of 1861?* Richmond, Va., 1907. Originally published, 1866.

BULLOCK, JOHN M. "President Lincoln's Visiting Card. The Story of a Parole of a Confederate Officer," *Century*, 55 (February, 1898), pp. 565–71.

BURGE, DOLLY S. L. *A Woman's Wartime Journal.* Macon, Ga., 1927.

BURROWS, J. LANSING. *Palliative and Prejudiced Judgments Condemned. A Discourse Delivered at the First Baptist Church, Richmond, Va., June 1, 1865... Together With an Extract From a Sermon, Preached on Sunday, April 23, 1865....* Richmond, Va., 1865.

BUTLER, BENJAMIN FRANKLIN. *Autobiography of Major-General Benjamin Franklin Butler. Butler's Book.* Boston, 1892.

CABLE, GEORGE WASHINGTON. *The Negro Question: A Selection of Writings on Civil Rights in the South*, ed. Arlin Turner. Garden City, N. Y., 1958. Collection of Cable's writings on government and racism in the South.

CAMPBELL, JOHN A. "Papers of Hon. John A. Campbell—1861–1865," *Southern Historical Society Papers*, NS 4 (October, 1917).

———. *Recollections of the Evacuation of Richmond, April 2, 1865.* Baltimore, Md., 1880.

CARR, JULIAN SHAKESPEARE. *The Hampton Roads Conference. A Refutation of the Statement that Mr. Lincoln Said If Union was Written at the Top the Southern Commissioners Might Fill in the Balance* [Durham, N. C.?, 1917].

CARSON, JAMES PETIGRU. *Life, Letters, and Speeches of James Louis Petigru, the Union Man of South Carolina.* Washington, D. C., 1920.

CATHEY, JAMES H. *Truth is Stranger than Fiction; or, the True Genesis of a Wonderful Man.* n.p., 1899. Asserts that Lincoln was the bastard son of a North Carolinian.

CHESNUT, MARY BOYKIN. *A Diary From Dixie*, ed. Ben Ames Williams. Boston, 1949.

CHITTENDEN, LUCIUS E. *Recollections of President Lincoln and His Administration.* New York, 1891. Includes account of the interview between Lincoln and the delegates to the Washington Peace Conference.

———. *A Report of the Debates and Proceedings in the Secret Sessions of the Conference Convention, for Proposing Amendments to the Constitution of the United States, Held at Washington, D. C., in February, A. D. 1861.* New York, 1864.

CHRISTIAN, GEORGE L. *Abraham Lincoln: An Address Delivered Before R. E. Lee Camp, No. 1, Confederate Veterans, at Richmond, Va., on October 29, 1909.* Richmond, Va., 1909.

CLAY-CLOPTON, VIRGINIA. *A Belle of the Fifties. Memoirs of Mrs. Clay, of Alabama, covering Social and Political Life in Washington and the South, 1853–66. Put into Narrative Form by Ada Sterling.* New York, 1905.

CLEVELAND, HENRY. *Alexander H. Stephens, In Public and Private, With Letters and Speeches, Before, During, and Since the War.* Philadelphia, 1866.

COGGINS, J. C. *Abraham Lincoln: A North Carolinian with Proof.* 2nd ed., revised. Gastonia, N. C., 1927.

COLEMAN, WILLIAM MACON. *The Evidence that Abraham Lincoln was not Born in Lawful Wedlock, or, the Sad Story of Nancy Hanks* [Dallas, Texas, 1899?].

Confederate Military History. A Library of Confederate States History, in Twelve Volumes, Written by Distinguished Men of the South, and Edited by Gen. Clement A. Evans of Georgia. Atlanta, 1899.

COOK, GILES B., G. W. B. HALE, AND LYON G. TYLER. *Confederate Leaders and Other Citizens Request the House of Delegates to Repeal the*

Resolution of Respect to Abraham Lincoln, the Barbarian. n.p., [1928?].

Cumming, Kate. *Kate: the Journal of a Confederate Nurse*, ed. Richard Barksdale Harwell. Baton Rouge, La., 1959.

Curry, Jabez L. M. *The Southern States of the American Union, Considered in Their Relation to the Constitution of the United States, and to the Resulting Union*. Richmond, Va., 1895. Originally published 1894.

Dabney, R. L. "Memoir of a Narrative Received of Colonel John B. Baldwin, of Staunton, Touching the Origin of the War," *Southern Historical Society Papers*, 1 (June, 1876), 443–55.

[Davidson, J. W.]. *Resolutions Adopted at a Meeting of the Officers of the Army and Navy and Citizens of Natchez on the Death of the President of the United States*. Natchez, Miss., 1865.

Davis, Jefferson. *The Rise and Fall of the Confederate Government*. 2 vols. New York, 1881.

———. *A Short History of the Confederate States of America*. New York, 1890.

Dawson, Sarah Morgan. *A Confederate Girl's Diary*. Bloomington, Ind., 1960.

Deering, John R. *Lee and His Cause; or, the Why and the How of the War Between the States*. New York, 1907.

DeLeon, T. C. *Belles, Beaux and Brains of the 60's*. New York, 1909.

———. *Four Years in Rebel Capitals: An Inside View of Life in the Southern Confederacy from Birth to Death*. Mobile, Ala., 1890.

Derry, Joseph T. *Story of the Confederate States; or, History of the War for Confederate Independence. . . .* Richmond, Va., 1895.

Dickinson, J. M. *A Voice From the South*. n.p., [1909]. Eulogy of Lincoln by a Mississippian.

Dodd, William E. *Lincoln or Lee. Comparison and Contrast of the Two Greatest Leaders in the War Between the States. The Narrow and Accidental Margins of Success*. New York, 1928. A distinguished Southern historian's praise of Lincoln and Lee resulted in what his biographer, Robert Dallek, called "the least satisfactory writings of Dodd's entire career."

———. "Some Difficulties of the History Teacher in the South," *South Atlantic Quarterly*, 3 (April, 1904).

[Dooley, John]. *John Dooley, Confederate Soldier. His War Journal*, ed. Joseph T. Durkin, S. J. Notre Dame, Ind., 1963.

Douglass, Frederick. *Oration of Frederick Douglass Delivered on the Occasion of the Unveiling of the Freedmen's Monument in Memory of Abraham Lincoln in Lincoln Park, Washington, D. C., April 14th, 1876*. Washington, D. C., 1876.

Early, Jubal A. *A Memoir of the Last Year of the War for Independence, in the Confederate States of America, Containing an Account of the Operations of His Commands in the Years 1864 and 1865*. Lynchburg, Va., 1867.

Edmondston, Catherine Devereux. *The Journal of Catherine Devereux Edmondston, 1860–1866*, ed. Margaret Mackey Jones (Mrs. George Lyle Jones). Privately published, 1954.

Eggleston, George Cary. *The American Immortals. The Record of Men Who by Their Achievements in Statecraft, War, Science, Literature, Art, Law, and Commerce Have Created the American Republic and Whose Names are Inscribed in the Hall of Fame*. New York, 1901. An appreciation of Lincoln is found on pp. 199–220.

———. *The History of the Confederate War; Its Causes and Conduct. A Narrative and Critical History*. London, 1910.

Experience of a Confederate States Prisoner, Being an Ephemeris Regularly Kept by a Officer of the Confederate States Army. Richmond, Va., 1862.

"The Final Reply to Westerner." n.p. [1928?]. This pamphlet is a compilation of letters, originally published in the *Richmond Times-Dispatch*, January 8, 1928, scourging Lincoln.

Foote, Henry S. *War of the Rebellion; or, Scylla and Charybdis, Consisting of Observations Upon the Causes, Course, and Consequences of the Late Civil War in the United States*. New York, 1866.

Fulkerson, H. S. *A Civilian's Recollections of the War Between the States*, ed. P. L. Rainwater. Baton Rouge, La., 1939.

Gay, Mary A. H. *Life in Dixie During the War*. 4th ed., enlarged. Atlanta, 1901.

A Gentleman of Mississippi. *Secession: Considered as a Right in the States Composing the Late American Union of States, and as to the Grounds of Justification of the Southern States in Exercising the Right*. Jackson, Miss., 1863.

GILBERT, C. E. *Two Presidents: Abraham Lincoln. Jefferson Davis. Origin, Cause, and Conduct of the War Between the States. The Truth of History Belongs to Posterity.* n.p., 1927.

GORDON, JOHN B. *Reminiscences of the Civil War.* New York, 1903.

HAMILTON, J. G. DEROULHAC, ed. *The Correspondence of Jonathan Worth.* 2 vols. Raleigh, N. C., 1909.

———. *Three Years in Battle and Three in Federal Prisons. The Papers of Randolph Abbott Shotwell.* 2 vols. Raleigh, N. C., 1929.

HARDIN, ELIZABETH PENDLETON. *The Private War of Lizzie Hardin. A Kentucky Confederate Girl's Diary of the Civil War in Kentucky, Virginia, Tennessee, Alabama, and Georgia*, ed. G. Glenn Clift. Frankfort, Ky., 1963. This ardent rebel was a cousin of Ben Hardin Helm, Lincoln's brother-in-law.

HARRIS, JOEL CHANDLER, ed. *Life of Henry W. Grady, Including His Writings and Speeches.* New York, 1890.

HARRIS, JULIA COLLIER, ed. *Joel Chandler Harris, Editor and Essayist. Miscellaneous Literary, Political, and Social Writings.* Chapel Hill, N. C., 1931.

———. *The Life and Letters of Joel Chandler Harris.* Boston, 1918. A memoir, with many letters, by his daughter.

HARRISON, MRS. BURTON. *Recollections Grave and Gay.* New York, 1911.

HAWLEY, J. M. "An Intellectual Giant," *Christian Advocate* (May 7, 1915), 9 (585). An appreciation of Albert T. Bledsoe's *Theodicy* by a contemporary.

HEARTSILL, WILLIAM W. *Fourteen Hundred and 91 Days in the Confederate Army; or Camp Life, Day by Day, of the W. P. Lane Rangers*, ed. Bell Irwin Wiley. Jackson, Tenn., 1954.

HERBERT, HILARY A., *et al. Why the Solid South? or, Reconstruction and its Results* (Baltimore, Md., 1890). Essays on Reconstruction in the several states by fourteen Southern legislators and public men and dedicated "to the business men of the North."

HERRICK, SOPHIA BLEDSOE. "Albert Taylor Bledsoe," *Virginia University Alumni Bulletin*, 6 (May, 1899), 1–6. A memoir by his daughter.

———. "Personal Recollections of My Father and Mr. Lincoln and Mr. Davis," *Methodist Review*, 64 (1915), 665–79.

HERRIOT, DAVID. "Abraham Lincoln. Some Hitherto Unpublished Correspondence," *The Dearborn Independent*, December 17, 1927, pp.

8–9, 26. Contains several letters to Lincoln from Southerners, threatening the President-elect with assassination. The same letters are in *Magazine of History With Notes and Queries. Extra Number—No. 149* (Tarrytown, N. Y., 1929), 36–41.

HESSELTINE, WILLIAM B., ed. *Three Against Lincoln: Murat Halstead Reports the Caucuses of 1860*. Baton Rouge, La., 1960.

HILL, BENJAMIN H., JR. *Senator Benjamin H. Hill, of Georgia: His Life, Speeches and Writings*. Atlanta, 1891.

JACKSON, H. W. R. *Confederate Monitor and Patriot's Friend, Containing Numerous Important and Thrilling Events of the Present Revolution*.... Atlanta, 1862.

[JACKSON, MARY NEILSON]. *A Fair Rebel's Interviews with Abraham Lincoln*. Privately printed, 1917.

JOHNSON, ROBERT E., AND CLARENCE CLOUGH BUEL, eds. *Battles and Leaders of the Civil War, Being for the Most Part Contributions by Union and Confederate Officers. Based Upon the "Century War Series."* 4 vols. New York, 1956. Published in *Century*, 1883–1887, and as a book in 1887.

JOHNSTON, JOSEPH E. *Narrative of Military Operations*. Bloomington, Ind., 1959. Originally published 1874.

JOHNSTONE, H. W. *Truth of the War Conspiracy of 1861*. Athens, Ga., 1921.

JONES, JOHN BEAUCHAMP. *A Rebel War Clerk's Diary at the Confederate States Capital*, ed. Howard Swiggett. 2 vols. New York, 1935.

JONES, KATHERINE M., ed. *Heroines of Dixie. Confederate Women Tell Their Story of the War*. Indianapolis, 1955. An anthology of writings, published and unpublished, of Confederate ladies, with some biographical material.

KEAN, ROBERT GARLICK HILL. *Inside the Confederate Government. The Diary of Robert Garlick Hill Kean, Head of the Confederate Bureau of War*, ed. Edward Younger. New York, 1957.

KNIGHT, LUCIAN LAMAR. *Memorials of Dixie-land. Orations, Essays, Sketches, and Poems on Topics Historical, Commemorative, Literary, and Patriotic*. Atlanta, 1919. Essay on Lincoln (1909), 383–87.

LEE, JAMES W. *Abraham Lincoln. A Tribute Delivered, February 14, 1909, Upon the Occasion of a Special Memorial Service*.... n.p., n.d. Contains text of Lee's address at Lincoln Commemorative Service in Trinity Methodist Episcopal Church, Atlanta.

The Lincoln Centenary. Program of the National Centenary Celebration Together With the Report of the Executive Committee of the Lincoln Farm Association and Other Matters in Connection With the Lincoln Birthplace Memorial. New York, 1909.

Lincoln Centenary Services, 1909, Temple Adath Israel, Louisville, Kentucky. Louisville, Ky., 1909.

LORD, WALTER, ed. *The Fremantle Diary. Being the Journal of Lieutenant Colonel Arthur James Lyon Fremantle, Coldstream Guards, on His Three Months in the Southern States.* Boston, 1954. Originally published 1863.

LUNT, DOLLY SUMNER (MRS. THOMAS BURGE). *A Woman's Wartime Journal. An Account of the Passage Over a Georgia Plantation of Sherman's Army on the March to the Sea, as Recorded in the Diary of Dolly Sumner Lunt*, ed. Julian Street. Macon, Ga., 1927.

LUTZ, RALPH HARWELL. "Rudolf Schleiden and the Visit to Richmond, April 25, 1861," *Annual Report of the American Historical Association for the Year 1915.* Washington, D. C., 1917.

MACCHESNEY, NATHAN WILLIAM, ed. *Abraham Lincoln. The Tribute of a Century, 1809–1909. Commemorative of the Lincoln Centenary and Containing the Principal Speeches Made in Connection Therein.* Chicago, 1910. Includes a number of speeches by Southerners in praise of Lincoln.

MCDONALD, MRS. CORNELIA. *A Diary, With Reminiscences of the War and Refugee Life in the Shenandoah Valley, 1860–1865*, annotated and supplemented by Hunter McDonald. Nashville, Tenn., 1934.

[MCDONALD, WILLIAM H.]. *The Two Rebellions; or, Treason Unmasked, by a Virginian.* Richmond, Va., 1865.

MCGUIRE, HUNTER, AND GEORGE L. CHRISTIAN. *The Confederate Cause and Conduct in the War Between the States, as Set Forth in the Reports of the History Committee of the Grand Camp, Confederate Veterans, of Virginia.* Richmond, Va., 1907.

MACMAHON, T. W. *Cause and Contrast. An Essay on the American Crisis.* Richmond, Va., 1862.

MAGRUDER, ALLAN B. "A Piece of Secret History: President Lincoln and the Virginia Convention of 1861," *Atlantic*, 35 (April, 1875), 438–45.

MAURICE, SIR FREDERICK BARTON, ed. *An Aide-de-Camp of Lee. Being the Papers of Colonel Charles Marshall. ...* Boston, 1927.

[MERIWETHER, ELIZABETH AVERY]. George Edmonds. *Facts and False-*

hoods Concerning the War on the South, 1861–1865. Memphis, Tenn., 1904.

MIERS, EARL SCHENCK, ed. *When the World Ended; The Diary of Emma LeConte.* New York, 1957.

MINOR, BERKELEY. *Lincoln.* Staunton, Va., 1909.

MINOR, CHARLES L. C. *The Real Lincoln. With Article by Lyon G. Tyler,* ed. Kate Mason Rowland. Richmond, Va., 1901.

———. *The Real Lincoln, From the Testimony of His Contemporaries.* 2nd ed., revised and enlarged. Richmond, Va., 1904.

MORDECAI, G. L. *A Tribute to Lincoln. "Happy to Serve an Enemy." An Ex-Confederate Writes in Praise of the Martyr President.* New York, 1910. Originally appeared in *New York Tribune*, February 12, 1901.

Observance of the Centennial Anniversary of the Birth of Abraham Lincoln, February Twelfth, 1909, Under the Inspiration of the Grand Army of the Republic. New York, 1910. Reports of the Centennial Celebrations held under auspices of GAR, and includes reports from several Southern states.

PAGE, THOMAS NELSON. *The Negro: The Southerner's Problem.* New York, 1904.

———. "A Southerner's View of Abraham Lincoln, February 12, 1909," *Proceedings of the Massachusetts Historical Society*, 69 (October, 1947–May, 1950), 308–30. According to Frederick H. Curtiss, this is the hitherto unpublished speech delivered by Page at the Lincoln Memorial Celebration at Masonic Temple, Washington, D. C.

PARRISH, EVA, AND MARY PARRISH. "What the South Thinks of Lincoln," *The Epworth Herald*, February 6, 1909, pp. 939–41. Tributes by prominent Southerners on Lincoln's Centennial.

PHILLIPS, ULRICH BONNELL, ed. *The Correspondence of Robert Toombs, Alexander H. Stephens, and Howell Cobb. Annual Report of the American Historical Association for the Year 1911*, II. Washington, D. C., 1913.

PICKETT, MRS. GENERAL [LASALLE CORBELL PICKETT]. "President Lincoln. Intimate Personal Recollections," *Lippincott's Magazine*, May, 1906, pp. 555–60.

———. *What Happened to Me.* New York, 1917.

A PLAIN FARMER. *Abraham Lincoln, Late President of the United States, Demonstrated to be the Gog of the Bible, as Foretold by the Prophet Ezekiel in the XXXVIII and XXXIX Chapters of His Book of*

Prophecy. The Thirteen Confederate States Shown to be the Mountains of Israel, and All the Predictions Concerning Them Literally Fulfilled in the Late War Between the North and the South. Memphis, Tenn., 1868.

POLLARD, EDWARD A. *Life of Jefferson Davis, With a Secret History of the Southern Confederacy....* Philadelphia, 1869.

———. *The Lost Cause: A New Southern History of the War of the Confederates....* New York, 1867.

———. *The Lost Cause Regained.* New York, 1868.

———. *Southern History of the War.* 2 vols. in one. New York, 1866. This edition combines, with appendices, the three volumes of war history which Pollard published during the conflict.

———. *The Southern Spy. Letters on the Policy and Inauguration of the Lincoln War. Written Anonymously in Washington and Elsewhere.* 2nd ed. Richmond, Va., 1861. Consists of ten open letters, five of them to Lincoln.

PRESTON, ROBERT J. *Southern Miscellanies No. 2.* Leesburg, Va., May, 1919. A long reply to Henry Watterson's praise of Lincoln and Yankee ways.

[PUTNAM, MRS. SALLIE A. B.]. *Richmond During the War: Four Years of Personal Observations. By a Richmond Lady.* New York, 1867.

QUATTLEBAUM, ISABEL. "Twelve Women in the First Days of the Confederacy," *Civil War History*, 7 (December, 1961), 370–85. Extracts from their writings and some biographical information.

REAGAN, JOHN H. *Memoirs, With Special Reference to Secession and the Civil War.* New York, 1906.

RICE, ALLEN THORNDIKE, ed. *Reminiscences of Abraham Lincoln by Distinguished Men of His Time.* New York, 1886.

ROSS, FITZGERALD. *Cities and Camps of the Confederacy*, ed. Richard B. Harwell. Urbana, Ill., 1958. Originally published 1865.

ROWLAND, DUNBAR, ed. *Jefferson Davis, Constitutionalist: His Letters, Papers, and Speeches.* 10 vols. Jackson, Miss., 1923.

RUSSELL, WILLIAM HOWARD. *My Diary, North and South.* Boston, 1863.

RUTHERFORD, MILDRED LEWIS. *Jefferson Davis, the President of the Confederate States, and Abraham Lincoln, the President of the United States, 1861–1865.* Richmond, Va., 1916.

———. *The Truths of History. A Fair, Unbiased, Impartial, Unprejudiced and Conscientious Study of History.* Athens, Ga., 1920.

SCRUGHAM, MARY. *Force or Consent as the Basis of American Government. The Debate on the Subject by the Author and Attorney W.H. Townsend.* Lexington, Ky., 1920.

———. *The Peaceable Americans of 1860–1861.* Columbia University Studies in History, Economics and Public Law. Volume XCVI. No. 219. New York, 1921.

Services in Commemoration of the One Hundredth Anniversary of the Birth of Abraham Lincoln, Arranged by Union and Confederate Veterans Under the Auspices of O.M. Mitchel Post No. 1, Grand Army of the Republic. Trinity Methodist Episcopal Church South, Atlanta, Georgia, Sunday Evening, February 14th, 1909. Atlanta, 1909. Includes program, text of addresses, and extracts from Atlanta newspapers on the event.

SHEPPARD, MORRIS. *Abraham Lincoln. Speech of Congressman Morris Sheppard of Texas. Republican Club Banquet, New York, February 12, 1908.* n. p. [1908].

SHRYOCK, RICHARD O., ed. *Letters of Richard D. Arnold, M.D., 1808–1876.* Papers of the Trinity College Historical Society, Double Series XVIII–XIX. Durham, N. C., 1929.

SHURTER, EDWIN DUBOIS, ed. *The Complete Orations and Speeches of Henry W. Grady.* New York, 1910.

SILVER, JAMES W., ed. *A Life for the Confederacy, as Recorded in the Pocket Diaries of Pvt. Robert A. Moore, Co. G, 17th Mississippi Regiment, Confederate Guards, Holly Springs, Mississippi.* Jackson, Tenn., 1959.

[SMITH, CHARLES HENRY]. *Bill Arp, From the Uncivil War to Date, 1861–1903* (Atlanta, 1903). Autobiographical ramblings by Smith, with a biographical sketch by his daughter.

SMITH, DANIEL E. HUGER, ALICE R. HUGER SMITH, AND ARNEY R. CHILDS, eds. *Mason Smith Family Letters, 1860–1868.* Columbia, S. C., 1950.

SNYDER, MRS. ANN E. *The Civil War From a Southern Stand-Point.* Nashville, Tenn., 1890. An "unreconstructed" history.

A SOUTH CAROLINIAN. *The Confederate.* Mobile, Ala., 1863. A rebel imitation of *The Federalist.*

The South in the Building of the Nation. A History of the Southern States Designed to Record the South's Part in the Making of the American Nation, to Portray the Character and Genius, to Chronicle the Achievements and Progress and Illustrate the Life and Traditions of the Southern People. 13 vols. Richmond, Va., 1909–1913.

THE SOUTHERNER. "Lincoln and Lee," *South Atlantic Quarterly*, 26 (January, 1927). Anonymous North Carolinian concludes that Lincoln and Lee share qualities of greatness. "Lincoln was a democratized Lee; Lee was an aristocratic Lincoln."

SPEER, EMORY. *Lincoln, Lee, Grant, and Other Biographical Addresses.* New York, 1909. Distinguished Georgia jurist praises Lincoln, pp. 19–44.

STEEL, S. A. "Albert Taylor Bledsoe," *Methodist Review*, 64 (April, 1915), 211–28.

STEPHENS, ALEXANDER HAMILTON. *A Constitutional View of the Late War Between the States; Its Causes, Character, Conduct, and Results Presented in a Series of Colloquies at Liberty Hall.* 2 vols. in one. Philadelphia, 1868, 1870.

———. *The Reviewers Reviewed. . . .* New York, 1872. A hip-and-thigh rebuttal to critics of his *Constitutional View.*

STONEBREAKER, J. CLARENCE. *The Unwritten South; Cause, Progress and Result of the Civil War. Relics of Hidden Truth After Forty Years.* 5th ed. n.p., 1908. Another "unreconstructed" history.

TAYLOR, JAY, ed. *Reluctant Rebel. The Secret Diary of Robert Patrick, 1861–1865.* Baton Rouge, La., 1959.

[TOWNSEND, JOHN]. *The South Alone Should Govern the South, and African Slavery Should be Controlled by Those Only Who are Friendly to it. Third Edition. Read and Send to Your Neighbor.* Charleston, S. C., 1860.

Tribute to the Late President Lincoln. Report of the Great Mass Meeting in Savannah, the Largest Ever Held in the City. . . . On Saturday, April 22, 1865. Savannah, Ga., 1865.

TUCKER, BEVERLEY. *Address of Beverley Tucker, Esq., to the People of the United States, 1865*, ed. James Harvey Young. Atlanta, 1948. Tucker's defense against the charges that he was involved in a conspiracy to murder Lincoln.

TYLER, LYON GARDINER. *Barton and the Lineage of Lincoln. Claim that Lincoln was Related to Lee Refuted.* 2nd ed. n.p. [1930?].

———. *A Confederate Catechism. The War of 1861–1865. November 20, 1930.* 5th ed., enlarged. Holdcroft, Va., 1930.

———. *General Lee's Birthday. Address by Lyon Gardiner Tyler at Hollins College on January 18, 1929.*... n.p., n.d.

———. *John Tyler and Abraham Lincoln. Who Was the Dwarf? A Reply to a Challenge.* Richmond, Va., 1929.

———. *The Letters and Times of the Tylers.* 2 vols. Richmond, Va., 1884–1885.

———. *Propaganda in History.* 2nd ed., revised. Richmond, Va., 1921.

UNDERWOOD, R. L. *The Women of the Confederacy.* New York, 1906. Tributes to and recollections of Southern women in war and reconstruction.

VANDIVER, FRANK E., ed. *The Civil War Diary of General Josiah Gorgas.* University, Ala., 1947.

VILLARD, HENRY. *Lincoln on the Eve of '61: A Journalist's Story*, ed. Harold G. and Oswald Garrison Villard. New York, 1941. Selections from the dispatches of German-born, 25-year-old Villard, correspondent of the *New York Herald*, who accompanied Lincoln on his journey to Washington in February, 1861.

WASHINGTON, BOOKER T. *An Address ... for Delivery at a Dinner Given by the Members of the Union League Club on February 12, 1899....* n.p., [1899].

———. *An Address on Abraham Lincoln Delivered Before the Republican Club of New York City on the Night of February Twelfth, 1909.* n.p., [1909].

———. "Lincoln and the Black Man," *Alexander's Magazine*, 7 (February, 1909).

WATTERSON, HENRY. "Abraham Lincoln," *Cosmopolitan Magazine*, 46 (March, 1909), 363–75.

———. *Abraham Lincoln. An Oration Delivered Before the Lincoln Union.... Chicago, February 12, 1895.* Louisville, Ky., 1899.

———. *The Compromises of Life, and Other Lectures and Addresses, Including Some Observations on Certain Downward Tendencies of Modern Society.* New York, 1903.

———. *The Editorials of Henry Watterson*, comp. with an introduction and notes by Arthur Krock. New York, 1923.

———. *"Marse Henry." An Autobiography.* 2 vols. in one. New York, 1919.

WELCH, SPENCER GLASGOW. *A Confederate Surgeon's Letters to His Wife.* New York, 1911.

Whitaker, J. S., comp. *Louisiana's Tribute to the Memory of Abraham Lincoln. . . . Public Demonstrations in the City of New Orleans.* New Orleans, La., 1881.

Williams, John Sharp. *Lincoln Birthplace Farm at Hodgenville, Ky. Address Delivered on the Occasion of the Acceptance of a Deed of Gift to the Nation by the Lincoln Farm Association of the Lincoln Birthplace Farm at Hodgenville, Ky. . . . September 4, 1916.* 64th Cong., 1st sess. Senate Document No. 345. Washington, D. C., 1916.

Wilson, Woodrow. *Division and Reunion. With Additional Chapters Bringing the Narrative Down to the End of 1918, by Edward S. Corwin.* New York, 1925. First edition, 1893. Wilson was selected to do this volume because he was a Southerner. For the period, it is remarkably detached in view.

———. *A History of the American People.* 5 vols. New York, 1903.

———. *Papers of Woodrow Wilson*, ed. Arthur S. Link, *et al.* 2 vols. to date. Princeton, N. J., 1966– .

———. *The Public Papers of Woodrow Wilson. Authorized Edition*, ed. Ray Stannard Baker and William E. Dodd. 6 vols. New York, 1925–1927.

Wise, John Sergeant. *The End of an Era.* New York, 1965. Originally published, 1899.

Wright, William E., ed. "The Bishop of Natchez on the Death of Lincoln," *Lincoln Herald*, 58 (Fall, 1956), 13–14. Pastoral letter of Bishop William Henry Elder.

BELLES-LETTRES

Abbott, Martin. "President Lincoln in Confederate Caricature," *Journal of the Illinois State Historical Society*, 51 (Autumn, 1958), 306–19. Selections of prose and cartoons from Confederate newspapers and periodicals.

Abram: A Military Poem, by a Young Rebelle, Esq. of the Army. Richmond, Va., 1863.

Alderman, Edwin Anderson, and Joel Chandler Harris, eds.-in-chief; Charles William Kent, literary ed. *Library of Southern Literature; Compiled Under the Direct Supervision of Southern Men of Letters.* 16 vols. New Orleans, La., 1908–1913. Selections from and biographical sketches of nearly 300 Southern writers; briefer biographies of many more.

ANDREWS, MARY RAYMOND SHIPMAN. *The Perfect Tribute.* New York, 1907. This short story first appeared in *Scribner's Magazine*, 40 (July, 1906), 17–24.

BIRCH, E. P. *The Devil's Visit to "Old Abe." Written on the Occasion of Lincoln's Proclamation for Prayer and Fasting After the Battle of Manassas. Revised and Improved Expressly for the LaGrange* [Ga.] *Reporter, by the Author.* n.p., [1862].

BOYD, LUCINDA. *The Sorrows of Nancy.* Richmond, Va., 1899.

DAVIDSON, NORA FONTAINE, comp. *Cullings From the Confederacy. Southern Poems Popular During the War, 1861–1865, Including the Doggerel of the Camp.* Washington, D. C., 1903.

DIXON, THOMAS. *The Clansman: An Historical Romance of the Ku Klux Klan.* New York, 1905.

———. *The Leopard's Spots: A Romance of the White Man's Burden —1865–1900.* New York, 1902.

———. *A Man of the People.* New York, 1920. The play is included in Edward Wagenknecht, ed., *Abraham Lincoln: His Life, Work, and Character. An Anthology of History and Biography, Fiction, Poetry, Drama, and Belles-Lettres* (New York, 1947), 385–458.

———. *The Southerner: A Romance of the Real Lincoln.* New York, 1913.

[FONTAINE, FELIX G.]. *Marginalia; or, Gleanings From an Army Note-Book, By "Personne."* Columbia, S. C., 1864.

HARRIS, GEORGE WASHINGTON. *High Times and Hard Times. Sketches and Tales by George Washington Harris*, ed. M. Thomas Inge. Nashville, Tenn., 1967.

———. *The Lovingood Papers*, ed. Ben Harris McClary. Knoxville, Tenn., 1962– . A project by "The Sut Society" to collect and publish all hitherto unpublished (except in newspapers) Sut Lovingood yarns. Good bibliography in Vol. I.

———. *Sut Lovingood*, ed. Brom Weber. New York, 1954. Weber has abridged Sut's vernacular and deleted a few passages.

———. *Sut Lovingood Travels With Old Abe Lincoln*, ed. Edd Winfield Parks. Chicago, 1937. The Sut pieces on Lincoln, which originally appeared in the *Nashville Union & American*, are here more faithfully rendered than in the Weber edition.

HARRIS, JOEL CHANDLER. *On the Wing of Occasions. Being the Authorized Version of Certain Curious Episodes of the Late Civil War,*

Including the Hitherto Suppressed Narrative of the Kidnapping of President Lincoln. New York, 1900.

HARWELL, RICHARD BARKSDALE, ed. *Songs of the Confederacy.* New York, 1951.

HEWITT, JOHN HILL. *King Linkum the First; a Musical Burletta, as Performed at the Concert Hall, Augusta, Georgia, February 23, 1863,* ed. Richard Barksdale Harwell. Emory University Publications, Sources & Reprints, Series IV. Atlanta, 1947.

LEISY, ERNEST E., ed. *Mark Twain: The Letters of Quintus Curtius Snodgrass.* Dallas, Texas, 1946. Ten Snodgrass letters, including the Lincoln piece, which appeared in the *New Orleans Crescent* in 1861.

MCCABE, JOHN D., JR. *The Aid-de-Camp: A Romance of the War.* Richmond, Va., 1863.

MCCLARY, BEN HARRIS. "Sut Lovingood Views 'Abe Linkhorn,'" *Lincoln Herald,* 56 (Fall, 1954), 44–45. Harris' Lincoln pieces briefly considered, with excerpts.

A MEMBER OF THE GAR. *The Picket Line and Camp Fire Stories. A Collection of War Anecdotes, Both Grave and Gay, illustrative of the Trials and Triumphs of Soldier Life, With a Thousand-and-One Humorous Stories, Told of and by Abraham Lincoln, Together with a Full Collection of Northern and Southern War Songs.* New York, [1864].

MERCER, S. C. *The Two Kentuckians, Read by Mrs. Irwin Dugan Before the Filson Club, Louisville, Ky.* Louisville, Ky., 1901. Poem about Jefferson Davis and Lincoln.

MILLER, STEPHEN FRANKS. *Ahab Lincoln: A Tragedy of the Potomac,* introduction by Richard B. Harwell. Chicago, 1958.

MOORE, FRANK, ed. *Anecdotes, Poetry and Incidents of the War: North and South, 1860–1865.* New York, 1866.

———, ed. *Rebel Rhymes and Rhapsodies.* New York, 1864.

———. *The Rebellion Record: A Diary of American Events, with Documents, Narratives, Illustrative Incidents, Poetry, Etc.* 11 vols. New York, 1861–1868.

———. *Songs and Ballads of the Southern People.* New York, 1866.

[SHEPPERSON, WILLIAM G.]. *War Songs of the South. Edited by "Bohemian."* Richmond, Va., 1862.

SILBERT, IRWIN. *Songs of the Civil War.* New York, 1960.

[Smith, Charles H.]. *Bill Arp, So Called: A Side Show of the War.* New York, 1866.

———. *Bill Arp's Peace Papers.* New York, 1873.

[Smith, William Russell]. *The Royal Ape: A Dramatic Poem.* Richmond, Va., 1863.

Songs of the South. Richmond, Va., 1863.

Volck, Adalbert J. "Confederate War Etchings, 1862–1863," *The Magazine of History with Notes & Queries. Extra Number—No. 16* (Tarrytown, N. Y., 1917).

War Lyrics and Songs of the South. London, 1866. A collection of poetry by Southern women, offered for sale in hopes that the proceeds would help crippled veterans, widows, and orphans.

Wellman, Manly Wade. *The Rebel Songster; Songs the Confederacy Sang.* Charlotte, N. C., 1959.

Williams, A. Dallas, comp. *The Praise of Lincoln: An Anthology.* Indianapolis, Ind., 1911. At least three Southern poets contributed to this anthology.

SECONDARY SOURCES

Abbott, Martin. "Southern Reaction to Lincoln's Assassination," *Abraham Lincoln Quarterly,* 7 (September, 1952), 111–27.

Baker, Ray Stannard. *Woodrow Wilson: His Life and Letters.* 8 vols. Garden City, N. Y., 1927–1940. Especially Vol. I, *Youth, 1856–1890.*

Baringer, William E. *A House Dividing: Lincoln as President-Elect.* Springfield, Ill., 1945.

Beale, Howard K. "What Historians Have Said About the Causes of the Civil War," *Theory and Practice in Historical Study: A Report of the Committee on Historiography* [of the Social Science Research Council]. Bulletin 54. New York, 1946.

Bennett, Lerone, Jr. "Was Abe Lincoln a White Supremacist?" *Ebony,* 23 (February, 1968).

Blair, Walter. *Horse Sense in American Humor, From Benjamin Franklin to Ogden Nash.* Chicago, 1942.

———. *Native American Humor (1800–1900).* New York, 1937.

Brands, Pearl Brown. "Music Written About Abraham Lincoln," *Étude,* February, 1938.

Brookes, Stella Brewer. *Joel Chandler Harris, Folklorist.* Athens, Ga., 1950. Primarily a study of the Uncle Remus stories.

Bryan, George S. *The Great American Myth.* New York, 1940. Explores the events and myths around Lincoln's assassination.

Buck, Paul H. *The Road to Reunion, 1865–1890.* New York, 1937.

Cash, W. J. *The Mind of the South.* New York, 1960. Originally published 1941.

Catton, Bruce. *The Coming Fury.* Garden City, N. Y., 1961.

Christie, Anne E. "Bill Arp," *Civil War History*, 2 (September, 1956), 103–19.

Cole, Arthur C. "Lincoln's Election an Immediate Menace to Slavery in the States?" *American Historical Review*, 36 (July, 1931), 740–67.

Cook, Raymond Allen. *Fire from the Flint: The Amazing Careers of Thomas Dixon.* Winston-Salem, N. C., 1968. A rather uncritical biography.

Coulter, E. Merton. *The Confederate States of America, 1861–1865.* Volume VII in *The History of the South.* Baton Rouge, La., 1950. Excellent bibliography and discussion of non-military affairs.

———. "What the South Has Done About Her History," *Journal of Southern History*, 2 (February, 1936), 3–28.

Cousins, Paul M. *Joel Chandler Harris. A Biography.* Baton Rouge, La., 1968.

Crenshaw, Ollinger. "The Psychological Background of the Election of 1860 in the South," *North Carolina Historical Review*, 19 (July, 1942), 260–79.

Current, Richard N. *Lincoln and the First Shot.* Philadelphia, 1963.

Davidson, James Wood. *The Living Writers of the South.* New York, 1869. Brief sketches of 241 living Southern writers.

Day, Donald. "The Life of George Washington Harris," *Tennessee Historical Quarterly*, 6 (March, 1947), 3–38. "Still the most extended record of Harris' life," according to Milton Rickels.

———. "The Political Satires of George W. Harris," *Tennessee Historical Quarterly*, 4 (December, 1945), 320–38. Stresses Harris' hatred for things Yankee and his "unreconstructed" writings after the war.

Eaton, Clement. *The Freedom-of-Thought Struggle in the Old South.* New York, 1964. An expanded version of *Freedom of Thought in the Old South* (Durham, N. C., 1940).

———. *A History of the Southern Confederacy*. New York, 1961.

———. "Mob Violence in the Old South," *Mississippi Valley Historical Review*, 29 (December, 1942), 351–70.

Fite, Emerson David. *The Presidential Campaign of 1860*. New York, 1911.

Frank, Seymour J. "The Conspiracy to Implicate the Confederate Leaders in Lincoln's Assassination," *Mississippi Valley Historical Review*, 40 (March, 1954), 629–56.

Gaines, Francis Pendleton. *The Southern Plantation: A Study in the Development and Accuracy of a Tradition*. New York, 1925. A study of the plantation tradition in literature.

Gaston, Paul Morton. *The New South Creed: A Study in Southern Mythmaking*. New York, 1970. An excellent study of the philosophy and programs of the New South leadership.

Gunderson, Robert Gray. *Old Gentlemen's Convention. The Washington Peace Conference of 1861*. Madison, Wis., 1961.

Hall, Wade. *The Smiling Phoenix: Southern Humor from 1865 to 1914*. Gainesville, Fla., 1965.

Hall, Wilmer. "Lincoln's Interview with John B. Baldwin," *South Atlantic Quarterly*, 13 (July, 1914), 260–69.

Hamilton, J. G. deRoulhac. "Lincoln's Election an Immediate Menace to Slavery in the States?" *American Historical Review*, 37 (July, 1932), 700–11. An answer to Cole's article of the same title (above).

———. "The Many-Sired Lincoln," *American Mercury*, 5 (June, 1925), 129–35. Disposes of many of the myths surrounding Lincoln's ancestry.

Harper, Robert S. *Lincoln and the Press*. New York, 1951.

Harwell, Richard Barksdale. "The Richmond Stage," *Civil War History*, 1 (September, 1955), 295–304.

Hobeika, John E. *The Sage of Lion's Den. An Appreciation of the Character and Career of Lyon Gardiner Tyler and of his Writings on Abraham Lincoln and the War Between the States*. New York, 1948. "Appreciation" is the right word to describe this worshipful eulogy of one of the South's most vociferous Lincoln-haters.

Hubbell, Jay B. *The South in American Literature, 1607–1900*. Durham, N. C., 1954. Biographical studies and bibliographies of leading Southern writers.

———. *Southern Life in Fiction. Eugenia Dorothy Blount Lamar Memorial Lectures, 1959; Delivered at Mercer University, on November 17, 18, and 19.* Athens, Ga., 1960.

JOHNSTON, RICHARD MALCOLM, AND WILLIAM HAND BROWNE. *Life of Alexander H. Stephens.* Philadelphia, 1884.

KEENE, JESSE L. *The Peace Convention of 1861.* Confederate Centennial Studies, No. 18. Tuscaloosa, Ala., 1961.

KIBLER, LILIAN ADELE. *Benjamin Perry: South Carolina Unionist.* Durham, N. C., 1946.

KINCAID, ROBERT L. *The Wilderness Road.* Indianapolis, 1947.

KIRKLAND, EDWARD CHASE. *The Peacemakers of 1864.* New York, 1927.

LEE, FITZHUGH. "The Failure of the Hampton Conference," *Century*, 52 (July, 1896), 476–78.

LINK, ARTHUR STANLEY. *Wilson.* 5 vols. to date. Princeton, N. J., 1947– . Especially Vol. I, *The Road to the White House.*

———, AND REMBERT W. PATRICK. *Writing Southern History. Essays in Historiography in Honor of Fletcher M. Green.* Baton Rouge, La., 1965. A superb compilation.

LIVELY, ROBERT A. *Fiction Fights the Civil War: An Unfinished Chapter in the Literary History of the American People.* Chapel Hill, N. C., 1957. Excellent bibliography of novels about the Civil War published up to 1949.

LOGAN, RAYFORD W. *The Negro in American Life and Thought. The Nadir, 1877–1901.* New York, 1954.

NEVINS, ALLAN. *The Emergence of Lincoln.* 2 vols. New York, 1950.

NEWBY, I. A. *Jim Crow's Defense: Anti-Negro Thought in America, 1900–1930.* Baton Rouge, La., 1965. Study of the development and application of racist ideas.

NICHOLS, ROY F. *The Disruption of American Democracy.* New York, 1948.

NIXON, RAYMOND B. *Henry W. Grady, Spokesman of the New South.* New York, 1943.

PHILLIPS, ULRICH B. "The Central Theme of Southern History," *American Historical Review*, 34 (October, 1928).

POTTER, DAVID M. *Lincoln and His Party in the Secession Crisis.* Yale Historical Publications. Studies XIII. New Haven, Conn., 1942.

———. *The South and the Sectional Conflict.* Baton Rouge, La., 1968.

PRATT, HARRY E. "Albert Taylor Bledsoe: Critic of Lincoln," *Illinois*

State Historical Society. Transactions for the Year 1934. Illinois State Historical Library Publication No. 41. Springfield, Ill., n.d. Pp. 153–83. Includes bibliography of works by and about Bledsoe.

PRESSLY, THOMAS J. *Americans Interpret Their Civil War.* Princeton, N. J., 1954.

QUARLES, BENJAMIN. *Lincoln and the Negro.* New York, 1962.

RAMSDELL, CHARLES W. "Lincoln and Fort Sumter," *Journal of Southern History*, 3 (August, 1937), 259–88.

RANDALL, JAMES G., AND DAVID DONALD. *The Civil War and Reconstruction.* 2nd ed. Boston, 1961.

RHODES, JAMES FORD. *History of the United States from the Compromise of 1850 to the Final Restoration of Home Rule at the South in 1877.* 8 vols. New York, 1907–1919.

RICKELS, MILTON. *George Washington Harris.* New York, 1965. Biography and criticism, with a useful bibliography.

SEAGER, ROBERT, II. *And Tyler Too. A Biography of John and Julia Gardiner Tyler.* New York, 1963.

SIMKINS, FRANCIS BUTLER. *A History of the South.* New York, 1953.

STAMPP, KENNETH M. *And the War Came. The North and the Secession Crisis, 1860–1861.* Baton Rouge, La., 1950. Focuses on reaction of Northern business community.

STEPHENSON, WENDELL HOLMES. *The South Lives in History: Southern Historians and Their Legacy.* Baton Rouge, La., 1955. Essays on William E. Dodd, Ulrich B. Phillips, Walter L. Fleming, and a survey of Southern historical scholarship from the 1880's to the present.

———. *Southern History in the Making. Pioneer Historians of the South.* Baton Rouge, La., 1964. Twelve essays on Southern historians.

THOMPSON, HOLLAND. *The New South. A Chronicle of Social and Industrial Evolution.* Volume 42 in The Chronicles of America Series. New Haven, Conn., 1920.

THOMPSON, LAWRENCE S. "The Civil War in Fiction," *Civil War History*, 2 (March, 1956), 83–95.

TOWNSEND, WILLIAM H. *Lincoln and His Wife's Home Town.* Indianapolis, Ind., 1929. More about Lexington, Ky., than about Lincoln.

VAN AUKEN, SHELDON. "The Southern Historical Novel in the Early Twentieth Century," *Journal of Southern History*, 14 (May, 1948), 157–91.

VAN DEUSEN, GLYNDON G. *William Henry Seward.* New York, 1967.

Von Abele, Rudolph. *Alexander H. Stephens: A Biography*. New York, 1946. Focuses upon Stephens as "a problem in the psychology of personality, motivation, and behavior."

Wall, Joseph Frazier. *Henry Watterson, Reconstructed Rebel.* New York, 1956.

Williams, Samuel Cole. *The Lincolns of Tennessee*. Harrogate, Tenn., 1942. The author believes he has found members of the Lincoln family who filtered down from Virginia to East Tennessee. Many were prosperous and most were Confederates.

Wilson, Edmund. *Patriotic Gore: Studies in the Literature of the American Civil War*. New York, 1962.

Wilson, James Southall. "Lyon Gardiner Tyler," *William and Mary College Quarterly Historical Magazine*, 2nd Ser. 15 (October, 1935).

Wise, Boyd A. "Lincoln in Drama," *Lincoln Herald*, 42 (October, 1939).

Woodward, C. Vann. *Origins of the New South, 1877–1913*. Volume IX in *A History of the South*. Baton Rouge, La., 1951.

———. *The Strange Career of Jim Crow*. 2nd ed., revised. New York, 1966.

Wyllie, Irvin G. *The Self-Made Man in America. The Myth of Rags to Riches*. New York, 1954.

Wynes, Charles E., ed. *The Negro in the South Since 1865. Selected Essays in American Negro History*. University, Ala., 1965. Includes an essay on Thomas Dixon by Maxwell Bloomfield originally printed in *American Quarterly*, 16 (Fall, 1964).

Index

The Image of Lincoln in the South was set on the Linotype in eleven point Granjon with two points spacing between the lines. Foundry Americana was selected for display. The book was designed by Jim Billingsley, composed manually and printed by Heritage Printers, Inc., Charlotte, North Carolina, and bound by Kingsport Press, Inc., Kingsport, Tennessee. The book is printed on paper designed for an effective life of at least three hundred years.

THE UNIVERSITY OF TENNESSEE PRESS : KNOXVILLE